rter

AFRICAN FILMMAKING

D1313269

TRADITIONS IN WORLD CINEMA
General Editors
Linda Badley (Middle Tennessee State University)
R. Barton Palmer (Clemson University)

Founding Editor
Steven Jay Schneider (New York University)

AFRICAN FILMMAKING
North and South of the Sahara

Roy Armes

EDINBURGH UNIVERSITY PRESS

© Roy Armes, 2006

Edinburgh University Press Ltd
22 George Square, Edinburgh

Typeset in 10/12.5 Adobe Sabon
by Servis Filmsetting Ltd, Manchester, and
printed and bound in Great Britain by
MPG Books Ltd, Bodmin, Cornwall

A CIP record for this book is available from the British Library

ISBN-10 0 7486 2123 7 (hardback)
ISBN-13 978 0 7486 2123 1
ISBN-10 0 7486 2124 5 (paperback)
ISBN-13 978 0 7486 2124 8

CONTENTS

ACKNOWLEDGEMENTS

Here, as with all my writings about African filmmaking, I owe a huge debt to Guido Aristarco, who organised a series of conferences in Bulgaria in 1978–9 in connection with a projected General History of World Cinema. This was the context in which I first met Ousmane Sembene, Paulin Soumanou Vieyra and Ferid Boughedir and discovered, much to my surprise, that there was indeed an African cinema, made by African filmmakers, happily far removed from the Tarzan films I had devoured as a child. The encounter with what was still unproblematically called 'third world cinema' changed for ever my hitherto wholly Euro-centric approach to writing about film.

This book owes its immediate existence to the persuasive powers of Steven Jay Schneider and R. Barton Palmer, the patience of Sarah Edwards and my own dislike of prime numbers (I have previously published seventeen books). My thanks go to John Flahive of the BFI for a VHS copy of *Aristotle's Plot*, to Dominique Sentiles of Médiathèque des Trois Mondes, Cornelius Moore and Gene Sklar of California Newsreel, and Renald Spech of ArtMattan for help in purchasing video tapes. I am also very grateful to Jeanik Le Naour for arranging Paris screenings at ADPF and to Kevin Dwyer for his invaluable support on many aspects of Moroccan cinema.

I must also thank the following individuals and organisations for permission to reproduce stills: the Montpellier International Festival for *Bye Bye Africa*, Duo Films for *Abouna*, *La Vie sur terre* (© Marie Jaoul de Poncheville and Anaïs Jeanneret) and *Heremakono* (© Kranck Verdier), California Newsreel for *Keita, L'héritage du griot*, ArtMattan Productions for *Sia*, Dani Kouyaté for *Ouaga Saga* (© Didier Bergounhoux), Nomadis Images for *Satin Rouge*, and Optimum Releasing for *Mille mois*.

LIST OF ACRONYMS

ACCT	Agence de Coopération Culturelle et Technique	France
ACE	Atelier du Cinéma Européen	France
ACT	Association des Cinéastes Tunisiens	Tunisia
ADCSud	Appui au Développement des Cinémas du Sud	France
ADPA	Association pour la Diffusion de la Pensée Française	France
AJCT	Association des Jeunes Cinéastes Tunisiens	Tunisia
ALN	Armée de Libération Nationale	Algeria
ANAF	Agence Nationale des Actualités Filmées	Algeria
ANPA	Agence Nationale de Promotion de l'Audiovisuel	Tunisia
BFI	British Film Institute	UK
CAAIC	Centre Algérien pour l'Art et Industrie Cinématographiques	Algeria
CAC	Centre Algérien de la Cinématographie	Algeria
CAI	Consortium Audiovisuel International	France
CAV	Centre Audio-Visuel	Algeria
CCM	Centre Cinématographique Marocain	Morocco
CDC	Centre de Diffusion Cinématographique	Algeria

CENACI	Centre National du Cinéma	Gabon
CIDC	Consortium Interafricain de Distribution Cinématographique	Burkina Faso
CIPROFILM	Consortium Inter-Africain de Production de Films	Burkina Faso
CIVCA	Compagnie Ivoirienne de Cinéma et d'Audiovisuel	Ivory Coast
CLCF	Conservatoire Libre du Cinéma Français	France
CNC	Centre National de la Cinématographie	France
CNC	Centre National du Cinéma	Burkina Faso
CNCA	(1) Centre National du Cinéma Algérien (1964–7)	Algeria
	(2) Centre National du Cinéma et de l'Audiovisuel (2004)	Algeria
CNPC	Centre National de Production Cinématographique	Mali
CNSAD	Conservatoire National Supérieur d'Art Dramatique	France
COMACICO	Compagnie Africaine Cinématographique Industrielle et Commerciale	France
DEA	Diplôme d'Etudes Approfondies	France
DEFA	Deutsche Film-AG	Germany
DNC	Direction Nationale du Cinéma	Burkina Faso
ENADEC	Entreprise Nationale de Distribution et d'Exploitation Cinématographiques	Algeria
ENAPROC	Entreprise Nationale de Production Cinématographique	Algeria
ENPA	Entreprise Nationale de Productions Audiovisuelles	Algeria
ENTV	Entreprise Nationale de Télévision	Algeria
ERTT	Etablissements Radio-Télévision Tunisiens	Tunisia
ESEC	Ecole Supérieure des Etudes Cinématographiques	France
ESRA	Ecole Supérieure de Réalisation Audiovisuelle	France
FACC	Fédération Algériennne des Ciné-Clubs	Algeria
FACISS	Fédération Africaine des Ciné-Clubs au Sud du Sahara	Black Africa

FAMU	Filmov Akademie Múzickych Umení (Film & Television Faculty of the Academy of Performing Arts)	Czech Republic
FAPCN	Fonds d'Aide à la Production Cinématographique Nationale	Morocco
FAS	Fonds d'Action Sociale	France
FED	Fonds Européen de Développement	EU
FEMIS	Fondation Européenne des Métiers de l'Image et du Son	France
FEPACI	Fédération Panafricaine des Cinéastes	
FESPACO	Festival Panafricain du Cinéma de Ougadougou	Burkina Faso
FIFAK	Festival International du Film Amateur de Kélibia	Tunisia
FIA	Fonds Images Afrique	France
FLN	Front de Libération Nationale	Algeria
FNCCM	Fédération Nationale des Ciné-Clubs au Maroc	Morocco
FODIC	Fonds pour le Développement de l'Industrie Cinématographique	Cameroon
FTCA	Fédération Tunisienne des Cinéastes Amateurs	Tunisia
FTCC	Fédération Tunisienne de Ciné-Clubs	Tunisia
GDR	German Democratic Republic	Germany
GPRA	Gouvernement Provisoire de la République Algérienne	Algeria
ICADI	Institut Communal des Arts Décoratifs et Industriels de Liège	Belgium
INAFEC	Institut Africain d'Education Cinématographique	Burkina Faso
IDHEC	Institut des Hautes Études Cinématographiques	France
IET	Institut d'Études Théatrales	France
IFC	Institut Français de Cinéma	France
IMA	Institut du Monde Arabe	France
INA	Institut National de l'Audiovisuel	France
INC	Institut National de Cinéma	Algeria
INSAS	Institut National des Arts du Spectacle et Techniques de Diffusion	Belgium

INSIC	Institut National des Sciences de l'Information et de la Communication	Algeria
ISADAC	Insitut Supérieur d'Art Dramatique et d'Animation Culturelle de Rabat	Morocco
JCC	Journées Cinématographiques de Carthage	Tunisia
MPEAA	Motion Picture Export Association of America	USA
NCO	Nationale Commissie Voorlichting Bewustworging Ontwikkelingssamenwerking	Holland
NFTVA	National Film and Television Academy	Holland
NOS	Nederlandse Omroepstichting	Holland
OAA	Office des Actualités Algériennes	Algeria
OAU	Organisation of African Unity	
OBECI	Office Beninois de Cinéma	Benin
OCAM	Organisation Commune Africaine et Mauritienne	France
OCIC	Organisation Catholique Internationale du Cinéma	Belgium
OCINAM	Office Cinématographique National du Mali	Mali
OCORA	Office de Coopération Radiophonique	Paris
ONACI	Office National du Cinéma	Congo
ONACIDA	Office National du Cinéma Dahoméen	Dahomey (Benin)
ONCIC	Office National du Commerce et de l'Industrie Cinématographiques	Algeria
ORTF	Office de Radiodiffusion et de Télévision Française	France
RTA	Radiodiffusion Télévision Algérienne	Algeria
RTM	Radio-Télévision Marocaine	Morocco
RTT	Radio-Télévision Tunisienne	Tunisia
SAC	Service Algérien du Cinéma	Algeria
SATPEC	Société Anonyme Tunisienne de Production et d'Expansion Cinématographiques	Tunisia
SCINFOMA	Service Cinématographique du Ministère de l'Information du Mali	Mali
SDC	Service de Diffusion Cinématographique	Algeria

SECMA	Société d'Exploitation Cinématographique Africaine	France
SEACI	Secrétariat d'Etat aux Affaires Culturelles et à l'Information	Tunisia
SIC	Société Ivoirienne du Cinéma	Ivory Coast
SIDEC	Société d'Importation, de Distribution et d'Exploitation Cinématographiques	Senegal
SNC	Société Nationale de Productions Cinématographiques	Senegal
SNED	Société Nationale d'Edition et de Diffusion	Algeria
SONACIB	Société Nationale Burkinabé du Cinéma	Burkina Faso
SONAVOCI	Société Nationale Voltaïque du Cinéma	Burkina Faso
STD	Société Tunisienne de Diffusion	Tunisia
TNB	Télévision Nationale du Burkina	Burkina Faso
TNP	Théâtre National Populaire	France
UCLA	University of California at Los Angeles	USA
UAC	Union Africaine de Cinéma	France
VGIK	Vsesoyuznyi gosudarstvennyi institut kinematografii (All-Union State Cinema Institute)	Russia

In memory of Lionel Ngkane
Friend and filmmaker

If Africans remain mere consumers of cinema and television images con-ceived and produced by others, they will become second-rate citizens of the world and be forced to accept a destiny which will not take into account their history, their basic aspirations and even less their values, their imaginary and their vision of the world.

If Africa does not acquire the capacity to forge its own gaze, so as to con-front its own image, it will lose its point of view and its self-awareness.

Gaston Kabore
FEPACI

INTRODUCTION

The progress of the means of communication and information have made Africa enter this 'global village' which the planet has become and which henceforth makes every country a house of glass where nothing is the same as before. Open to the world's evolution and aware of belonging to a public opinion more and more sure of its rights, Africans desire henceforth to participate in the administration of their society.

Émile Mworoha and Bernard Nantet[1]

I. THE AFRICAN EXPERIENCE

The contradictions of modern Africa which stem from the co-existence of widely differing values are still the inescapable reality.

Shatto Arthur Gakwandi[2]

THE POSTCOLONIAL SITUATION

Filmmaking in Africa by Africans is fundamentally a postcolonial activity and experience, and nowhere is this more the case than in the two contiguous but variously colonised geographical areas dealt with in this book. The first area comprises the North African countries forming the Maghreb: Tunisia and Morocco, which both became independent in 1956, and Algeria, whose independence was achieved only after a long and bloody war of liberation in 1962. The second area comprises the states formed south of the Sahara from the two giant colonies of French West Africa and French Equatorial Africa, which were divided at independence into the twelve separate countries now known as Benin (formerly Dahomey), Ivory Coast, Guinea, Senegal, Mali, Mauritania, Niger, Burkina Faso (formerly Upper Volta), Chad, Central African Republic, Gabon and Congo. To this list we may add the two West African states which were formerly German colonies but had become French protectorates after the First World War: Togo and Cameroon. These two were granted their independence in 1960, along with all the other West African States apart from Guinea, which had proclaimed its independence in 1958. The two contiguous areas north and south of the Sahara together provide a continuous unbroken land mass of just under 11 million square kilometres (about 16.5 per cent larger than the United States). About a third of this area (3.2 million square kilometres) is in the Maghreb and just over two thirds (7.7 million square kilometres) in the south. The whole stretches from the Mediterranean to the banks of the Congo, and from the Atlantic coast of Senegal to the borders of the Sudan. This huge area is home to some 175 million people, 65 million in the Maghreb and 110 million to the south.

A good starting point for an understanding of the contemporary situation of this area is to consider the nature of the independence achieved in the startlingly brief time span between 1958 and 1962. In the words of Roland Oliver, the title of whose book I have borrowed for this section, most modern African nations inherited a colonial structure:

> Their frontiers were all colonial frontiers, agreed in the 1880s and 1890s. Their capitals were the colonial capitals, from which radiated the colonial infrastructures of roads and railways, posts and telecommunications. All retained, in some measure, the languages of the colonizers as languages of wider communication.[3]

As a result, he adds that 'for 97 per cent of the population, independence as such made little practical difference'.[4] Writing in 1980, Richard W. Hull advanced similar views, arguing that 'behaviour and status systems of the former colonialists have been adopted by African elites as their own', while 'social stratification has increased since independence in nearly all African nations'.[5]

Hull also claims that regardless of their actions, 'most African nationalists were sincerely interested in building a modern nation state'.[6] As a result, despite the somewhat doubtful beginnings, each new independent African state has become fully a 'nation' in the terms defined by Benedict Anderson, namely 'an imagined political community'. It is 'imagined' because 'the members of even the smallest nation will never know most of their fellow-members, meet them, or even hear of them'. It is 'political' in the sense that it is both limited (all nations have boundaries) and yet sovereign within those boundaries. And it is a 'community' because, whatever the real social divisions, 'the nation is always conceived as a deep, horizontal comradeship'.[7] The latter idea, Anderson argues, allows one of the most amazing aspects of a national state, namely that it makes it possible 'for so many millions of people, not so much to kill, as willing to die for such limited imaginings'.[8] When we look at the current problems faced by so many African states, it is too easy to blame outside factors, such as postcolonial dominance. Cruise O'Brien and Rathbone's reminder about West African states applies equally to the countries of the Maghreb: 'These states have . . . reached maturity.

Each has an adult generation which grew up in a sunlight unshaded by the *tricolore* or the Union Jack'.[9] But the heritage of the colonial era is none the less crucial.

While the newly independent African ex-colonies have undoubtedly become nation states in the conventional Western sense, the particular state form which they inherited – the structure of the colonial state – is deeply flawed. The colonial state is necessarily characterised by 'autocratic centralism', since, in such a state, all real power of policy and decision was gathered at the executive summit, embodied in a supreme governor appointed in London or Paris. Hence, as Basil Davidson points out, the phenomenon of nationalism becomes much more complex than it first seemed, being 'the ambiguous fruit of an opposition or a counterpoint between the themes of the African past and those of the cultures of the imperialist nations which colonized the continent'.[10] Davidson sets out the current dilemma with striking clarity: is the African nation state vowed, as in Europe, 'to a history of international conflict, rivalry, and mutual destruction?' Or does it contain the seeds of 'a development toward regional and even subcontinental systems of organic union, and therefore toward new modes of cultural emancipation?'.[11] Such ambiguities were not anticipated at the moment of independence, and Frantz Fanon's celebrated essay 'On National Culture: Reciprocal Bases of National Culture and the Fight for Freedom'[12] could serve as both an inspiration for the first African filmmakers and a means by which critics could assess their work.[13]

The leaders of the newly independent states of Africa in the 1950s saw themselves as the enemies of colonialism and its tyrannies and, as Roland Oliver observes, like most educated Africans, 'virtually all were, in European and American terms, people of the left'.[14] Most of them sought – and many claimed to have found – 'a kind of indigenous socialism inherent in African tradition'.[15] The political tool to be used as the instrument of 'African socialism' was the 'party', 'seen not as a contender for power at successive elections, when its record and programme was presented to the people for approval, but as the animating mind and purpose of the whole nation, established and irreplaceable.'[16]

The model for this party was not, however, the Western democratic system under whose auspices the new national constitutions had been written, but 'the Marxist-Leninist tradition of eastern Europe'.[17] The result was the typical African single-party state where, as Richard W. Hull notes,

> the executive, administrative and legislative cadres are intertwined. The one-party states tend to be monolithic and absorb the youth movements, trade unions, and the cooperatives. Opposition is permitted, but only within the context of the party organs and within the general framework of the national ethos, as defined by the party.[18]

As in eastern Europe, this form of autocratic rule has not favoured economic growth or development, and the resulting social discontent is at least partly responsible for the successive military coups which are such a feature of African political rule. Where Islam is the dominant religion, the situation is perhaps even more extreme, since the distinction in the Christian West between church and state is not matched by a similar split within Islam. There is no Muslim state in Africa or the Arab world as a whole which functions as more than a notional democracy. African filmmakers – like African cultural workers as a whole – have therefore to find means to operate – that is to say, to find necessary freedoms – under political systems where autocracy is the norm.

<h2 style="text-align:center">FRENCH INFLUENCE</h2>

It is generally agreed that traditional African social organisation and development resulted in 'clusters of small states sharing a common language and culture',[19] some of which were later incorporated into larger states. From this pattern stems the huge linguistic, ethnic and cultural diversity of contemporary Africa, which in turn makes generalisation about 'Africa' (or 'African cinema' for that matter) so hazardous. As a UNESCO report of 1993 noted, 'whenever there has been near confrontation and competition between the forces of ethnicity on the one side and the forces of class-consciousness on the other, ethnicity has almost invariably triumphed in Africa.[20] Associated with these ethnic groups were specific religious practices, since, 'as everywhere in the world, African statecraft was much involved with religion and magic'.[21] Though early post-independence filmmakers – often strongly influenced by Marxist thinking – were largely hostile to religion (viewed as mere superstition), traditional African religious practices and beliefs do find expression from the mid-1980s in an increasing number of very striking films.

Superimposed upon the traditional pattern of social organisation and religion was the reorganisation of Africa into forty or so large colonies in which an educational system which favoured Europeanised teaching was offered to the talented few. The French system, in West Africa as elsewhere, produced 'educated Africans who were known as *assimilés* – those who could be assimilated into the superior culture and administration which France had brought to Africa'.[22] By the 1940s these *assimilés* had acquired the right to vote in French elections, and it was from their ranks that the first leaders of the independent states of the late 1950s and early 1960s emerged. As Hull notes, such a system meant that 'the leaders of the newly independent governments of French-speaking Africa tended to have closer emotional ties to their former colonial master than did their English-speaking counterparts'.[23] French cultural policies – including those concerning cinema – can be seen, in part, as a response to this emotional connection. But this should not mask the underlying reason for France's continued involvement with its former colonies, its self-interest. As Donal B. Cruise O'Brien aptly observes, 'the true justification for France's investment in post imperial Africa, an investment much more substantial than was provided by Britain for her African ex-colonies, was the maintenance of French national prestige.[24]

In the colonies – for the emerging African elites as well as for the whites – European languages became the languages of politics, administration and commerce, and the focus was on communication with the revelant capital in Europe rather than with any neighbouring colony. The question of language is crucial in any colonial or postcolonial situation. As Albert Memmi notes, the majority of the colonised will 'never have anything but their native tongue; that is, a tongue which is neither written nor read, permitting only uncertain and poor oral development'.[25] But even the child 'who has the wonderful good luck to be accepted in a school will not be saved nationally'.[26] The mastery of two languages creates, for many, a painful duality, since 'the colonized's mother tongue, that which is sustained by his feelings, emotions and dreams, that in which his tenderness and wonder are expressed, that which holds the greatest emotional impact, is precisely the one which is least valued.[27]

For writers using the language of the coloniser in their work, this duality can impose real tensions (which, in creative terms can be positive as well as merely negative). But the technology of film offers a very different solution. Film dialogue in the native tongue can be followed easily by even an illiterate (if limited) African public, while, at the same time, subtitles can make the film accessible to a Western audience (with the local language adding that touch of 'otherness' so prized on the art house circuit). This is one reason why the vast majority of films both north and south of the Sahara use local variants of Arabic and regional or national languages, even if – for the purposes of obtaining vital foreign aid or co-production finance – the film has had originally to be scripted and dialogued in French.

But though European languages were imposed on Africa, there was no matching transfer of Western technology. Noting that 'the only non-European society that borrowed effectively from Europe and became capitalist is that of Japan', Walter Rodney argues that a similar development was impossible for Africa because 'the very nature of Afro-European trade was highly unfavourable to the movement of positive ideas and techniques from the European capitalist system to the African pre-capitalist (communal, feudal, and pre-feudal) system of production'.[28] But even for a society like Japan, the necessary adaptations proved difficult. In an essay written in 1933, the Japanese novelist Junichiro Tanizaki describes the transition in words that have equal resonance for Africa:

> The Westerner has been able to move forward in ordered steps, while we have met superior civilisation and have had to surrender to it, and we have

had to leave a road we have followed for thousands of years. The missteps and inconveniences this has caused have, I think, been many.[29]

Tanizaki's specific comments on film and the sound media have equal applicability to the African situation:

One need only compare American, French, and German films to see how greatly nuances of shading and colouration can vary in motion pictures . . . If this is true even when identical equipment, chemicals, and film are used, how much better our own photographic technology might have suited our complexion, our facial features, our climate, our land. And had we invented the phonograph and the radio, how much more faithfully they would reproduce the special character of our voices and our music.[30]

We must never forget that the technology of filmmaking introduced after independence was a borrowed technology and that the prestige of existing Western applications of this technology could not fail to impress emergent African filmmakers.

The basic contradictions of the postcolonial situation – political independence within a colonial social structure, a bilingual adminstrative culture, the coexistence of the trappings of a modern state (a seat at the United Nations, a national flag and anthem, a national airline, and so on) with a life for the majority of the population unchanged since at least the nineteenth century – form the context for any aspect of postcolonial culture, including filmmaking. As part of the small but slowly expanding élite of relatively educated and upwardly mobile people, the African filmmakers we are considering here are totally caught up – in their lives and work – within the ambiguities of this process. Indeed with their bilingual culture, their university degrees (often at postgraduate or doctoral level) and their foreign technical training, they are among the brightest members of this élite.

The two areas north and south of the Sahara were colonised in quite different ways. French West and French Equatorial Africa were territorial groupings administered as colonies, Togo and Cameroon were mandates administered on behalf of the League of Nations (and subsequently trusteeships under the United Nations), Tunisia and Morocco were French protectorates (the latter with Tangier as 'an international zone'), while Algeria after 1881 was technically part of metropolitan France (comprising three 'départements' electing representatives to the French parliament). It is a reflection of this colonial situation that Maghrebian and Sub-Saharan filmmakers are often referred to as belonging to a francophone African cinema (as opposed to an anglophone or a lusophone one). Yet in their films they use almost exclusively local or national languages: Moré for Gaston Kabore and Idrissa Ouadraogo

from Burkina Faso, Bambara for Cheick Oumar Sissoko from Mali, colloquial Arabic for the Maghrebian filmmakers, and even Tamzight (the Berber
language) for films set in the High Atlas mountains made by Algerian directors in the mid-1990s, when use of this language finally became legal in
Algeria. Even after independence, French influence has remained strong
throughout the areas north and south of the Sahara and, as Denise Brahimi
notes, the term 'francophone' is useful to denote countries where French continues to be used as both a written and a cultural language and where extensive literatures in French – poetry, novels and drama – continue to thrive.
Brahimi's definition is the one that will be used here: 'Concretely, the so-called
francophone countries are those whose cultural orientation, comprising
several sorts of exchange, is much more towards France than towards the
anglophone countries'.[31]

The reasons for the persistence of French-language literatures are complex.
Jacqueline Kaye notes, in the introduction to a recent collection of new
writing from North Africa translated from both French and Arabic, that bi-
or multilingualism can be a fruitful context for a writer's creativity: 'Writers
and speakers in these countries exist in a constant linguistic flux . . . creating
an everyday awareness of the historicity of language'.[32] As Kaye also points
out, French-educated Berber writers, such as Driss Chraïbi in Morocco
and Mouloud Feraoun in Algeria, 'may have had other than purely pragmatic
reasons for preferring French over Arabic', since French was 'the first
"choice" language for those who wished to disassociate themselves from the
postcolonial ruling classes'.[33] Language use always carries complex implications. As Cruise O'Brien has noted, a Senegalese individual 'in choosing to
speak Wolof most of the time, principally in town, seems in the long run to
be making an ethnic and even a national choice', but this may well be a strategy of avoiding confrontation, 'skulking across a no man's land of identity',
in a state dominated by Wolof speakers.[34] Elsewhere, in Cameroon for
example, the multiplicity of local languages has made the use of the French
language an inevitability for novelists, and Mongo Beti has given a strong
defence of such a stance:

> The totally free creation of French-language works by Africans is the ideal
> means of imposing their imagination, their genius, their sensibility, and
> the natural tendencies of their pronunciation on a language which would
> otherwise remain a foreign dialect, a mere instrument to keep them in
> their place, a new pretext for their secular servitude.[35]

While Cameroonian filmmakers have been similarly compelled to use French dialogue in their work, the use of their local or national languages has at least saved
most African filmmakers from what is, so often, an ambiguous compromise.[36]

ISLAM

In addition to the common heritage of French colonization, another unifying factor is the shared influence of Islam. Roland Oliver points out that, when looked at from the traditional standpoint of both European and Middle Eastern history, 'the part of Africa to the north of the central Sahara is not really African at all. Egypt and the Mahrib, conquered in the seventh and eighth centuries and fully Islamised by the tenth, belong almost to the Islamic heartland. They are the Muslim "west" ' (this is the meaning of the Arab term 'Maghreb'). Yet seen from the Islamic south, from countries where 'Islam has been established for six to eight centuries, and where the main direction of trade, travel, forced migration and cultural influence has been northwards across the desert', the perspective is very different: 'It is the Islamic factor in all its historical depth that makes North African countries inescapably a part of Africa, whatever other affiliations may be claimed for them.[37] The anthropologist Jacques Maquet also argues that the division of Africa into two cultural areas, one north and one south of the Sahara, is arbitrary: 'The great desert, though in some respects a barrier, has also been a communication route, witness the map of caravan trails linking the Mediterranean coast to Niger and Chad'.[38] In a similar way, 'Islam, a religion with scriptures, is not confined to North Africa but extends widely south of the Sahara from coast to coast'.[39]

David Robinson, who notes that 50 per cent of all Africans are Muslims (making up a quarter of the world's total), sees two processes at work over the past 1,400 years: the islamisation of Africa and the africanisation of Islam.[40] One of the major paths by which Islam spread into Sub-Saharan Africa was along the East African coast – what Robinson calls the 'Swahili gateway'. The other was via the various trade routes through the Sahara desert, mainly controlled by Berber tribesmen who acted as traders and guides for camel caravans. Some of these Berbers were welcomed by non-Muslim rulers 'to reinforce the wealth and strength of their dominions'.[41] Others, such as the Almoravids, adopted a more militant stance and imposed Islam by military conquest (as Mohamed's early Bedouin followers had done). But in spreading south of the Sahara, Islam was appropriated or articulated in a variety of societies which 'created "Muslim" space or made Islam their own'.[42] As David Robinson further notes, 'Muslims in different parts of Africa were eager to express their faith in concrete terms, what academics often call visual culture'.[43] Today's filmmakers – caught between their French education and their Islamic heritage – offer an ambiguous, but totally contemporary – African visual culture.

All the states considered here have either Muslim majorities or significant Muslim minorities and, as Richard W. Hull observes, 'the independence period has been characterised by the accelerating growth in Islam. It has been estimated that for every one convert to Christianity, there are nine converts to

Islam'.[44] Cruise O'Brien makes further clear that the interaction between contemporary Islam and the inherited structures of French colonial rule has been extremely complex. While developing its own institutional forms, Islam has 'helped to give substance to institutions of Western importation, in the institutions of the colonial and of the postcolonial state'.[45] As a result, we need to see the outcome as 'less a clash of civilisations, pitting Islam against the West or the rest, than a negotiation of civilisations, Islam coming to the rescue of the Western institutional legacy in Africa'.[46]

There is a distinction too to be made between those African Muslims who, while accepting Arabic as the sacred language of the Koran, continue to use in their everyday lives one of the multitude of indigenous languages of Sub-Saharan Africa, and those – such as the bulk of the population of the Maghreb – who have become arabised. Yet the split between the language of family and the language of external communication typical south of the Sahara does find a parallel in the linguistic situation in the Arabic-speaking countries of the Maghreb. If anything, the situation there is even more complex since the term 'Arabic' is used to describe three different forms of the same language: 'classical Arabic, which is the language of the Koran, the holy book of Islam; colloquial, or spoken, Arabic, as used in the daily lives of the people of the Arab countries; and modern standard Arabic, sometimes also called modern literary Arabic'.[47]

The Koran, written around AD 650, has been the key unifying factor in the Islamic world. Modern standard Arabic also serves to bring Arabs together, since it is the form in which most newspapers, magazines and books are written. It is also, in its spoken version, the language of radio and television throughout the Arab world, with the result that 'every Arab who is literate reads modern standard Arabic' and 'nearly every Arab, even if illiterate, will understand the spoken version of modern standard Arabic to some extent'.[48] But spoken colloquial Arabic, which is inevitably used in films depicting ordinary people's everyday lives, is very different in each Arab country. This creates considerable difficulties of inter-Arab communication and exchange particularly for the Maghreb 'where the influence of the Berber languages and French has rendered the contemporary colloquial almost incomprehensible to Eastern Arabs'.[49] As a result, very few Maghrebian films receive wide distribution in the Arab world. The linguistic, as well as political, difficulties faced by the Organisation of African Unity, founded in 1963, have been paralleled by those of the Pan-African Federation of filmmakers (Fédération Panafricaine des Cinéastes, or FEPACI), set up in 1970 and aligned to it.

The importance of Islam in African literature is explored in *The Marabout and the Muse*, in which the editor, Kenneth W. Harrow, deals with a wide range of issues: developments in key geographical areas such as Nigeria and the Maghreb, the novels of internationally known European-language novelists such as the

Somalian Nuruddin Farah, the Moroccan Driss Chraïbi and the Algerian Assia Djebar, and the work of the host of lesser-known writers working in a variety of forms in African languages. As Harrow observes, the volume bears witness to 'Islam's pluralist heritage' in such a way that 'we see emerging a view of Islam that sets pluralism against mono-culturalism, and that locates these opposing poles at the heart of Islam itself'.[50] Widely differing attitudes to Islam – and indeed to Christianity and traditional beliefs – are to be found in post-independence African films. Early Sub-Saharan filmmakers, led by the Marxist Ousmane Sembene, were generally hostile to what were seen as tyrannical abuses of Islam, while in the north, as the Tunisian director Mahmoud Ben Mahmoud has noted, 'virtually all well-heeled intellectuals have no roots in Muslim culture'.[51] But because of the filmmakers' concern with the everyday realities of life in a Muslim culture, Islam has been a constant factor in films north and south of the Sahara.

A WORLD OF CONTRADICTIONS

The co-existence of the diverse influences of France and Islam points to a fundamental factor about African life and culture: to be an African is to live in seemingly contradictory worlds. Jacques Maquet looks at the whole history of Africa, from prehistoric times to the industrial era, in terms of six successive 'civilisations', and he points to the continued existence of all six in contemporary Africa. But they now exist in very modified forms. Huntsmen now use money 'to buy shirts and soap', cultivators' children 'learn to read in rural schools', hereditary chiefs 'must account for their administration to the Ministry of the Interior', herdsmen 'make cheese and butter in collective dairies', cotton is woven, leather is cut, wood is worked, 'but in textile factories, shoe factories and carpenters' shops'.[52]

A second example of the co-existence of seeming opposites is the rural – urban divide. Oliver points out that in 1998 over half of the African population still lived mainly from the land and that 'of these the majority, and of women the *large* majority, still followed a pattern of life not very different from that of their pre-colonial ancestors'.[53] In rural areas, the division of labour remained that of a typical agrarian society over the centuries, 'whereby the men were responsible for clearing, building, herding, hunting and defence, whereas women hoed, planted, harvested, cooked, carried water and went to market'.[54] But, at the same time, the period since independence has seen an enormous growth in urbanisation, with its totally different demands on men and women, and on their relationships. For Muslims, with their distinctive concepts of space and separation between the sexes, life in cramped modern urban accommodation presents particular problems. All these issues find expression in contemporary African cinema, both as debates to be pursued thematically in a film and as shaping factors in film narrative. The depiction of time, for example, is very distinctive in those African films which respond creatively to the lived, every-day fact that modernity and tradition are not successive temporal states, but co-existing and inter-related contemporary situations.

Urban growth which was already underway in the Maghreb under French colonisation, when the coastal towns became ever more important centres for international trade, has continued unabated since independence. Thus Casablanca, a small medina of 20,000 inhabitants at the beginning of the French protectorate in 1912, had grown to a city of over 2.8 million by 1994, and was closely followed by Algiers (2.4 million), Tunis (2 million) and Rabat (1.2 million).[55] Similar growth has occurred south of the Sahara. During the colonial era, as Oliver points out, a typical capital had just 50,000 inhabitants, and probably half of these were domestic servants.[56] But since independence the rate of urbanisation has been staggering. The population of Sub-Saharan Africa tripled in the latter half of the twentieth century, but the numbers living in towns increased ninefold. While in 1940, scarcely 10 per cent of Africans were town dwellers,[57] now over half the population of the Maghreb lives in towns,[58] and that figure is expected to be reached in the rest of Africa by 2010.[59] African cinema tends on the whole to be a cinema of urban problems, and when rural issues are discussed, it is usually in relation to the lure and influence of city life. But urban existence itself is not usually depicted as exclusively modern, but rather as deeply impregnated with traditional values brought in from the coun-tryside by the floods of new migrants. Within the towns there is that juxtapo-sition of opposites, dating from the colonial period and well characterised by Frantz Fanon in *The Wretched of the Earth*: 'This world divided into com-partments, this world cut into two is inhabited by two different species. The originality of the colonial context is that economic reality, inequality and the immense difference of ways of life never come to mask the human realities'.[60] In terms of urban life, this inequality is clearly visible:

> The zone where the natives live is not complementary to the zone inhab-ited by the settlers . . . The settler's town is a well-fed town, an easy-going town; its belly is always full of good things. The settler's town is a town of white people, of foreigners . . . The native town is a crouching village, starved of bread, of meat, of shoes, of coal, of light. The native town is a crouching village, a town on its knees, a town wallowing in the mire. It is a town of niggers and dirty arabs.[61]

With independence most of the settlers have vanished, but the social inequal-ities remain, with the former white settlements now inhabited by the new native ruling elite. This contrast – together with its implications – forms the subject matter for the short film by Ousmane Sembene with which Sub-Saharan African cinema can arguably be said to begin: *Borom Sarret* (1963).

The contrast in two modes of life within the same town is most evident in the Maghreb, which had a higher degree of urbanisation before colonisation and where the traditional Arab medinas, largely unchanged since the Middle Ages, still exist, though now surrounded by modern urban settlements. To enter the medina is to go back in time, to a world with a labyrinth of streets and cul-de-sacs too narrow for modern transport, anonymous shop fronts and windowless house exteriors, and with the souks (or markets) arranged in hierarchical order in relation to the mosque, which forms the central feature of any medina. The medina is a timeless world with none of the marks of modernity: no cars, no telephone kiosks, no modern street furniture, no lighted shop windows, no post offices or banks. The Moroccan director Mohamed Abderrahmane Tazi makes witty use of this disparity in his comedy *Looking for My Wife's Husband/A la recherche du mari de ma femme*, where the medina interiors are furnished as they would have been in the 1970s, while the wider urban scenes show life as it was when the film was shot (in 1993). The medina features in much Maghrebian cinema as a focal point of contemporary contradiction or the locus of nostalgia for lost or threatened values.

African societies have coped surprisingly well with the rural exodus and with these enormous changes and contradictions. Taking perhaps an unduly optimistic view, Oliver argues that urban migration 'was not seen as flight, but as a life-enhancing progression',[62] undertaken initially by young men in search of a better life. What is certainly true is that the social gaps between town and countryside, which might be expected to have opened up, have not occurred. When settled in the town, the young men did not cut off their links with their home villages, 'they returned for holidays, to help with the harvest, to woo their brides and, at last, to retire. They sent money to their rural relatives, and they provided temporary accommodation in town for those seeking to follow their example'.[63] The journey – from countryside to the big city or from urban sophistication to the purifying atmosphere of traditional life – is a key motif in African cinema.

Perhaps the ability of Africans to cope with such a dual existence stems from the fact that, long before the advent of the colonisers, Africans were accustomed to plural identities in a form of social organisation for which the Western term 'tribe' (often pejoratively used) is a gross oversimplification. The notion of the 'tribe' is just one example of the widespread colonial practice of 'the invention of tradition in colonial Africa', so excellently chronicled by Terence Ranger. Traditional societies 'had certainly valued custom and continuity, but custom was loosely defined and infinitely flexible. Custom helped to maintain a sense of identity, but it also allowed for an adaptation so spontaneous and natural that it was often unperceived'.[64] Recent studies of nineteenth-century pre-colonial Africa have emphasised that far from there being a single 'tribal' identity, most Africans moved in and out of multiple identities, defining themselves at one moment as subject to this chief, at another as a member of that cult, at another moment as a part of that clan, and at yet another moment as an initiate of that professional guild.[65]

This same situation persists in postcolonial society which, Achille Mbembe notes, 'is made not of one coherent "public space", nor is it determined by any single organising principle'.[66] Instead we find 'a plurality of "spheres" and areas, each having its own separate logic yet nonetheless liable to be entangled with other logics when operating in certain specific contexts'.[67] As a result, the individual (what Mbembe terms 'the postcolonial "subject"') 'mobilises not just a single "identity", but several fluid identities which, by their very nature, must be constantly "revised" in order to achieve maximum instrumentality and efficacity as and when required'.[68]

In his study of Islamic society, *The Multiple Identities of the Middle East*, Bernard Lewis notes that 'the primary identities are those acquired at birth': by blood (family, clan, tribe), by place (village, neighbourhood, district, quarter, province or city) and by religion.[69] In this connection it is worth noting two observations made by Jolayemi Solanke about contemporary Africa as a whole. For Solanke, 'the key concept in understanding African social organisation is that of the corporate group. Every individual belongs to several overlapping groups which provide the frame of reference for his daily life'.[70] This has important implications for the way in which Africans see themselves as individuals. Social control within African society is based on the individual as part of a corporate group: 'The perception of belonging to a group – whether family, age-grade, village, clan or nation – is almost always paramount of a sense of individuality. One acts as a member of a group and is responsible to that group'.[71]

For those Africans who live in Islamic societies, the relationship between the individual and the collectivity is even more complex and in many ways yet further removed from that which is to be found in hierarchically organised ('pyramidal') Western societies. Fuad I. Khuri points out that in Arab ideology, 'reality is perceived as a series of non-pyramidal structures, a matrix composed of discrete units inherently equal in value'.[72] Three 'principles of action and organisation' follow from a non-pyramidal image of reality, namely, the vulnerability of isolation, the need to seek protection in groups, and the importance of tactics, rather than status.[73] The individual has, therefore, a very distinctive role in Arab culture: 'caught between "the fear of being alone", on the one hand, and the drive to be "first among equals", an imam or emir, on the other'.[74] Success in social terms, becoming first among equals, means building a group around yourself, so that you will never be left alone. The only viable alternative for the individual unable to do this is to join the group for which kinship makes him eligible, because 'the isolated are vulnerable'.[75] In the Arab world, Khuri argues, 'the strategy is to act in groups'.[76]

There are clear differences in emphasis between Khuri's arguments about acquiring power and those of Solanke about achieving social inclusion. But what is crucial is that Africans – whether Muslims or not – do not define themselves as notionally free individuals responsible ultimately only to themselves, which is the way that Westerners have operated for centuries. This is reflected in the narrative structures and the shaping of protagonists of African cinema, as it is in much African literature. As Tunisian film theorist Tahar Cheriaa has noted, in African films 'the individual is always pushed into the background, and the hero – African films are rich in characters in the classic sense – never occupies the foreground. The principal character in African films is always the group, the collectivity, and that is the essential thing'.[77]

NOTES

1. Émile Mworoha and Bernard Nantet, 'Des raisons d'espérer', in Rémy Bazenguissa and Bernard Nantet (eds), *L'Afrique: Mythes et réalités d'un continent* (Paris: Le Cherche Midi Éditeur, 1995), p. 193.
2. Shatto Arthur Gakwandi, *The Novel and Contemporary Experience in Africa* (London, Lusaka, Ibadan and Nairobi: Heinemann, 1977), p. 1.
3. Roland Oliver, *The African Experience* (London: Weidenfeld & Nicolson, 1999), p. 259.
4. Ibid.
5. Richard W. Hull, *Modern Africa: Change and Continuity* (Englewood Cliffs, NJ: Prentice-Hall, 1980), p. 243.
6. Ibid., p. 189.
7. Benedict Anderson, *Imagined Communities: Reflections on the Origin and Spread of Nationalism* (London and New York: Verso, 1991, revised edition), pp. 6–7.
8. Ibid., p. 7.
9. Donal B. Cruise O'Brien and Richard Rathbone, 'Introduction', in Donal B. Cruise O'Brien, John Dunn and Richard Rathbone (eds), *Contemporary West African States* (Cambridge: Cambridge University Press, 1989), p. 2.
10. Basil Davidson, *The Search for Africa* (London: James Currey, 1994), p. 254.
11. Ibid.
12. Frantz Fanon, *The Wretched of the Earth* (Harmondsworth: Penguin Books, 1967), pp. 166–99.
13. I have discussed 'national culture' in Roy Armes, *Third World Filmmaking and the West* (Berkeley: University of California Press, 1987), pp. 24–8.
14. Oliver, *The African Experience*, p. 277.
15. Ibid.
16. Ibid., p. 278.
17. Ibid.
18. Hull, *Modern Africa*, p. 192.
19. Oliver, *The African Experience*, p. 302.
20. Cited in John Reader, *Africa: A Biography of the Continent* (Harmondsworth: Penguin Books, 1998), p. 627.
21. Reader, *Africa*, p. 627.
22. Ibid.

23. Hull, *Modern Africa*, p. 184.
24. Donal B. Cruise O'Brien, *Symbolic Confrontations: Muslims Imagining the State in Africa* (London: Hurst & Co., 2003), pp. 142–3.
25. Albert Memmi, *The Colonizer and the Colonized* (London: Souvenir Press, 1974), p. 106.
26. Ibid., pp. 104–5.
27. Ibid., p. 107.
28. Walter Rodney, *How Europe Underdeveloped Africa* (London: Bogle-L'Ouverture, 1972), p. 116.
29. Junichiro Tanizaki, *In Praise of Shadows* (London: Vintage, 2001), p. 16.
30. Ibid., pp. 16–7.
31. Denise Brahimi, *Cinémas d'Afrique francophone et du Maghreb* (Paris: Nathan, 1997), p. 7.
32. Jacqueline Kaye, *Maghreb: New Writing from North Africa* (York: Talus Editions, 1992), p. 5.
33. Ibid., p. 6.
34. Cruise O'Brien, *Symbolic Confrontations*, p. 15.
35. Mongo Beti, cited in Richard Bjornson, *The African Quest for Freedom and Identity: Cameroonian Writing and the National Experience* (Bloomington: Indiana University Press, 1994), p. 329.
36. Cf. Jacqueline Kaye and Abdelhamid Zoubir, *The Ambiguous Compromise: Language, Literature and Identity in Algeria and Morocco* (London and New York: Routledge, 1990).
37. Oliver, *The African Experience*, p. 305.
38. Jacques Maquet, *Civilisations of Black Africa* (New York: Oxford University Press, 1972), p. 17.
39. Ibid.
40. David Robinson, *Muslim Societies in African History* (Cambridge: Cambridge University Press, 2004), p. 27.
41. Ibid., p. 39.
42. Ibid., p. 42.
43. Ibid.
44. Hull, *Modern Africa*, p. 233.
45. Cruise O'Brien, *Symbolic Confrontations*, p. 178.
46. Ibid.
47. Nicholas Awde and Putros Samano, *The Arabic Language* (London: Saqi Books, 1986), p. 14.
48. Ibid.
49. Viola Shafik, *Arab Cinema* (Cairo: The University of Cairo Press, 1998), p. 83.
50. Kenneth W. Harrow (ed.), *The Marabout and the Muse: New Approaches to Islam in African Fiction* (Portsmouth, NH and London: Heinemann and James Curry, 1996), p. xxiii.
51. Mahmoud Ben Mahmoud, cited in Michel Amarger, M'Bissine Diop and Catherine Ruelle, 'Islam, croyances et négritude dans les cinémas d'Afrique', Paris: *Africultures* 47 (2002), p. 11.
52. Maquet, *Civilisations*, p. 171.
53. Oliver, *The African Experience*, p. 304.
54. Ibid., p. 303.
55. Jean François Troin, *Maghreb Moyen-Orient: Mutations* (Paris: Sedes, 1995), p. 217.
56. Oliver, *The African Experience*, p. 283.
57. Roland Pourtier, *Villes Africaines* (Paris: La Documentation Française, 1999), p. 1.

58. Troin, *Maghreb-Moyen Orient*, p. 218.
59. Oliver, *The African Experience*, p. 304.
60. Fanon, *The Wretched of the Earth*, p. 30.
61. Ibid.
62. Oliver, *The African Experience*, p. 283.
63. Ibid.
64. Eric Hobsbawm and Terence Ranger (eds), *The Invention of Tradition* (Cambridge: Cambridge University Press, 1983), p. 247.
65. Ibid., p. 248.
66. Achille Mbembe, cited in Richard Werbner and Terence Ranger (eds), *Postcolonial Identities in Africa* (London: Zed Books, 1996), p. 1.
67. Ibid.
68. Ibid.
69. Bernard Lewis, *The Multiple Identities of the Middle East* (London: Weidenfeld and Nicolson, 1998), p. 4.
70. Jolayemi Solanke, 'Traditional Society and Political Institutions', in Richard Olaniyan (ed.), *African History and Culture* (Lagos: Longman, 1982), p. 27.
71. Ibid., p. 28.
72. Fuad I. Khuri, *Tents and Pyramids: Games and Ideology in Arab Culture from Backgammon to Autocratic Rule* (London: Saqi Books, 1990), p. 11.
73. Ibid., p. 11.
74. Ibid., p. 14.
75. Ibid., p. 13.
76. Ibid., p. 11.
77. Tahar Cheriaa, 'Le Groupe et le héros', in CESCA, *Camera nigra: Le Discours du film africain* (Brussels: OCIC, 1984), p. 109.

PART I

CONTEXT

If we are to address questions of the history and culture of nationhood, the particular form taken by the intersection of contemporary history, culture and politics which manifestly is a crucial question for the recent experiences of most of the world's population, we ought similarly to consider not what 'identity' is . . . but how actual, specific, socially and historically located people, and groups of people, themselves articulate their self-conceptions, their historical experience and their place in society.

James McDougal[1]

PART I

CONTEXT

2. BEGINNINGS

North Africa has given us better wines than we could have imagined. I see no reason why she should not, tomorrow, give us the best French films.[2]

French actor Harry Baur, 1937

COLONIAL CINEMA

The cinema reached Africa at much the same time as it spread across Europe and the United States. There were film shows in Cairo and Alexandria as early as 1896, in Tunis and Fez in 1897, Dakar in 1900 and Lagos in 1903. The initial impulse behind this worldwide spread was purely commercial: the desire to exploit to the full the commercial potential of what its inventors, like the Lumière Brothers, feared might be just a passing novelty. But as film narrative developed in length and complexity, the export of film took on a new significance. As Ferid Boughedir has observed: 'Cinema reached Africa with colonialism. Its principal role was to supply a cultural and ideological justification for political domination and economic exploitation'.[3] In many ways cinema succeeded in this role: 'A native worker performs better when he believes that the representatives of colonial power are his betters by race, and that his own civilisation is inferior to that of the whites'.[4]

Little one-minute films were also shot in Africa at the turn of the century, as the Lumière operators made a habit of shooting local 'views' (a comparatively simple procedure since Lumière's cinematograph was both camera and projector combined).The aim was both to increase the attractiveness of the

Lumières' local screenings and to provide films for subsequent worldwide distribution. The Lumière catalogue of 1905 contains over fifty such views shot in North Africa. One of Lumière's leading operators, whose career is of particular interest, is Alexandre Promio (1868–1926). He shot little scenes in Algiers and Tlemcen as early as 1896, and worked in Cairo and elsewhere in Egypt in 1897, returning to North Africa once more in 1903. Promio, who discovered the East on his first trip to Algeria, remained fascinated by it, but, as Jean-Claude Seguin notes, his gaze 'may be subtle, but it is nonetheless obviously orientalist'.[5] Promio went on in 1912 to work for the film and photographic service of the French government in Algiers, where he stayed for twelve years. Seguin sees a continuity in his thirty-year career, which can serve as an exemplar for the development and use of cinema in colonial Africa as a whole in the early years of the twentieth century. Working for the Lumière company for ten years, Promio 'had explored the planet to reveal its comical, surprising or simply exotic aspects'. For the French administration he had subsequently 'journeyed across the colony, travelling in the service of the vast propaganda project inspired by the French authorities'.[6]

The arrival in Tunisia in 1919 of the director Luitz-Morat – a former stage partner of Sarah Bernhardt in *La Dame aux camélias* and of Réjane in *Madame Sans-gêne* – to shoot scenes for his feature film *The Five Cursed Gentlemen/Les Cinq gentlemen maudits*, [7] marked a new stage in the exploitation of the African colonies, namely their use as locations for foreign feature films. Of the handful of films set in West Africa, most – such as Léon Poirier's *Brazza or The Epic of the Congo/Brazza ou l'épopée du Congo* (1939) and Jacques de Baroncelli's *The Man of the Niger/L'Homme du Niger* (1939) – dealt with the French colonial experience in West Africa seen through the eyes of a heroic European protagonist. The tone of the latter film – and its ideological message – is clear from a 1940s French review:

> Thus, as you see, French cinema during recent years has done its utmost to show the true face of Africa and the true face too of France in the African domain. Through this magic lantern, the world has been able to perceive that France has accomplished the remarkable feat of making itself loved like a mother in its colonies, because everywhere and always it has shown itself to be just and humane.[8]

The overwhelming bulk of the colonial films were, however, set in North Africa. Even the Pierre Loti novel *The Novel of a Colonial Soldier/Roman d'un spahi*, which is set in Senegal, was filmed in 1935 by Michel Bernheim with the location changed to Southern Morocco. A mythical North Africa became the location for a succession of notable films. As David Henry Slavin observes, 'colonial films are melodramas, simple stories of individual lives and loves. But they are suffused with racial and gender privilege'.[9] In comparison with other mainstream European and Hollywood films, they also contain a very high proportion of tales of defeat. The flavour of this cinema is excellently captured by Dina Sherzer. The colonies are presented as 'territories waiting for European initiatives, virgin land where the White man with helmet and boots regenerated himself or was destroyed by alcoholism, malaria, or native women'. The films 'displayed the heroism of French men, along with stereotypical images of desert, dunes and camels, and reinforced the idea that the Other is dangerous'. But what is most remarkable about this body of films is what they omitted: 'They did not present the colonial experience, did not attach importance to colonial issues, and were amazingly silent on what happened in reality'. In this way they 'contributed to the colonial spirit and temperament of conquest and to the construction of White identity and hegemony'.[10] Common to all such colonial melodramas is a single ideology, well defined, from a South African viewpoint, by Keyan Tomaselli five years before the advent of black rule:

> For Africa as a whole, cinema has always been a powerful weapon deployed by colonial nations to maintain their respective spheres of political and economic influence. History is distorted and a Western view of Africa continues to be transmitted back to the colonized. Apart from the obvious monetary returns for the production companies themselves, the values Western cinema imparts and the ideologies it legitimates are beneficial for western cultural, financial, and political hegemony.[11]

Pépé le Moko (1936) is the archetypal French colonial film, though very little of the film was actually shot in North Africa – the Casbah was reconstructed by designer Jacques Krauss at the Joinville studios in Paris. Made by Julien Duvivier, one of French cinema's most successful technicians who was then at the height of his powers, the film tells of the doomed love of the Parisian jewel thief Pépé le Moko (played by Jean Gabin), who has taken refuge in the casbah, and Gaby (Mireille Balin), a high-class prostitute (*poule de luxe*), who is visiting Algiers with her rich champagne-merchant lover. Though Pépé is aware that he will be arrested if he leaves the Casbah, he nonetheless tries to accompany Gaby when she leaves. Captured and handcuffed, he stabs himself on the dockside, as the unsuspecting Gaby sails away.

Like most colonial films, this is a purely European drama, to which the inhabitants of Algiers (and to a considerable extent the setting itself) are irrelevant. What is very striking from a present-day standpoint is the handling of the setting and the Arab characters. When the local French police chief, Slimane, describes the Casbah, he mentions nine national or racial types as making up the Casbah's 40,000 inhabitants, but the word 'Arab' does not occur. There are, as most commentators on the film have noted, no Arabs in the Casbah! Slimane is stereotyped as a wily and treacherous oriental, detested by his French superiors, and Pépé's girlfriend Inès (French actress Line Noro) is depicted not as an Arab, but as a gypsy, complete with dark make-up, black frizzy hair and large earrings. As the Algerian critic Abdelghani Megherbi notes, 'Duvivier did not think it worthwhile to give even the slightest role to Algerians. The latter, as was the custom, formed an integral part of the decor on which colonial cinema fed so abundantly'.[12] The sole Arab name in the credits is that of Mohamed Iguerbouchen, who supplied the 'oriental' music to supplement Vincent Scotto's effective but fundamentally Western score.

TUNISIA

The only pioneer filmmaker to work independently in either the Maghreb or West Africa under colonialism was the Tunisian Albert Samama Chikly (1872–1934), a remarkable figure in every respect to be a pioneer of Arab and African cinema. For one thing Chikly was a Jew, son of the Bey of Tunis's banker, who had acquired French citizenship. Chikly's Italian wife and his only child, his daughter Haydée, both converted to Islam, and there can be no doubt about his personal sense of his Tunisian identity. But after running away to sea as a teenager, Chikly remained fascinated with the West and its technology. He was one of the first Tunisians to own a bicycle, which he used to explore the Tunisian South. He then set up the first X-ray laboratory in Tunis and imported radio equipment within a few months of Marconi's invention becoming known and while it was still an experimental technology. As an active photographer, he was inevitably fascinated by the Lumières' invention of the cinematograph in 1895, and his daughter Haydée claims he organised a first film show in Tunis in 1896. Certainly, he and a fellow photographer, Soler, organised public ten-minute screenings for a week or so in 1897, to great acclaim according to his nephew Raoul Darmon: 'Every showing was greeted with acclamation by the audience and the enthusiasm was such that when the programme finished, half the audience regularly refused to leave and paid for a second screening'.[13]

Ever the enthusiast, Chikly explored underwater photography in a submarine designed by the vicar of Carthage, the abbé Raoul, and aerial photography in collaboration with the aeronaut Valère Lecomte. He also attached his camera to both a microscope and a telescope. Continuing to use both his still and movie cameras, Chikly became a reporter, recording local issues for Paris newspapers and the Gaumont newsreels, and then embarking on a filmic documentation of all aspects of Tunisia. As Guillemette Mansour notes, his photographs are not orientalist compositions, but works that display 'an acute sense for framing an image and a remarkable mastery of light'.[14] His first experience as war reporter came when he filmed and reported on the Italian invasion of Libya in 1911, from the Turkish side. When the First World War began, Chikly became one of the dozen cameramen employed by the French Army film service (along with Abel Gance – future creator of *Napoléon* – and Louis Feuillade – author-to-be of the *Fantômas* and *Judex* series), filming at the front at Verdun in 1916. His services, in a war in which 10,000 Tunisian volunteers and conscripts died in the trenches, earned him the Military Medal.

The extensive use of North African locations by French filmmakers began soon after the end of the First World War, and Chikly served as cameramen for one of these films, *Tales of the Arabian Nights/Les Contes des mille et une nuits* (1922) directed by the Russian émigré Victor Tourjansky. The same year Chikly directed his own first fictional film, *Zohra*, scripted by and starring his daughter Haydée. This short film tells the story of a young French woman shipwrecked on the coast of Tunisia and rescued by Bedouin tribesmen, with whom she lives for a while. Captured by bandits while travelling in a caravan taking her to a French settlement, she is again rescued, this time by a dashing French aviator, and restored to her parents. This simple tale reflects two of Chikly's passions, Bedouin life and aviation, and Haydée's performance earned her a part in Rex Ingram's *The Arab* (1924), which starred Ramon Navarro.

Chikly's second, feature-length, film, *The Girl from Carthage/La Fille de Carthage/Aïn El-Ghazel* (1924), was also scripted by Haydée who again took the leading role and also edited the film. If *Zohra* was, as Guillemette Mansour observes, 'a semi-documentary',[15] *The Girl from Carthage* is the full fictional story of a young woman, under pressure to marry her father's choice of husband (a rich and brutal landowner), who runs away to the desert and is followed by the gentle young teacher she loves. When he is killed by their pursuers, she stabs herself and falls dead across his body. Chikly's personal friend, the Bey of Tunis, provided extras, allowed the use of one of his palaces, and even visited the shooting on several occasions. The film's theme of forced marriage and the use of a female protagonist (together with the particularly important role in the production played by Haydée Chikly) make *The Girl from Carthage* a fascinating precursor of the kind of Tunisian cinema which would come into being over forty years later.

Chikly refused to allow his daughter Haydée (later Haydée Tamzali) to take up Rex Ingram's invitation to Hollywood (she was a teenager, taking her baccalaureate at the time), so her film career effectively ended with *The Girl from Carthage*, though she did appear, in old age, in Mahmoud Ben Mahmoud's documentary about her father and in Ferid Boughedir's feature film *One Summer in La Goulette/Un été à La Goulette*. Since large portions of both his films are preserved, Chikly's own place in film history – anticipating the first Egyptian-made feature by three years – is assured. But, like so many film pioneers, he was to die in poverty, succumbing in 1934 to lung cancer contracted at the front in a gas attack during the First World War and aggravated by his smoking.[16]

SOUTH AFRICA

At the time of independence in the Maghreb and French colonial Africa – when the new African cinemas were about to come into being – there were only two film industries in Africa. One of these – that located in South Africa – could obviously be of no relevance, despite the state subsidy scheme established in 1956 and the existence of 1,300 or so feature films produced there between 1910 and 1996,[17] since it was a white cinema constructed for a white audience. Writing in 1989, Keyan Tomaselli notes the strategic ideological importance of South African cinema: 'Repression has to be legitimised in some way, and cinema has historically played an important role in presenting apartheid as a natural way of life'.[18] South African cinema during the apartheid era continued the traditional role of cinema in colonial societies. Though South Africa's filmmakers 'feel that their films lie outside politics, that they are merely entertainment', Tomaselli argues that the films in fact serve the state through 'their class position, their underlying social and cinematic assumptions', as well as 'their displacement of actual conditions by imaginary relations which delineate an apartheid view of the world'.[19]

In the one of the first comprehensive surveys of African filmmaking – Guy Hennebelle's *Les Cinémas africains en 1972* – the white Zimbabwean (at that time, before independence, Rhodesian) filmmaker Michael Raeburn gave an interesting introduction to South African cinema, pointing out that these films are 'made by whites, for whites. The financing of this production is made possible by the extremely high standard of living of the white minority privileged by shameful racial laws'.[20] Raeburn characterises the 100 feature films shot since 1945 as 'just pale imitations of Anglo-American archetypes',[21] noting a striking resemblance to Western colonial cinema: 'in the white films, the nonwhites are only extras. If the script requires a non-white to talk to or touch a white, the role has to be played by a blacked-up white'.[22]

The one South African feature film to become an international success was *The Gods Must Be Crazy* (1980), made by one of South Africa's leading directors, Jamie (Jacobus Johannes) Uys. A former school teacher, Uys had been active as a film director for thirty years and was to be awarded South Africa's highest civil award, the Order of Merit, for services to the film industry, in 1983.[23] On the surface, the film – known in France as *Les Dieux sont tombés sur la tête* – is simply a very amusing comedy about a bushman, !Ky, who sets out to return an empty Coke bottle which he thinks is a gift from the gods. The other plot strand concerns a white scientist (whose speciality is elephant dung), who involves !Ky in his effort to help save a white school teacher who has been kidnapped – along with her class of black schoolchildren – by a black guerrilla leader. Though the film is seemingly innocuous, poking fun at blacks and whites alike, it is in fact, as the English documentary filmmaker Peter Davis demonstrates, 'impregnated with the spirit of apartheid'.[24] The film masquerades as a Botswanan production, but the 'Botswana' where the bushmen lead their idyllic life in no way resembles the real landlocked republic of the same name. Significantly, the film could not have been set in South Africa, since there the pass laws restricting the movement of blacks would have rendered its plot impossible. The commentary accompanying the opening travelogue is highly condescending, and the name of the black guerrilla villain, Sam Boca, has curious connotations, since the sambok is the leather whip regularly used by white South African police to disperse black demonstrations. The name also recalls that of Sam Nujoma, leader of the SWAPO liberation movement in neighbouring Namibia, and indeed the film has disturbing echoes of the actual political situation there, since the South African authorities had enlisted the bushmen in their fight against SWAPO.[25] Davis concludes that, whatever his intentions, Uys has created 'an imaginary country which the architects of apartheid would like us to believe in, a South Africa well-intentioned to all'.[26] If the plot is read metaphorically, it shows that 'the blacks are like children led astray by agitators coming from outside (the black liberation forces). But they are not the only ones under threat: the white race, personified by the heroine, is also threatened too'.[27]

   The Gods Must Be Crazy embodies a particular moment in African history. Three years later (though still nine years before the end of apartheid in 1994), the filmmaker John van Zyl could already look towards the emergence of a very different South African cinema, which would relate more closely to developments elsewhere in the continent, a cinema 'whose vigour and inspiration will have to come from the same roots as the vigour and inspiration of its theatre'. He recognises that 'the real industry of the future will be a predominantly black one, and will link itself to the energy of other Third World film industries'.[28] There were indeed interesting co-production links with West African filmmakers (Souleymane Cisse, Idrissa Ouedraogo and Jean-Pierre Bekolo) in the mid-1990s, and by the beginning of the new millennium, some steps at least had been taken to transform South African cinema itself.[29]

EGYPT

The second African film industry in existence at the time of independence in the Maghreb and Sub-Saharan Africa was that in Egypt, which also had a very different political and economic history from that of its neighbours. Notionally independent since 1922 – though with British dominance persisting from 1882 until the 1952 military coup against King Farouk – Egypt had a history of industrial development going back to the early part of the nineteenth century, when, as Tom Kemp points out, Mohamed Ali 'initiated a state programme, designed to strengthen the economy of his country, not unlike that of Peter the Great in Russia a century before'. For various reasons, not least the Anglo-Turkish Treaty of 1838 which insisted on the ending of state monopolies, Mohamed Ali's project failed and 'for the rest of the nineteenth century Egypt became a primary-exporting, predominantly agricultural country'. But with the attempts at industrialisation came – for the élite at least – a growing sense of national identity. Fresh attempts at modernisation were made in the twentieth century when 'some import-substitution industries were established', the trend being 'assisted by the two world wars and the slump in export prices during the 1930s'.[30]

This was the context in which Egyptian cinema came into being. Initially, developments were the work of isolated pioneers, many belonging to Cairo's thriving expatriate communities. As Kristina Bergmann puts it, 'at first financed by Lebanese and Greeks, shot by Italians, designed and acted by the French, films then became Egyptian'.[31] The key date was the founding of the Misr Studios in 1935, after which Egyptian cinema became a genuine film industry, capable of producing a dozen films in 1935 and building continuously so as to reach over forty a year by 1945. The vision and drive behind this development was that of Talaat Harb, director of Bank Misr, who envisaged a company 'capable of making Egyptian films with Egyptian subjects, Egyptian literature and Egyptian aesthetics, worthwhile films that can be shown in our own country and in the neighbouring countries of the East'.[32] Since Bank Misr was the leading Egyptian bank, the film industry was at the heart of the development of Egyptian capitalism. As Patrick Clawson has explained, 'Bank Misr was established precisely to foster local industry . . . Through such firms as one of the world's largest textile mills, printing presses, button factories, linen-spinning mills, Bank Misr dominated the entire Egyptian economy until its nationalisation in 1960.[33] The film industry itself was nationalised, to become the General Organisation of Egyptian Cinema, a year later.

In her foreword to a volume celebrating 100 years of Egyptian cinema, Magda Wassef notes the existence of 3,000 fictional feature films with which millions of Arabs could identify: 'several dozen unforgettable titles, some outstanding filmmakers and, above all, an impact that exceeds the aim fixed at the outset: "entertainment".'[34] Through its stars and singers, Egyptian cinema became 'an object of Arab desire and pride. Through it they feel reconciled with their identity, ridiculed and crushed by the destructive and often castrating colonial presence'.[35] Egypt's dominant genre, the melodrama, is worth considering briefly, not because of its direct influence on post-independence filmmakers elsewhere in Africa, which was virtually nil, but as a fascinating contrast to the European colonial film, and as another kind of baseline against which the particular approaches of the post-independence filmmakers north and south of the Sahara can be assessed. It is the form through which all future Arab filmmakers discovered cinema as children.

Three basic features of melodrama are common to both the Egyptian film and the European or Hollywood colonial feature. The first is the focus on emotional intensity and calamitous events to which, from an Egyptian perspective, Ali Abu Shadi draws attention. Plots are 'marked by the sudden movement between highly exaggerated situations in which coincidence plays a major role', and melo-dramatic style 'uses emotionalism in the writing and the directing and exploits any device to manipulate the feelings of the audience'.[36] The second element shared with the colonial film is the use of 'a succession of stereotypes and clichés', and characters whose progress and relationships are structured so as to meet the needs of accessible dramatic patterns.[37] The third shared feature is the manichean world, which Khémais Khayati sees as particularly characteristic of Egyptian cinema: 'There is good and evil. There is God and the Devil. Between them no reconciliation is possible. Values are total and never relative . . . Nothing usurps the absolute nature of God'.[38] There is immense comfort for the audiences – in the West as much as in the Arab world – in such a black-and-white world of total certainties. We know how people should behave and can appreciate when the accepted norms are violated. There is no ambiguity about how the world should be. The ambiguity for us comes from empathy with characters who transgress, but it is a comfortable ambiguity, because we know that they will, in the end, have to face up to the consequences of their actions.

The key difference between Egyptian melodrama and the colonial film, whether European or Hollywood, lies in the treatment of character. In Egyptian cinema, as Ali Abu Shadi demonstrates, the characters 'do not change or grow emotionally, and the lines between good and evil are clearly demarcated. There is a relative absence of human will, with fate determining the outcome of events'.[39] This view is supported by Abbas Fadhil Ibrahim in his analysis of three melodramas from the years 1959–60: 'Fatality, fate and chance make and undo the happiness and misfortune of the characters. Accidents, incidents and slips multiply, modifying the course of their lives'.[40] According to Khayati, in Arab-Muslim culture, 'the submission of the individual is complete and the alle-giance of the community to God is total. Every revolt against the community is a revolt against God. And every revolt against God is an assault on the immutable order of the world and, for this reason, merits punishment'.[41] This is, of course, the very opposite of the Western ideology underlying Hollywood and European films, colonial or not, where the key assumption about characters is that they are individuals, able to make choices as the basis for action. Whatever the pressures or dangers, these choices are ultimately freely made by the individual, and cannot be blamed on background, family upbringing, heredity, social or economic pressures, and certainly not on fate. In contrast Egyptian tradition-based drama is 'a drama of fatality and happy endings, a drama which does not know the anguish of free choice and which works in blocks and never by nuances'.[42]

The ideological differences between Egyptian and Hollywood melodrama result in a very different sense of temporality and plot structure. Sayed Saïd argues that in Egyptian melodramas 'the time measured by the calendar' is drowned out by 'everything which is linked to the past: lessons, meanings, values, traditions, ideas, illusions, even myths'.[43] In the Western film, by contrast, time moves swiftly forward and, in conventional Hollywood cinema at least, the final part of a film is a veritable rush towards closure. In contrast, 'the future is almost absent from Egyptian cinema and the exceptions can be counted on the fingers of one hand. As for an optimistic vision of the future, that is even rarer'.[44] This difference in temporality – Egyptian cinema locked immutably in the past, Western cinema looking relentlessly forward – is reflected in a very different notion of identity. In Egyptian cinema, as defined by Saïd, the national Self is 'implicitly defined by a whole series of urban and rural traditions under threat' while the Other 'is the source of all evil, the source of all threats'. According to Saïd, 'you cannot understand meanings in Egyptian cinema without locating the struggle with Western cultures and civilisations'. The struggle with the colonialist Other 'is not just one of the subjects dealt with by cinema. It is its principal background'.[45]

A perfect example of the Egyptian approach to melodrama is Henry Barakat's *The Sin/Al-haram*, produced by the General Organisation for Egyptian Cinema in 1965. *The Sin* is widely regarded as the prolific Cairo-born director's best work, and it figures in at least one list of the ten best Arab films of all time.[46] Adapted from a novel by Youssef Idriss, the film deals with the sufferings of migrant farm workers, whose lives are precarious, since they are hired only by the day at crucial seasons of the year and forced to work far from their homes. Though filmed on location and including many villagers in its cast, the film's stance is far from that of the Italian neorealists. The subject is softened and sentimentalised, the action is set safely back in 1950 (the Farouk era) and, in the central role, Faten Hamama gives a glittering star performance. What is fascinating is the way in which the film shapes its story of a woman who inadvertently kills her own newborn child, so that while its personal emotional impact is maintained, it is, at the same time, swallowed up, as it were, in the eternal, unchanging life of the peasantry. *The Sin* brings together all the key elements of Egyptian melodrama: a circular narrative structure using a long central flashback through which the past weighs down upon the present, a pattern of images and music that enhances the audience's emotional response, a protagonist who suffers but lacks any individual responsibility for what happens to her, an overall sense of unchallengeable fatality, and the portrayal of an unchanging traditional community which is barely touched by the ripple of personal tragedy.

ALGERIA

The final potential model of pre-independence filmmaking in Africa is to be found during the bitter Algerian war for independence (1954–62), when 16mm militant film was used as part of the liberation struggle. As the Algerian sociologist Mouny Berrah notes, 'from 1957–1962, Algerian cinema was a site of solidarity, exchange and expression between members of the Algerian *maquis* and French intellectuals who sympathised with the liberation movement'.[47] The catalyst for this was the French communist documentary filmmaker René Vautier (born 1928), who had been decorated with the *croix de guerre* at the age of sixteen for his resistance activities against the German occupiers in his native France. But in 1952 he had been imprisoned by the French government for violating the 1934 Laval law by filming without authorisation in Africa, where he had made the first French anti-colonialist film, *Africa 50/Afrique 50* (1950).[48] Vautier had already made an independent short (now lost), *One Nation, Algeria/Une nation, l'Algérie*, when he began filming with Algerian resistance fighters in 1957–8 under the auspices of the National Liberation Front (FLN) leader Abbane Ramdane. The result was the widely seen twenty-five- minute documentary *Algeria in Flames/Algérie en flammes* (1959), of which the technicians in East Germany, where it was edited, made 800 copies.[49] Unfortunately for the director, by the time the film was complete, Ramdane had been murdered in one of the internecine disputes which characterised the FLN, and Vautier himself was imprisoned by the Algerians, without trial and largely in solitary confinement, for twenty-five months.

The first film collective which Vautier set up in the Tebessa region in 1957, the Farid group, comprised a number of Algerians, including the future feature director Ahmed Rachedi. It aimed 'to show the methods used by the French administration and army to deal with the Algerian population'.[50] In 1958 the group was transferred to Tunis, then the base for the leaders of the Algerian liberation movement, where it became the film service of the Algerian Republican Provisional Government in exile (GPRA). The GPRA thought the role of film important enough for it to send another young filmmaker, Mohamed Lakhdar Hamina, to study film at FAMU in Prague in 1959. Vautier himself, who was wounded three times in his various frontier crossings into Algeria, set up a film school, whose pupils made two collective documentaries in 1957–8. But before the end of the hostilities, four of the five students had been killed.

A number of documentaries were made within the context of the liberation struggle,[51] and, as Mouny Berrah notes, these were all 'collective and committed films, immediate films devoted to their project with the intention of rehabilitating a self-image deconstructed and devalued by the occupier and arguing for the justice of a war condemned as "butchery" by the enemy'.[52] For the Algerian film historian Lotfi Maherzi, the films have a double value: recording the precise reality of the situation in Algeria, and showing the close support of the Algerian people for the struggle.[53] They found an audience not only in the Arab countries and eastern Europe, but also on Western television, where they served to counter French propaganda efforts. Though they could not, of course, be shown at the time in Algeria, Abdelghani Megherbi notes that they were frequently projected there during the first years of independence.[54]

In post-independence Algiers, in 1962, Vautier and Rachedi went on to set up the short-lived audio-visual centre (CAV), in the context of which *A People on the March/Peuple en marche* (1963) was made. But their particular form of committed militant filmmaking had no part to play in the totally bureaucratised mode of film production that emerged in Algeria in the mid-1960s. Considering the post-liberation career of Ahmed Rachedi, Claude Michel Cluny notes what he considers a 'fundamental error' in Algeria cinema: 'They had not worked out what role cinema could play in the elaboration of a new society; they gave priority to a celebration of past battles, rather than to a militant cinema with a revolutionary vocation'.[55] Rachedi, like Lakhdar Hamina, became both a prominent feature filmmaker and a bureaucrat, and only René Vautier retained his stance as an independent militant filmmaker (making, among other committed films, the highly praised *Being Twenty in the Aurès Mountains/Avoir vingt ans dans les Aurès* in 1972).

CONCLUSION

This chapter has set out to show the nature of the varying strands of film production which existed in Africa at the time when post-independence feature filmmaking was established, in both the Maghreb and Sub-Saharan West Africa, in the mid-1960s. Foreign producers from Europe and the United States still use the rural landscapes of the Maghreb as locations for their films and, though the old colonial ideology no longer prevails, the works produced have as little relevance as ever to the realities of African life. A number of filmmakers in Morocco and Tunisia have taken the opportunity to gain some experience by working on these foreign features, but only very subordinate roles – as production managers or assistant directors – are open to them. In any case this is a form of production beyond their aspirations, since the sheer size of the financial resources behind international productions such as *Lawrence of Arabia* or *Raiders of the Lost Ark* makes this model of production irrelevant to indigenous African producers.

The nature of the African industries which emerged in Egypt and South Africa show clearly how filmmaking is of necessity shaped both by overall national industrial development and by ideological factors: Islamic beliefs about morality, social responsibilities and gender relations, on the one hand, apartheid assertions and assumptions about race, on the other. Both film industries continue with varying degrees of success to face new challenges in a very different world, confronting the very real threats to freedom of expression posed by Islamic fundamentalism in Egypt, and responding to the equally real opportunities of shaping a black cinema for a black-governed society in the new

South Africa. But in the absence of the kinds of industrial infrastructures which were developed in Egypt and South Africa, the models of production developed there remain largely irrelevant to other African filmmakers north and south of the Sahara.

Equally, the increasingly autocratic one-party states that emerged after independence throughout Africa made the Vautier model of militant documentary filmmaking – a perfect example of the 'third cinema' advocated by Fernando Solanas and Octavio Getino and theorised by Teshome H. Gabriel[56] – totally impossible. The situation of post-independence filmmakers instead echoes that of Samama Chikly in Tunisia in the 1920s, in that they have no option but to work totally independently but within strict, state-defined limits, finding finance where they can, working as total creators (producing, directing, scripting) in a context lacking in technically trained local collaborators. It is to the very different contexts, constraints and opportunities facing the filmmakers of the Maghreb and francophone Sub-Saharan West Africa that we now turn.

NOTES

1. James McDougal, 'Introduction', in James McDougal (ed.), *Nation, Society and Culture in North Africa*, (London: Frank Cass Publishers, 2003), pp. 2–3.
2. Harry Baur, quoted in Maurice-Robert Bataille and Claude Veillot, *Caméras sous le soleil: Le Cinéma en Afrique du nord* (Algiers: 1956), p. 9.
3. Ferid Boughedir, 'Report and Prospects', in Enrico Fulchignoni (ed.), *Cinema and Society* (Paris: IFTC, 1981), p. 101.
4. Ibid.
5. Jean-Claude Seguin, *Alexandre Promio ou les énigmes de la lumière* (Paris: L'Harmattan, 1999), p. 250.
6. Ibid., p. 254.
7. Bataille and Veillot, *Caméras sous le soleil*, pp. 13–14.
8. Rémy Carrigues, 'L'Homme du Niger', in *L'Almanach Ciné-Miroir*, 1940.
9. David Henry Slavin, *Colonial Cinema and Imperial France, 1919–1939* (Baltimore: The Johns Hopkins University Press, 2001), p. 17.
10. Dina Sherzer, *Cinema, Colonialism, Postcolonialism: Perspectives from the French and Francophone Worlds* (Austin: University of Texas Press, 1996), p. 4.
11. Keyan Tomaselli, *The Cinema of Apartheid* (London: Routledge, 1989), p. 53.
12. Abdelghani Megherbi, *Les Algériens au miroir du cinéma colonial* (Algiers: SNED, 1982), p. 247.
13. Cited in Guillemette Mansour, *Samama Chikly: Un Tunisien à la rencontre du XXème siècle* (Tunis: Simpact Editions, 2000) (from which most of the information given here is derived), p. 29.
14. Ibid., p. 64.
15. Ibid., p. 254.
16. Ibid., p. 268.
17. Arnold Shepperson and Keyan G. Tomaselli, 'Le Cinéma sud-africain après l'apartheid: La restructuration d'une industrie', in Samuel Lelièvre (ed.), *Cinémas africains, une oasis dans le désert?* (Paris: Corlet/Télérama/CinémAction 106, 2003), p. 252.
18. Tomaselli, *Cinema of Apartheid*, p. 11.
19. Ibid., p. 81.

20. Michael Raeburn, 'Prétoria veut construire un "Hollywood" sud-africain . . .', in Guy Hennebelle (ed.), *Les Cinémas africains en 1972* (Paris: Société Africaine d'Edition, 1972), p. 261.
21. Ibid., p. 263.
22. Ibid.
23. Keyan Tomaselli, 'Le Rôle de la Jamie Uys Film Company dans la culture afrikaner', in Keyan Tomaselli (ed.), *Le cinéma sud-africain est-il tombé sur la tête?* (Paris: *L'Afrique littéraire*, 78/CinémAction 39, 1986), p. 26.
24. Peter Davis, '*Les dieux sont tombés sur la tête*, de Jamie Uys: Délices et ambiguités de la position du missionnaire!', in Tomaselli (1986), p. 53.
25. Ibid., p. 57.
26. Ibid., p. 56.
27. Ibid., pp. 57–8.
28. John van Zyl, cited in Tomaselli, *Cinema of Apartheid*, p. 127.
29. See Gibson Boloko, 'La Situation de l'industrie cinématographique Sud-africaine (1980–2000)', in Lelièvre, *Cinémas africains*, pp. 258–63.
30. Tom Kemp, *Industrialization in the Non-Western World* (London and New York: Longman, 1983), p. 189.
31. Kristina Bergmann, *Filmkultur und Filmindustrie in Ägypten* (Darmstadt: Wissenschaftliche Buchgesellschaft, 1993), p. 6.
32. Samir Farid, 'Les Six générations du cinéma égyptien', Paris: *Écran* 15, 1973, p. 40.
33. Patrick Clawson, 'The Development of Capitalism in Egypt' (London: *Khamsin* 9, 1981), p. 92.
34. Magda Wassef (ed.), *Egypte: Cent ans de cinéma* (Paris: Institut du Monde Arabe, 1995), p. 14.
35. Ibid.
36. Ali Abu Shadi, 'Genres in Egyptian Cinema', in Alia Arasoughly (ed.), *Screens of Life: Critical Film Writing from the Arab World* (Quebec: World Heritage Press, 1998), p. 85.
37. Khémais Khayati, *Cinémas arabes: Topographie d'une image éclatée* (Paris and Montreal: L'Harmattan, 1996), p. 204.
38. Ibid., p. 202.
39. Shadi, 'Genres', p. 82.
40. Abbas Fadhil Ibrahim, 'Trois mélos égyptiens observés à la loupe', in Mouny Berrah, Victor Bachy, Mohand Ben Salama and Ferid Boughedir (eds), *Cinémas du Maghreb* (Paris: CinémAction 14, 1981), p. 123.
41. Khayati, *Cinémas arabes*, p. 203
42. Ibid., p. 204.
43. Sayed Saïd, 'Politique et cinéma', in Magda Wassef (ed.), *Egypte: Cent ans de cinéma*, p. 192.
44. Ibid.
45. Ibid., p. 193.
46. Khayati, *Cinémas arabes*, pp. 77–87.
47. Mouny Berrah, 'Algerian Cinema and National Identity', in Arasoughly, *Screens of Life*, p. 64.
48. The script of this rarely shown film has been published: René Vautier, *Afrique 50* (Paris: Editions Paris Expérimental, 2001).
49. René Vautier, *Caméra citoyenne* (Rennes: Éditions Apogées, 1998), p. 156.
50. Lotfi Maherzi, *Le Cinéma algérien: Institutions, imaginaire, idéologie* (Algiers: SNED, 1980), p. 62.
51. See Mouloud Mimoun (ed.), *France-Algérie: Images d'une guerre* (Paris: Institut du Monde Arabe, 1992), pp. 68–71.

52. Mouny Berrah, 'Histoire et idéologie du cinéma algérien sur la guerre', in Guy Hennebelle, Mouny Berrah and Benjamin Stora (eds), *La guerre d'Algérie à l'écran* (Paris: Corlet/Télérama/*CinémAction* 85, 1997), p. 160.
53. Maherzi, *Le cinéma algérien*, p. 64.
54. Megherbi, *Les Algériens au miroir du cinéma colonial*, p. 269.
55. Claude Michel Cluny, *Dictionnaire des nouveaux cinémas arabes* (Paris: Sindbad, 1978), p. 264.
56. See Fernando Solanas and Octavio Getino, 'Towards a Third Cinema', in Michael Chanan (ed.), *Twenty-Five Years of the New Latin American Cinema* (London: British Film Institute, 1983), and Teshome H. Gabriel, *Third Cinema in the Third World* (Ann Arbour, MI: UMI Research Press, 1982).

3. AFRICAN INITIATIVES

The current philosophy of filmmakers is in fact that the state should sustain production by helping its financing and distribution, but by regularising the market. The state should protect rather than take everything on board.

Ferid Boughedir, 1987[1]

This study is largely concerned with post-independence filmmaking in four adjoining areas astride the Sahara, all of which were colonised by the French up to the end of the 1950s or the beginning of the 1960s. Three of these – Algeria, Morocco and Tunisia – are independent states, and there is no critical problem in making general claims about them as unified contexts for filmmaking (though this is not to assume, a priori, that film production there constitutes a 'national cinema'). To see the fourth area as a single unit is perhaps more controversial, since it comprises fourteen independent states in francophone West Africa south of the Sahara, all of which were either former French protectorates (Cameroon and Togo) or previously formed part of the two French supercolonies, French West Africa and French Equatorial Africa (the remaining twelve). The unifying factor here is that most of the impetus and finance for filmmaking here has come from France, as part of the French government's policy of maintaining close cultural and economic links with its former African colonies. A further argument, which I hope will be shown to be correct by what follows, is that there is a unity linking filmmakers north and south of the Sahara, though these are generally regarded as quite separate worlds by Western, particularly US, critics. I share with the Tunisian critic Hédi Khelil the belief that 'filmmakers from Tunisia, Morocco, Algeria, Mali, Burkina Faso and Senegal are very close to each other in the questions they pose and the ways in which they pose them'.[2] Certainly, despite the diversity in history and the ways in which independence was acquired, filmmaking began in all four areas at the same time, in the late 1960s, with twenty features in all made between 1965 and 1969.

In Sub-Saharan Africa, Ousmane Sembene led the way with his Senegalese features *Black Girl/La Noire de . . .* (1966) and *The Money Order/Le Mandat* (1968), accompanied by one feature from Guinea in 1966 and two from the Ivory Coast (by the French-based filmmakers Désiré Ecaré and Bassori Timité) in 1969. During the 1970s, production continued in these three states, and filmmakers from a further eight states produced features: Benin, Burkina Faso, Cameroon, Congo, Gabon, Mali, Mauritania and Niger. Chad and Togo followed belatedly in the 1990s, and Didier Ouenangare co-directed the first feature film in the Central African Republic in 2003. In the Maghreb, feature filmmaking began in Algeria in 1965 with Ahmed Rachedi's masterly documentary *Dawn of the Damned/L'Aube des damnés*, which was quickly followed by eight fictional features in the 1960s, among them Mohamed Lakhdar Hamina's *The Wind from the Aurès/Le Vent des Aurès* (1966). Tunisian cinema was inaugurated by Omar Khlifi with the appropriately named *The Dawn/L'Aube* (1966), and three further Tunisian features were made in the late 1960s. Morocco followed with three features – all produced by the state film organization, the CCM – in 1968–9.

With two major (on-going) African film festivals established – the Journées Cinématographiques de Carthage (JCC) in Tunis in 1966 and the Festival Panafricain du Cinéma de Ouagadougou (FESPACO) in Ouagadougou in 1969 – filmmakers were able to meet and organise. The result was the founding of the Pan-African Filmmakers' Federation (FEPACI) which met first in Tunis in 1970 and again in Algiers in 1975. Other meetings of filmmakers followed – at Mogadishu in 1981 and Niamy in 1982 – and a number of statements and charters were produced. Ferid Boughedir, a true cinéaste (filmmaker, academic, historian, critic), has traced the initial stage of the filmmakers' thinking. The basis of their strategy was that 'the viability of production was linked to the viability of the four other sectors: exhibition, technical infrastructure, professional training and, of course, the import and distribution of films. Only states could control these areas, so the state became the fairy godmother'.[3] This was a policy the newly independent African states were broadly willing to follow and many of them set out to exercise tight control over all aspects of film through the local variant of the Ministry of Information and/or Culture. In all cases, their attempts to confront the major international distributors (such as Hollywood's MPEAA) were unsuccessful and indeed, south of the Sahara, distribution remained largely in the hands of two French organisations (COMACICO and SECMA), themselves subsidiaries of Monaco-based holding companies, until 1974.[4] National state film organisations, structured on the lines of the French Centre National Cinématographique (CNC) and each provided with a typically French-language acronym, were established. But apart from the CNPC in Mali and the CCM in Morocco, few of these state organisations survive today, having been closed down as a result of the state's gradual withdrawal from direct involvement in film production.

In most francophone African countries the government has at some time or another offered financial support for at least some filmmakers, and in certain states the list of government-supported films is virtually the total list of films produced (in Algeria up to the mid-1990s, for example, or in contemporary Morocco). But the involvement in film finance has been paralleled by state control of expression. Everywhere censorship, open or concealed, is to be found, with certain films never finding a release at home unless and until the demands of the government censor have been met. Throughout the region finance for investment in film production has always been scarce, with the result that almost half the filmmakers have made only a single feature film in their whole careers, and only a handful have completed, say, half a dozen films in a dozen years. Even Souleymane Cisse from Mali, internationally recognised as a major filmmaker, has completed only five features since his debut in 1975.

ALGERIA

Film had been seen to form a vital part of the liberation struggle by the FLN and in the immediate aftermath of the war it seemed briefly as if Algeria might develop a distinctive set of national film institutions based on this experience. The first context of production for post-independence Algerian cinema, the film collective CAV, led by the activists René Vautier and Ahmed Rachedi, was set up in 1962. But CAV's closure after the completion of a small number of documentaries and just one feature-length work, *A People on the March/Peuple en marche* (1963), showed that this was not to be. For a while in the 1960s there was a certain diversity of production organisations supporting filmmaking. Algerian Television (RTA), for example, co-produced the first Algerian fictional feature and initially pursued an ambitious programme of feature-length film production for television, with its directors usually working in black and white and on 16mm film and often on location. A number of these productions received showings in cinemas and at foreign festivals. But RTA's co-production activities gradually petered out in the 1970s. A further production context was the OAA, set up in 1963 by the Ministry of Information to produce its own regular weekly newsreel. But OAA in fact quickly became the production base for the early fictional features of one of the most forceful and influential figures in Algerian cinema, the OAA's first and only director, Mohamed Lakhdar Hamina. There was even one private company, Casbah Films, founded by the former FLN activist Yacef Saadi, whose own story formed the basis of the company's best known feature, *The Battle of Algiers/La Bataille d'Alger* (1965), directed by the Italian Gillo Pontecorvo. The first major state film production organisation, the CNCA, was set up in 1964 with a remit that largely mirrors that of the colonial film service set up by the French in 1947. It even established a short-lived professional film training programme (INC), where the students in its sole year of operation included a number of the future feature filmmakers.

Then in 1967–8 came a reorganisation of film structures, when the OAA and CNCA were disbanded and three new organisations – the CDC, CAC and ONCIC – were set up. CDC took over the ciné-bus role initially established by the French colonial SDC, and CAC took took charge of the administrative roles. But ONCIC, initially granted just the monopoly of film production in 1967, steadily absorbed all the other functions, to become a total state monopoly. From this point on, it was evident that Algerian cinema was not to have a revolutionary role, but instead would serve a propagandistic function in support of government policies. Stylistic innovation was not sought and, as the Algerian film historian Lotfi Maherzi writes, 'cinema was still seen with the same commercial vision. No other codes, no other models of production or programming than those provided by Western cinema were proposed'.[5] Maherzi further notes that though 'the official texts constantly affirm the educative and ideological function of Algerian cinema',[6] ONCIC was in fact set up to be an industrial and commercial operation. But as has usually been the case throughout the world, the state bureaucracy proved to be a very inefficient film producer and the organisation's structures stifled creativity. Despite this, Algeria remained the leading film producing country in the Maghreb until the early 2000s, with over 120 films produced by about fifty directors.

ONCIC's production monopoly meant that it was responsible for virtually all Algerian feature-film production for cinema release from 1968 until it was dissolved in 1984. Film directors became salaried state employees, paid irrespective of whether they made films or not. As the director Mohamed Chouikh has observed: 'Making a film outside the state structures was a counter-revolutionary act. It just didn't happen, you couldn't even get permission to shoot. That's why all the filmmakers, myself included, were integrated into the state sector'.[7] Though the CNCA had contributed two features, the OAA four and RTA six, it was ONCIC which produced or co-produced forty-six of the sixty-one Algerian feature films made in the period up to 1984. It was responsible for the greatest

Algerian success of the 1970s, Mohamed Lakhdar Hamina's *Chronicle of the Years of Embers/Chronique des années de braise*, which won the Palme d'or at Cannes in 1975. Despite ONCIC's overall predominance, some of the key films of the period were produced on the margins (among them, the fascinating sole features of Farouk Beloufa and Mohamed Zinet).

From the mid-1980s Algerian cinema underwent a series of bewildering bureaucratic reorganisations which had a very negative effect on the level and quality of production. In 1984 ONCIC was dissolved and its functions split between two separate organisations, one set up for production (ENAPROC) and one for distribution (ENADEC). The three features produced by ENAPROC before its rapid demise were very much the kind of works which ONCIC had previously produced. Then in 1987 the two organisations were fused again to form CAAIC. Simultaneously RTA's television resources were regrouped to form ENPA and the boundaries which had hitherto clearly separated film and television production became blurred. Between them, in the period 1986–96, CAAIC and ENPA were responsible for twenty-two features (an average of two a year), with Amar Laskri's Vietnamese co-production, *Lotus Flower/Fleur de lotus* (1998), which was much delayed in production, emerging several years later. Many of these films were joint productions between the two companies and most were low-budget works – some in 16mm – primarily directed at a television market.

The violent 1990s political turmoil in Algeria – what Benjamin Stora has called 'the invisible war', in which as many as 100,000 people may have died[8] – drove many directors into exile in France and Italy. As a result, co-productions not involving the state sector made their appearance for the first time, with films shot in Algeria but funded from Europe. In October 1993 a further radical step was taken by the Algerian government: the CAAIC state-employed directors had their contracts terminated. CAAIC was to continue in existence only to offer limited production support and to administer a new funding scheme based on scripts submitted to a state commission. Finally, in 1997, the government closed down CAAIC, ENPA and the newsreel organisation, ANAF, effectively leaving Algeria without any film production structures.

Since this 1997 closure, the production situation in Algeria has remained parlous, and the director of the Algerian Cinémathèque, Boujemaa Karèche, was hardly exaggerating when he stated: 'Algerian cinema in 2000: zero production, zero film theatres, zero distributors, zero tickets sold'.[9] No Algerian feature films were made between 1997 and 2002: there was simply no film finance available in the country. Though the film editor-turned-director Yamina Bachir-Chouikh had remained in Algeria, her internationally acclaimed *Rachida*, which ended the drought in 2002, was made totally with French money.[10] A funding scheme based on a tax on box-office receipts dried up (there were virtually no box office receipts to tax) and had to be supplemented by the Ministry of Culture with the aim of producing five films to celebrate the 1,000-year history of Algiers, but only one of these has emerged, Ghaouti Bendeddouche's *The Neighbour/La Voisine*. The joint Algerian-French partial funding of nine further projects to celebrate 'The Year of Algeria in France 2002' has proved more successful, with seven films (but just two by Algerian-based directors) having appeared. Only in 2004 was a new national film centre (CNCA) re-established. With just eleven films (all wholly or partly French-funded and seven of them directed by filmmakers resident in Europe) released between 2000 and 2004, the extent to which one can now talk meaningfully of an Algerian cinema is doubtful, with the work of the exiled directors being particularly problematic. Rachid Benhadj's *Mirka* (2000), for example, was shown at the JCC festival in Tunis as an 'Algerian' film. But Benhadj currently lives in Italy and his film is a truly international co-production: Italian-French-Spanish funding, Vanessa Redgrave and Gérard Depardieu as its stars, cinematography by the internationally renowned Vittorio Storaro, and a luxuriant Hollywood-style score by the Algerian composer Safi Boutella.

MOROCCO

After a slow start. Moroccan film output has grown steadily for almost forty years, and with 150 features made by some sixty directors in the period to the end of 2004, Morocco is now the leading film producer in the area. The Moroccan Film Centre (CCM) had a considerable experience of short film-making, but feature film production did not begin until 1968, twelve years after independence, with the government seemingly indifferent initially to the wider potential of the film medium. The CCM had been created by the French in the 1940s as an essentially colonial organisation, yet it was allowed to continue in existence with virtually unchanged functions after independence – though with Moroccan technicians gradually replacing the French expatriates and with the newsreel service restructured as an independent production facility, the Actualités Marocaines, in 1958. Significantly the CCM was responsible not to the Ministry of Culture – as is the case with most state film production organisations – but to the Ministry of Information and the Interior. At independence the state took no powers to control film import, distribution or exhibition, and Morocco's 250 35mm cinemas, mostly situated in urban centres, were left in the private sector. Inevitably they favoured imported foreign films.

Though the CCM funded or co-funded the first three Moroccan feature films in 1968–9, it did not immediately continue this support in the following decade. It was not until 1977 that at least partial funding by the CCM became the norm, with seven features supported in the period 1977–9. But the films of the early 1970s, on which Morocco based its first international reputation, were all privately financed. The advances in the provision of studios and facilities for laboratory and dubbing work had little or no impact on the level of Moroccan domestic production, which remained low throughout the 1970s. During the whole period since 1968, foreign-produced films, shot using Moroccan locations, have far outweighed local initiatives in terms of both finance and resources.[11]

The local production situation changed radically in 1980 when the Moroccan government introduced a system of assistance for production (the so-called 'fonds de soutien'), which though paying no attention to quality, did have the effect of greatly stimulating production activity. As a result the 1980s saw an upsurge in filmmaking, with the production of thirty-eight feature films, twenty-one of them made by new directors. The plan was undoubtedly well-intentioned, but the sums offered were small and they were paid only after the completion of the film. Moreover the scheme was not supported by any system to control imports or to organise distribution, so that the result was the production of a large number of films for which there was virtually no audience, either inside Morocco or abroad.

In 1988 the aid scheme was modified again (acquiring the acronym FAPCN) to lay a greater emphasis on quality and to offer funding largely on the basis of scripts submitted by filmmakers. The level of funding increased further in the 1990s and new tax concessions were offered to film producers. As a result, six or seven features have been made each year since the beginning of the 2000s (thirty-three in all), a level almost three times that achieved in the 1970s and 1980s. For the first time Moroccan films have begun to attract substantial local audiences with several achieving audiences of over 200,000, and the record being held by two comedies, Mohamed Abderrahman Tazi's *Looking for My Wife's Husband/A la recherche du mari de ma femme* (1993) and Saïd Naciri's *Crooks/Les Bandits* (2004), both of which drew over 1 million spectators in Morocco alone.

The strength of the Moroccan system is that it is eclectic, with money given both to those who achieve box-office hits at home and to those who are more successful with festival audiences abroad. Each year at least one newcomer receives funding for a first feature film, usually after completing two or three short films. The weakness of the system is that government aid is virtually the only source of film finance in Morocco. Films that do not receive state support are simply not made. In general, films made by Moroccan-born filmmakers resident abroad – even Fatima Jebli Ouazzani's *In My Father's House*, which won the top prize at the 1998 National Film Festival – do not receive distribution in Morocco.

In the 1990s, the CCM in Morocco made interesting co-productions with filmmakers from Mali, the Ivory Coast and Tunisia, but its own production has focused very largely on the domestic market, and films made as foreign co-productions are unusual. As in Algeria under the monopoly of ONCIC in the 1980s, there seems to be some trade-off between quantity and quality in the

Moroccan system. Although the CCM has produced twice as many films as Tunisian producers since 1990, these works have attracted nowhere near the same level of international critical attention.

TUNISIA

Although it is by far the smallest of the Maghrebian states, Tunisia's forty or so directors have produced over eighty features in forty years, twenty of them between 2000 and 2004. After independence, the two key organisations which shaped film production, and film culture in general, in Tunisia were SEACI and SATPEC. SEACI was the government organisation set up to supervise culture and information, the cinema division of which was headed by the distinguished critic Tahar Cheriaa from 1961 to 1969. In the early 1960s, SEACI followed the French colonial pattern of rural distribution of films, setting up a number of cultural centres equipped with 16mm projectors and organising a ciné-bus distribution system. It also produced two films directed by foreign filmmakers, and three of the first six Tunisian feature films released between 1967 and 1970.

SATPEC was the state-owned company set up in 1957 to manage the production, import, distribution and exhibition of films. In the early 1960s SATPEC's attempts to confront the multinational distribution companies which dominated the Tunisian domestic film market were unsuccessful, but, undeterred, it established an ambitious film production complex at Gammarth in 1966. Unfortunately this could process only black-and-white films until 1983, and as a result incurred costs and losses which were to lead eventually to the virtual bankruptcy of the parent company. SATPEC ceased its involvement in feature production at the end of the 1980s and was closed down in 1994, when it was absorbed into the television company Canal Horizon. During the years of its involvement in Tunisian feature film production (1969–90), SATPEC did not have a monopoly of film production. But, usually acting as co-producer with the director's own production company, it was jointly responsible for twenty-nine of the forty-nine Tunisian features produced over this period, a dozen of which also involved foreign co-production companies.

Though Tunisia has the smallest number of film theatres among the three Maghrebian states (150 at independence, declining to just thirty-six in the year 2000), it has always had a rich film culture, exemplified by the bilingual film revue *Goha* (later *SeptièmArt*), which was founded in 1964 and reached its 100th issue in 2002. The leading Arab film festival, the biennial Carthage Film Festival (the JCC), was founded in Tunis in 1966 and continues into the 2000s. There has been a flourishing amateur film movement since the 1960s, when the on-going amateur film festival at Kélibia, FIFAK, was established. It was from this amateur film movement that half a dozen or so of the new Tunisian feature film directors emerged.

Despite the closure of SATPEC, the Tunisian government has continued to support film production. In 1981 it introduced system of aid for film producers based on a 6 per cent levy on all box-office receipts (akin to that in Morocco). Since 1990 the state television service (ERTT) has also served as co-producer of one film a year (twelve in all up to 2002), and the Tunisian Ministry of Culture has contributed directly to half a dozen others. Because of the limitations of the Tunisian domestic market, filmmakers have had to look abroad for production finance, and of the thirty-six features released since 1990, twenty-eight have been international co-productions. Most of the co-producing companies have been in France or Belgium (where many filmmakers received their training), but there have also been links with Morocco (six features). A key event in the mid-1980s was the emergence of Ahmed Attia as a major independent producer, responsible through his company Cinétéléfilms for many of the best recent Tunisian features, which achieved wide success and an international distribution.

SUB-SAHARAN FRANCOPHONE WEST AFRICA

There are several reasons for treating these fourteen states as a single unit in terms of their filmmaking. As former colonies, all were given special treatment by French ministries concerned with foreign affairs and cultural cooperation (indeed the Ministry of Cooperation was set up specifically to develop post-independence ties with Africa). It is difficult to imagine that many of the films considered here could have been made and obtained wide international showings without French government support. The need for foreign showings is very clear, since often the number of cinemas in the filmmaker's home country is derisory: Mahamat Saleh Haroun films a visit to what he claims is Chad's only existing film theatre in his quasi-documentary Bye Bye Africa (1999).

The total number of films produced by individual states over thirty or forty years is very small, on average about six feature films annually, shared between the fourteen states. Often, as is the case with Benin, Cameroon and Gabon, there is a ten-, fifteen- or even twenty-year gap between the work of the mainly 16mm pioneers of the 1970s (mostly directly funded by the French Ministry of Cooperation) and that of the 35mm 'new cinema' practitioners of the 1990s (also dependent on foreign funding). The whole impetus for the change from 16mm to 35mm came from French sources, even in Senegal, which has a history of continuous production, if only at the rate of a single film a year, since 1966. Nowhere – neither in the Maghreb nor in francophone West Africa – has there been the kind and level of general investment in infrastructure equivalent to that which allowed a genuinely autonomous film industry to emerge in Egypt. Nor has such a project been attractive to successive French governments, which have never shown any real interest in African infrastructional development.

The number of cinemas in any given state has never reached a level which would allow it to sustain financially a local production with a local audience. An invaluable survey by Jacques Roitfeld for Unifrance Film in 1980 estimated the total number of film theatres in francophone West Africa as 337,[12] and there is a broad correlation between the number of films produced and the national total of cinemas. This is very apparent if we consider the five countries which have produced twenty or more films:

> Senegal: forty-seven films; third equal in number of cinemas (fifty-two)
> Burkina Faso: forty films; seventh in number of cinemas (twelve)
> Cameroon: thirty-one films; third equal in number of cinemas (fifty-two)
> Ivory Coast: twenty-six films; second in number of cinemas (fifty-nine)
> Mali: twenty-five films; fifth in number of cinemas (thirty).

The anomalies are Guinea, whose output (fourteen films) does not match its number of cinemas (sixty-five), perhaps because of the autocratic rule and particular cultural policies of President Sekou Touré, and Burkina Faso, which became the externally funded 'capital' of francophone African cinema, despite its paucity of film theatres.[13]

The argument that these francophone West African films are best seen as a single group does not mean, however, that specifically African initiatives were unimportant or that the types of filmmakers in specific African countries – and the films they have produced – do not have characteristics that differentiate them from production in neighbouring states. There are huge distinctions between the newly independent states of Sub-Saharan Africa in terms of history, language and ethnicity, and indeed there are equally wide differences within them. The most extreme case is perhaps **Cameroon** with a population of just 15 million, who belong to 200 different ethnic groups and speak over 100 different languages.[14] Not surprisingly, Cameroon's feature films consistently use the French language (apart, that is, from Jean-Pierre Bekolo's *Aristotle's Plot/Le Complot d'Aristote* (1996), which uses English and is in other ways quite distinctive, having been shot in Zimbabwe with South African actors and with the post-production work being undertaken in Zimbabwe, France and Canada).[15] Cameroon's output (thirty-one films by thirteen directors, most of them French film school graduates, with five from the CLCF alone) is boosted by eight Alphonse Béni features in the period 1975–85, aptly described by Ferid Boughedir as 'films policiers érotico-disco'.[16] Jean-Pierre Dikongue-Pipa's classic 'cultural' feature, *Muna Moto* (1975), pointed to one possible direction for Cameroonian production, but the actual course taken by the Cameroonian filmmakers has been a distinctly commercial orientation with real efforts to reach a wide audience through the use of comedy. In 1973 the government set up a funding body, FODIC, which supported four features between 1978 and

1982. But only one film was made in the nine years between 1987 and 1996, when a new group of young French-funded directors working in 35mm began to make their appearance and international reputations.

Another French-language cinema of the 1970s, that of **Gabon** (nine films from six directors), displays a similar discontinuity. Though Gabon had just eight cinemas, the president, Omar Bongo, took a highly personal interest in film, establishing a film centre (CENACI) and encouraging a couple of 1970s productions. In the late 1970s the president's own company produced versions of two plays written by his wife and an adaptation of his own memoirs. Subsequently there was a twenty-one year gap before the production of *Dôlè*, made by the young FEMIS graduate Léon Imunga Ivanga and winning the top prize at the JCC in Tunis in 2000. The output of **Benin** (formerly Dahomey), which nationalised its six cinemas in 1974, is smaller and even more fragmented (just nine features from five directors). The initial film organisation, the ONACIDA, changed its name in 1974 (when the country was renamed by its Marxist-Leninist government) to OBECI. According to Victor Bachy, nationalisation 'raised great hopes, but OBECI, badly directed and badly managed, led Benin cinema to disaster'. There were just two features in the mid-1970s from filmmakers who subsequently went into exile, and a further feature in 1985, then a fourteen-year gap, as the first two directors born after independence made their appearance.

Congo's tiny output (five films by four filmmakers, all of whom were trained in Paris) is equally disjointed. Initially, there was a French-funded pioneering feature in 1973, followed in 1979 and 1981 by two features produced by the state organisation ONACI. Then there was a thirteen-year gap until the first films of younger filmmakers were shown. **Guinea**, with fourteen films from seven filmmakers plus two collectively made features, nationalised its cinemas – through the state company Syli-Cinéma – as soon as it claimed its independence in 1958, and produced a first feature in 1966. Subsequently, Guinea's cinema comprises essentially three stages: a trio of films by Dansogho Mohamed Camara and a dance film by Moussa Kemoko Diakite between 1977 and 1990; three films directed between 1991 and 2002 by Cheik Doukouré, who has lived in France for forty years; and debut films by three new younger directors since 1997.

Niger has less than a dozen cinemas and its output of twelve films (all but one in 16mm) are the work of just five directors, four of whom are self-taught. Indeed, the distinctive feature of Niger's cinema, according to Ferid Boughedir, is that its filmmakers 'represent African cinema from inside',[17] not with the kind of distance found in the work of European-trained intellectuals. Niger was a favoured location for the French documentarist and ethnographer Jean Rouch, and he discovered and helped two 1960s pioneers of African cinema: the animator Mustapha Alassane and Oumarou Ganda, who played the lead in

Rouch's documentary *Moi un noir*. Most of their work comprises short or medium-length films, but Alassane did direct three 16mm features and Ganda two – the first in the early 1970s and the second, *The Exile/L'Exilé*, shortly before his death in 1981, at the age of just forty-six.[18] In the early 1980s Niger television (ORTN) briefly became the focus of local filmmaking and also participated in the production of the Mauritanian Med Hondo's pan-African epic, *Sarraounia*. No feature films have been made in Niger since 1989.

Four other 'national' cinemas comprise just one or two filmmakers, most of whom live in exile. Feature filmmaking in **Mauritania**, for example, is represented by just two Paris-based filmmakers, but both in their very different ways are major figures in African cinema. The veteran Med Hondo has produced seven politically committed features and a number of long documentaries since 1970, while Abderrahmane Sissako, who trained at the Moscow film school (VGIK), is one of the great hopes of the new African cinema. **Chad** was the birthplace of two Paris-trained and French-based filmmakers whose careers began in 1999–2000: Mahamat Saleh Haroun, who made two French-produced features at the turn of the millennium, and Issa Serge Coelo, who made one. **Togo**'s sole filmmaker, Kilizou Blaise Abalo, made his only feature, *Kawilasi*, co-produced by Togo's Ministry of Cooperation and Culture, in 1992. In the **Central African Republic (Centrafrique)** Didier Ouenangare co-directed a first feature, *The Silence of the Forest/Le Silence de la forêt*, (with the Cameroonian Bassek Ba Kobhio) in 2003.

There are just four Sub-Saharan francophone African cinemas – in addition to Cameroon – that have a sufficient level of continuous production to enable any sort of meaningful statements to be made about trends or tendencies, but it is doubtful whether the films can be said to constitute a 'national' cinema. The four states are Ivory Coast (twenty-six films from thirteen filmmakers), Mali (twenty-five films from eleven filmmakers), Burkina Faso (forty films from twenty filmmakers) and Senegal (forty-seven films from twenty-one filmmakers).

Ivory Coast cinema has a double origin, in the 1960s work of the IDHEC graduates Désiré Écaré and Bassori Timité in Paris and in the state organisation, SIC, set up in 1962 and in existence (though with little real impact) until 1979. The two – very different – major directors, who have contributed half the films, are both 1970s pioneers trained at French film school: Henri Duparc, who has made six features, most of them exuberant comedies, and Roger Gnoan Mbala, who has made five and has specialised of late in village dramas treating themes of power and religion. None of the other eleven directors has made more than a couple of films, so it is difficult to give this cinema a focus, beyond the fact that most of its directors (nine out of thirteen) are Paris film school graduates.

Though a first feature film in **Mali** was not made until 1975, government concern with cinema as a social force began a dozen years earlier with the creation in 1963 by the Ministry of Information of a national film organisation, OCINAM, with key technical assistance from Yugoslavia. Five of Mali's future feature film directors were sent for training in Moscow and one to East Germany. In 1967 the production unit was separated off from OCINAM to become SCINFOMA, which produced a dozen shorts, before being in turn dissolved into the CNPA which (particularly under the leadership of Cheick Oumar Sissoko who joined it in 1981) became a focus for Malian production from the 1970s through to the 2000s. Sissoko has followed the same pattern of socially committed filmmaking as the pioneer Souleymane Cisse, who was shaped by his training at the VGIK film school in Moscow in the 1960s. With five features each, they dominate Malian filmmaking, jointly setting its tone and, in the case of Cisse, changing the whole course of Sub-Saharan African filmmaking with *Yeelen* in 1987. Their efforts have been supported more recently by the work of other younger Moscow graduates. With most of its directors professionally trained and several of them professional writers, Malian cinema is particularly rich in the range and texture of its films. Though the state provides some support through CNPA, most films are international co-productions. Ferid Boughedir wrote in 1984 that 'Malian cinema possesses the men. The helping hand of a few legislative measures would certainly allow it to become one of the great African cinemas of tomorrow'.[19] Since the arrival of Sissoko in 1986, the appearance of Cisse's *Yeelen* in 1987, and the emergence of five other newcomers between 1989 and 2002, this promise has been at least partially fulfilled.

In **Senegal**, which makes up about a fifth of francophone West African cinema in terms of both films and directors, nine features were produced before a state production organisation was created. Leading the way was Ousmane Sembene with his first three features, *Black Girl/La Noire de . . .* (1964), *The Money Order/Mandabi* (1968) and *Emitai* (1971). Though the first two of these were completed partly thanks to French financing, *Emitai*, with its denunciation of French colonialism, was independently financed. From 1970 Sembene was supported by Mahama Traore (generally known as Johnson Traore), who made three 16mm fictions in four years through his company Sunu Films, Ababacar Samb-Makharam (with *Kodou*) and Momar Thiam. In 1973 Djibril Diop Mambety made his feature appearance, after a couple of shorts, with his wonderfully inventive first feature, *Touki Bouki*. Two years later Safi Faye, francophone West Africa's first woman feature director, made the widely seen, feature-length, black-and-white 16mm, *Letter from My Village/Lettre paysanne/Kaddu Beykat* (1975), a mix of documentary and fiction.

The state production organisation, SNC, which began operations in 1973, provided up to 90 per cent of the production costs of five features – a mix of 16mm and 35mm works – before its demise in 1977. The decade ended strongly with three good but very varied features: Sembene's *Ceddo*, Moussa Yoro

Bathily's *Tiyabu Biru* and Safi Faye's *Fad'Jal*, the latter co-funded by the French Ministry of Cooperation and the Paris-based INA. The institution of a new funding structure (the Fonds d'aide à l'industrie cinématographique) led to a brief burst of early 1980s filmmaking, with three debut features, including that of the veteran film historian and documentarist Paulin Soumanou Vieyra. Three other directors – Thierno Faty Sow, Samb-Makharam and Thiam – made their second or third features. Then there was a four-year gap (1984–7) before, as elsewhere in Africa, a new generation, mostly born in the 1950s, made their appearance. These new filmmakers included Amadou Saalum Seck, who had studied in Munich, Clarence T. Delgardo, who trained in Algeria and Portugal, and four Paris film school graduates – Moussa Sene Absa, Samba Félix N'Diaye, Joseph Gaye Ramaka and Mansour Sora Wade – who made a wider impact.

Burkina Faso (previously known, until 1984, as Upper Volta) occupies a paradoxical position in African filmmaking. As Victor Bachy put it in 1983, the country is 'filmically speaking, an exceptional country, a sort of African lighthouse'.[20] Ferid Boughedir goes even further calling it, in 1984, 'a symbol at the heart of African cinema'.[21] Since 1969, the country and its capital Ouagadougou have been home to Black Africa's premier biennial film festival, FESPACO, and it is there too that the African filmmakers' association, FEPACI, has its headquarters. Thanks to French funding from 1979, attempts were also made to build an inter-African film distribution organisation (CIDC) and a parallel production consortium (CIPROFILM), both of which carried great hopes that they were unable to fulfil. The first Sub-Saharan African film school (INAFEC) was set up in 1976, but though its graduates include major figures such as Idrissa Ouedraogo, Dani Kouyaté and Régina Fanta Nacro, it attracted few foreign students and closed in 1986. It was in Ouagadougou too that the African film library (the Cinémathèque Africaine) was established in 1995.

Though Burkina Faso possessed only six cinemas at the time of independence, its government was the first in Sub-Saharan Africa to nationalise film exhibition in 1970, giving the administration of the six cinemas over to a new state organisation, SONAVOCI. It also led the struggle to free francophone Africa from the stranglehold of foreign distribution companies. But feature filmmaking was slow to develop and initially lacked a clear focus, partly because the first ten films were directed by ten different directors, with a mix of film school graduates and autodidacts. But in a fascinating book-length 'close-up' on Burkina Faso's cinema from 1960 to 1995, Teresa Hoefert de Turégano demonstrates, from a 2005 perspective, a clear double pattern of Burkinabè production. In the films which were dominated by the local authorities or made as African co-productions (though financing still often comes largely from France), the features produced are 'highly socio-educative, didactic and melodramatic'.[22] Though wholly laudable in their aims and intentions, these films have received virtually no screenings abroad and at the same time have proved unpopular with audiences at home. The second tendency – pioneered by Gaston Kabore with *Wend Kuuni* (1982) – comprises films that 'have narratives that are universally tuned, and in some cases play with an exotic dimension'.[23] Here the financing is overtly European and the filmmakers resident or regularly present in France. Yet these films have proved most popular with Burkinabè audiences (with *Wend Kuuni* attracting over 100,000 spectators).[24] This tendency contains the work of the three key figures who have given Burkinabè cinema its international cinema: Gaston Kabore, Idrissa Ouedraogo and S. Pierre Yaméogo. These three, who are together responsible for half the national output, were all born in the 1950s, studied filmmaking in Paris, and began their careers in the 1980s. The period since 1990 has seen the appearance of eight younger directors, mostly born in the 1950s or 1960s and all working in 35mm with largely French funding, but apart from Dani Kouyaté they have had far less impact than their elders.

CONCLUSION

As can be seen from the above overview, there were a number of general factors which influenced filmmaking in all four geographic areas. Firstly, there was the persistence into the post-independence period of Western film dominance over African screens, a situation that African governments were largely unable to control. Speaking specifically about Cameroon, but describing a situation common throughout Africa, Richard Bjornson has noted that foreign films and pulp fiction appealed to Cameroonians for the same reason as soccer matches: 'All three forms of entertainment provide a vicarious escape from the monotony of everyday life. They also enabled people momentarily to forget the country's pressing social and economic problems'.[25] African filmmakers wishing to confront serious national issues in their films have therefore faced real problems in creating a popular audience for their work, since they are proposing a quite different function for cinema from that to which film audiences are accustomed.

Secondly, the heritage of the colonial period played a key role in the structural organisation of African film production. In the Maghreb, the influence of the French was crucial because of the important infrastructures that were left in place at the time of independence: over 300 cinemas in Algeria, 250 in Morocco, 155 in Tunisia. The interest in cinema which had been developed by the French before independence is reflected in the existence of the same kind of unified federation of national ciné-clubs as exists in France, each equipped with the characteristic French acronym: FTCC in Tunisia, FACC in Algeria, FNCCM in Morocco. South of the Sahara there was no such infrastructure, though a cross-national federation of film clubs, the FACISS, did exist. France's prestige led the new African governments to turn their attention to film and to create national film organisations modelled on the lines of the French CNC.

Thirdly, in all four areas, filmmaking was initially regarded as first and foremost an affair of the state, which played a crucial role in fostering film production and ordering its financing. Throughout the Maghreb it was – unsurprisingly – the indigenous governments in Algeria, Morocco and Tunisia which took on the role of organising film production. But south of the Sahara, many of the key governmental inputs into film production itself were made in Paris, with results that are inevitably ambiguous in their national status and indeed Africanness. These ambiguities are well captured in Ferid Boughedir's observation that 'one can say, broadly, that African cinema, in francophone Africa at least, exists thanks to France and also does not exist thanks to France'.[26]

Fourthly, in virtually all four areas, the attitude of the state towards film production shifted radically in the 1980s and early 1990s, a move exemplified by the closing down of numerous state production organisations and the introduction of new schemes of aid in Morocco and Tunisia. Equally important were the shifts in French aid to African film production, which transformed production south of the Sahara. One sign of this new French approach is the resumption of feature filmmaking in most francophone West African states. Another is the production between 1989 and 1999 of over fifty 35mm short and medium-length films (many works by new directors which have no immediately obvious commercial possibilities).[27] It is to these French aid programmes that we must now turn.

NOTES

1. Ferid Boughedir, *Le Cinéma africain de A à Z* (Brussels: OCIC, 1987), p. 28.
2. Hédi Khelil, *Resistances et utopies: Essais sur le cinéma arabe et africain* (Tunis: Editions Sahar, 1994), p. 4.
3. Ibid., p. 26.
4. For a fuller discussion of distribution and exhibition, see Manthia Diawara, *African Cinema: Politics and Culture* (Bloomington: Indiana University Press, 1992), pp. 104–15.
5. Lotfi Maherzi, *Le Cinéma algérien: Institutions, imaginaire, idéologie* (Algiers: SNED, 1980), p. 66.
6. Ibid.
7. Mohamed Chouikh, 'On croyait être le cheval de Troie qui ferait bouger les choses de l'intérieur', in *Où va le cinéma algérien?*, *Cahiers du Cinéma*, special issue (Paris, February–March 2003), p. 72.
8. Benjamin Stora, *La Guerre invisible: Algérie, années 90* (Paris: Presses de Sciences PO, 2001), p. 7.
9. Boujemaa Karèche, interview in *Où va le cinéma algérien?*, p. 36.
10. As Tewfik Farès asks, 'Is *Rachida* an Algerian film? Is *Rosemary's Baby* a Polish film?', in *Où va le cinéma algérien?*, p. 70.
11. In 1996–7 the disparity was over forty to one ($2.4m Moroccan investment, $98.2m foreign investment) (Rabat: *Cinémaroc* 8, December 1998).
12. Jacques Roitfeld, *Afrique noire francophone* (Paris: Unifrance, 1980).
13. The general decline in African cinemas is illustrated by a more recent survey: twenty-two in Senegal and just seven in Cameroon (both down from fifty-two),

twenty-five in Ivory Coast (down from fifty-nine), twenty-three in Mali (down from thirty). Only the special case of Burkina Faso (up from twelve to thirty-four active cinemas) bucks this trend, in *L'Atlas du Cinéma*, *Cahiers du Cinéma*, special issue (Paris, April 2003), p. 33.

14. Guy Jérémie Ngansop, *Le Cinéma camerounais en crise* (Paris: L'Harmattan, 1987), p. 13. Richard Bjornso, notes that 'the definition of language is a vexed question in this context and depends to a large extent on the way one distinguishes between languages and dialects. Estimates on the number of Cameroonian languages range from sixty to 250', in *The African Quest for Freedom and Identity: Cameroonian Writing and the National Experience* (Bloomington: Indiana University Press, 1994), p. 485.

15. Jonathan Haynes, 'African Filmmaking and the Postcolonial Predicament: *Quartier Mozart* and *Aristotle's Plot*', in Kenneth J. Harrow (ed.), *African Cinema: Postcolonial and Feminist Readings* (Trenton, NJ and Asmara, Eritrea: Africa World Press, 1999), p. 25.

16. Ferid Boughedir, *Le Cinéma en Afrique et dans le monde* (Paris: *Jeune Afrique Plus*, 1984), p. 72.

17. Ibid., p. 76.

18. Though their work does not fit with the 'traditions' traced here, both were important pioneers of African cinema. For Ganda, see Maïzama Issa, *Omarou Ganda, Cinéaste nigérien: Un regard de dedans sur la société en transition* (Dakar: Ena-Édition, 1991), and for Alassane, see Gaêl Teicher, *Moustapha Alassane Cinéaste* (Paris: Les Éditions de l'Oeil, 2003).

19. Boughedir, *Le Cinéma en Afrique*, p. 75.

20. Victor Bachy, *La Haute Volta et le cinéma* (Brussels: OCIC, 1983), p. 7.

21. Boughedir, *Le Cinéma en Afrique*, p. 74.

22. Teresa Hoefert de Turégano, *African Cinema and Europe: Close-up on Burkina Faso*, Florence: European Press Academic, 2005, p. 228.

23. Ibid., p. 229.

24. Ibid., p. 256.

25. Bjornson, *The African Quest*, p. 311.

26. Ferid Boughedir, in Philippe J. Maarek (ed.), *Afrique noire: quel cinéma?* (Actes du colloque, Université Paris X Nanterre, December 1981) (Paris: Association du Cinéclub de l'Université de Paris X, 1983), p. 32.

27. See the *Guide du cinéma africain (1989–1999)* (Paris: Ecrans Nord-Sud, 2000).

4. THE FRENCH CONNECTION

It is less the case of a French aid policy serving the cinemas of the South, than of the latter being used to assist French cultural policy.

Raphaël Millet, 1998[1]

FRENCH AID (1): 1963–79

Filmmaking south of the Sahara has long been a matter of concern for the French government. As a result, although we are dealing with films that often have a distinctly anti-colonial edge and a clear insight into postcolonial realities, it is impossible to understand the existence of these films without considering first the attitudes and policies of the former colonising power, France. A good starting point is the concept of 'Francophonie'. The word itself dates from the nineteenth century, but its modern political sense of a union of those countries where the French language is used in government, commerce, administration and culture has a part-African origin, in the thinking and policies of three post-independence presidents: Léopold Sédar Senghor (Senegal), Habib Bourguiba (Tunisia) and Hamani Diori (Niger). These national leaders were 'preoccupied with maintaining privileged links with the former colonising power within the perspective of postcolonialism'.[2] In world political terms, 'la Francophonie' is an organisation comparable with the British Commonwealth, present in all five continents and with forty-nine member states (twenty-six of them African) and three observers.

Africa has always been a key concern, since, as J. Barrat has observed, 'Africa allows France truly to be a world power, and not just a European one'.[3] As far as cinema is concerned, Raphaël Millet captures the rationale of the French aid programme perfectly:

> The French concept of patrimony is sufficiently wide to encompass cultural productions from the francophone area. Thus the francophone 'cinemas from elsewhere' (*cinémas d'ailleurs*) – even if they are in another language: Baoule, Wolof, Dioula, etc – become 'French' (the shift is easy), and can therefore be statistically integrated into the evaluation of the spread of French culture in the world.[4]

It must always be borne in mind that the relationship between France and its former African colonies is not one between equals. As Alphonse Mannée-Batschy and Berthin Nzélomona stress: 'When one considers the economic exchanges between the members of "la Francophonie", one is struck by the frightening imbalance benefiting the rich countries which are members'. As a result, Africa will 'continue to play the traditional role of supplier of basic products and strategic raw materials in the process of globalisation and the international division of labour'.[5]

It is within such a framework that one needs to evaluate the multiplicity of bilateral and multilateral cultural links which bind the francophone countries, of which those specifically concerning cinema form just one part. Though French aid has been absolutely vital to the creation of African cinema, the actual sums involved are tiny in the context of the overall budgets of the ministries concerned (the French Ministry of Culture receives no less than 1 per cent of the overall French government revenues).[6] In 1963 the French Ministry for Cooperation and Development, set up specifically to oversee cooperation between France and the African states, established a film bureau in Paris, headed by Jean-René Debrix. Like the parallel newsreel production set-up (the CAI), it was staffed by professional editors (among them Andrée Davanture), but it was equipped only with 16mm post-production facilities. Debrix ran the unit till 1978 and during his time the level of African production was so low that every film project could be given backing. An individual filmmaker simply had to turn up at the bureau. But Debrix's successor, Jacques Gérard, found that, with both filmmakers and projects multiplying, choices had to be made and, as he says, 'it was extremely strange for a French administrator to have to make choices about whether or not an African film should be produced'.[7] In all, during the period 1963–75, 125 of the 185 feature and short films made in francophone Africa received French technical and financial support. Debrix claims that, none of these 125 films has been subject to censorship or rejection by the Ministry of Cooperation and its Bureau de cinéma.[8] But he admits that he did refuse to back Ousmane Sembene's *Black Girl/La Noire de . . .* , a bleak picture of French postcolonial attitudes, though the Ministry did subsequently buy the non-commercial distribution rights.

It was through the purchase, at a higher than normal price, of these non-commercial distribution rights – for showings in educational establishments in France and at French cultural centres in Africa – that the French government funding was organised. Any aid before production involved the employment of a French producer, who would control the finance, and post-production aid had to be spent in Paris laboratories or at the bureau's editing facilities: a typical example of an aid programme where the money returns to the donor nation and does nothing to create an infrastructure in the recipient nation. The initial result was also a curiously ghettoised body of films, made by individuals, often without reference to their respective national governments and cut off from normal commercial exhibition outlets in Africa (which were generally equipped for 35mm projection). Instead, the films were at the time available for viewing (in 16mm film or Umatic and VHS copies) through the film library of the Ministry of Cooperation and subsequently through Audecam. Now (a wonderful irony!) the archive is held by the Association pour la Diffusion de la Pensée Française (the Association for the Diffusion of French Thought), which conceals its identity under the acronym ADPF. In general, the films have seldom been available on African screens: this is, in a very real sense, a cinema of which France is 'the *principal* producer and consumer'.[9]

It is hard to dispute Claire Andrade-Watkins's harsh judgement on sixteen years of French aid. She points out that the primary objective of France's post-colonial support was 'to maintain the colonial legacy of assimilation, perpetrating and strengthening a Franco-African cultural connection through newsreels, educational documentaries and films of *cultural expression* produced by Africans and distributed and shown in non-commercial venues such as ciné-clubs, cinémathèques and French embassies throughout francophone Africa'.[10] Debrix talks of the aim of 'an African cinema free in its expression and creativity',[11] but even he seems doubtful of real achievements after a dozen years of administering the scheme, observing that 'everything remains to be done in Africa in the area of cinema'.[12] At times he even seems disparaging, describing African cinema as 'a cinema of ideologues, a cinema for festivals'.[13] Certainly this is a neutered cinema from which any real critique of French neo-colonialism or African corruption must of necessity be absent. It is ostensibly a cinema of cultural identity, but the definition of this identity is distinctly limited in social and political terms. A good example of what could nevertheless be achieved within this system of French aid is Jean-Pierre Dikongue-Pipa's picture of African traditional values in a rural society, *Muna Moto* (1975), which was shot in 16mm but blown up to 35mm, won prizes at festivals in Geneva and Paris, at FESPACO and the JCC, but was seen by only 3,000 spectators when it was shown commercially in Paris.[14]

FRENCH AID (2): 1980–2004

The first French scheme for aid to African filmmaking through the Ministry of Cooperation's film bureau was closed down in the last years of the Giscard presidency, but found new life in 1980 with the advent of President François Mitterand. Initially the French gave support to a number of pan-African projects: the leading African film festival (FESPACO), an African film school (INAFEC), an African film library (the Cinémathèque Africaine), a pan-African distribution organisation (CIDC) and its corresponding production consortium (CIPROFILM). Since all of these initiatives were located in the capital of Burkina Faso, Ouagadougou, this country became in effect the heart of African filmmaking. Aid for film production also resumed, but the focus of post-production facilities in Paris after 1980 was the independent company Atria, set up by Andrée Davanture specifically to support filmmakers north and south of the Sahara and funded by the Ministry of Cooperation and the French film centre (the CNC).

This decentralisation was typical of the way in which French aid was organised from the 1980s onwards. A key development was the establishment in 1984 of the Fonds Sud, funded jointly by the Ministries of Foreign Affairs, Cooperation and Culture, together with the CNC, with a specific brief to finance (with aid of up to 1 million francs per project) features for distribution in film theatres in France and abroad. In the first twenty years of its existence (to the end of 2004) the Fonds Sud helped fund some 322 films worldwide, in Latin America, Asia, Africa, the Middle East and Eastern Europe. Its impact on African filmmaking north and south of the Sahara has been enormous, with no less that 105 films receiving production assistance. By far the greatest amount of aid has gone to Tunisia (twenty-three films), followed at some distance by Burkina Faso (fourteen), Morocco (twelve), Algeria and Senegal (both eleven), Cameroon and Ivory Coast (both six). Guinea, Mauritania, Congo and Chad have each had two films funded; Togo, Benin, Central African Republic and Gabon one each. Fonds Sud funding has been crucial for the development of the careers of certain filmmakers: Nouri Bouzid (Tunisia) has received aid for all five of his features, Idrissa Ouedraogo (Burkina Faso) and Cheick Oumar Sissoko (Mali) for four each of theirs.[15]

That funding from the Fonds Sud has been additional to that which could be obtained directly from the Ministry of Cooperation, from the Fonds d'Action Sociale (FAS), the Agence de Coopération Culturelle et Technique (or ACCT, later reshaped as the Agence Intergouvernementale de la Francophonie) and various other French sources such as the Fondation Gans pour le Cinéma, the Fondation Beaumarchais and the television organisation Canal+. Other European sources which have aided African production include the European Union itself (through the Fonds Européen de Développement (FED), part of whose funding – thanks to French efforts – is reserved for filmmaking). There are also a number of private foundations such as the Dutch Fonds Hubert Bals and the Swiss foundations, Montecinemaverita and Stanley Thomas Johnson, to which filmmakers can apply. In addition, there is also a Canadian funding scheme, linked to the Montreal 'Vues d'Afrique' festival, the 'Programme to Incite North-South Co-operation', and further possibilities of funding from various European television companies. Success with one governmental agency often opens the door to others and encourages private foundations and French production companies to become involved. All of these multiple funding opportunities are in addition to whatever may be available locally in the filmmaker's own country. It is not unusual to find that an African film lists, in its credits, production companies from two or three different countries and support from half a dozen or more funding bodies.

Any African film that achieves funding therefore needs to satisfy a number of divergent foreign needs and interests. It must conform partly at least to European criteria as to what constitutes an 'African' film. From a Burkina Faso perspective, Teresa Hoefert de Turégano argues that 'in essence the Franco-African exchange is far from one-directional and reveals a negotiated new Africanness'.[16] But she ignores the most crucial of the demands made on African filmmakers, namely that, whatever language will be used in the eventual film, a full, dialogued production script in a European language (usually French) will be required by foreign backers. Until very recently it has also been helpful for an African filmmaker to have a production base in Paris in order to take full advantage of all available funding and distribution possibilities. The danger of such procedures is that what will result is a kind of internationalised 'author's cinema' (*cinéma d'auteur*), in which the crucial role the cinema can play in the affirmation of African identity is called into question or at least neutralised.

As far as French-funded productions were concerned, the arrangements after 1990 initially seemed to proceed as before. In 1991 three African features, all funded by the Ministry of Cooperation, shot in 16mm and edited at Atria, were shown in the 'Un certain regard' section of the Cannes festival. But later, Andrée Davanture notes, the situation changed: 'in the 1990s, it seemed that the only films they favoured were those able to "meet" a French audience, to be presented at European film festivals, above all at Cannes. It's a defensible point of view, but it shouldn't be the only one'.[17] Davanture's view is supported by Raphaël Millet, writing in 1998, who notes that 'a selection for Cannes or a large [Parisian] audience is a symbolic success for the Agence de la Francophonie or the Fonds Sud, whose prestige and visibility are thereby increased'.[18]

In 1999 the whole pattern of French aid to African filmmaking took yet another turn. The Ministry of Cooperation was reabsorbed into the Ministry of Foreign Affairs, and the Ministry's previous direct aid scheme now became the Appui au Développement des Cinémas du Sud (ADCSud), which held its first funding meeting in December 2000. Within this new governmental structure African filmmakers no longer had a privileged place and several collaborating organisations which had received funding through the 1990s – such as Atria – now found themselves abandoned. The level of aid (about 20 million francs a year) remained unchanged from the 1990s, but the fund was now open to a new and much wider 'priority' group, the so-called Zone de Solidarité Prioritaire (ZSP). Grants were given to filmmakers from other parts of Africa (Angola, Mozambique, Ghana, South Africa and Ethiopia), and also to directors from Lebanon, Iraq, Cuba, Vietnam and the Palestinian territories. Francophone Africa remained a priority, however, and sixty-five of the eighty-five films given funding between 2001 and 2003 were produced in the francophone countries north and south of the Sahara with which we are concerned here. In January 2004 the ADCSud was itself dissolved and replaced by the Fonds Images Afrique (FIA), targeted specifically at Sub-Saharan Africa. The new programme's stated aims are to enrich the programme rosters of television channels in the countries concerned (funding all types of production – telefilms, sitcoms, animation, video-clips, pilots for magazine programming, documentaries) and to increase the share of African fictional feature films in cinemas in Africa. The new scheme drew its funding from a range of sources: the French Ministry of Foreign Affairs, the Intergovernmental Agency of the Francophonie, the European Commission and the French national film centre (CNC).

The official emphasis continues to be on the development of African cultural identities and once more there are no plans for any investment in African infrastructure. But in fact the work produced can be described as 'exotic film with French cultural affinities' and defined as 'an adjunct to French cinema within a global struggle for existence in the film markets'.[19] In furnishing funding for African film, the French government is indeed attempting to assert for itself a central role in world cinema. To quote Raphaël Millet again: 'Going beyond the defence of its own national cinema (the French "cultural exception"), France affirms itself as a dynamic player in the whole landscape of world cinema'.[20] This view is echoed by the government's own official justification for this aid programme. For example, Dominique Wallon, head of the short-lived organisation set up to promote and distribute African films, 'Ecrans Nord-Sud' (1998–2001), stresses the usefulness of such a scheme for French domestic film production:

> Whether we're talking about Europe, the Maghreb or Black Africa, whatever the differences in cultural identity, there exist cultural familiarities, especially filmic ones, which mean that spectators who go to see *Halfaouine* [Ferid Boughedir's highly successful Tunisian feature of 1990] are more willing to see French films. It's evidence of the absolute solidarity of national cinemas resisting American pressure. Hence the strategy of helping co-productions, the projects with Africa and Eastern Europe.[21]

THE AFRICAN FILMMAKER

How does the individual filmmaker fare in this context so much defined by French government policies? If we look at the overall output of films in the francophone countries north and south of the Sahara, we find that just over 580 films have been made by about 270 filmmakers. The following tabulation – which ignores films shot and distributed on video – lists all fictional feature films to the end of 2004 in accordance with the filmmaker's nationality. It is based on commonly accepted listings and includes a few feature-length documentaries, which were widely seen and are regarded as particularly important, and a few works which, strictly speaking, are shorter than conventional feature length. The listing is shown in Table 4.1.

Table 4.1 African Film Production

Country	Population	Filmmakers	Films	First Feature
Benin	6.0m	5	9	1974
Burkina Faso	10.6m	20	40	1971
Cameroon	14.3m	13	31	1975
Central African Rep	3.5m	1	1 [co-prod]	2003
Chad	7.5m	2	3	1999
Congo	2.8m	4	5	1973
Gabon	1.3m	6	9	1971
Guinea	7.1m	7 [2 collectives]	14	1966
Ivory Coast	14.5m	13	26	1969
Mali	10.9m	11	25	1975
Mauritania	2.5m	2	9	1971
Niger	10.4m	5	12	1972
Senegal	9.2m	21	47	1964
Togo	4.5m	1	1	1992

Sub-Saharan Africa Total		Filmmakers	Films	
		111	232 (48% first films)	

Country	Population	Filmmakers	Films	First Feature
Algeria	27.0m	53	125	1965
Morocco	26.0m	61	149	1968
Tunisia	8.5m	44	82	1966

Maghreb Total		Filmmakers	Films	
		158	356 (45% first films)	

OVERALL TOTAL		Filmmakers	Films	
		269	588 (46% first films)	

The tabulation of production to the end of 2004 allows us to see the strict limitations in film output throughout the four areas in the forty years since Sembene's feature debut in 1966: on average barely two films per filmmaker, and in total about fourteen films a year split between seventeen sovereign states with a total population of over 166 million. Aside from Ousmane Sembene, who has managed to combine nine completed feature films with a parallel output of ten novels and volumes of short stories, only a handful of Maghrebian filmmakers have been able to make a real career in African cinema. Perhaps because of the paucity of output, it is seldom possible to trace any kind of creative development over time in the work of an African filmmaker. Few can be said to have surpassed the qualities of their first features in their later work (though some have undoubtedly equalled it). As a result, in this study which looks at major works, most of the films discussed are debut features, with all the particular excitements and constraints that this implies. Indeed, over half of all francophone African filmmakers north and south of the Sahara have failed to complete a second feature. Where a second feature film has been completed, this has often been long delayed: twenty years (1982–2002) for Kollo Daniel Sanou from Burkina Faso, twenty-one years (1972–93) for the Algerian Djafar Damardjji, twenty-two years (1980–2002) for the Tunisian Abdellatif Ben Ammar, twenty-five years (1970–95) for the Moroccan Hamid Benani. For this reason, the order of discussion of a filmmaker is in accordance with the decade in which s/he made a first feature or switched to a radically difference form of filmmaking.

Gaps similar to those in individual careers occur in the 'national' outputs of Sub-Saharan states, with no films between 1985 and 1999 for Benin, between 1982 and 1995 for Congo, or between 1978 and 1999 for Gabon. Even if we treat the Sub-Saharan states as a single block, the average output is still less than six feature films a year, and there are only three years when the collective output rose above ten films a year (twelve features were produced in 1982, and eleven in both 1992 and 2002). The same pattern is largely true of the Maghreb, where Algeria averages under three features a year and peaked at eleven features in 1972 and twelve in 1982, and Morocco averages just over three features a year and has reached ten only twice (in 1982 and 1995). The smallest Maghrebian cinema, Tunisia, averages just over two films a year and reached its highest annual figure (seven) in 2002. Since much of this tiny output – even some of the work of the most prestigious filmmakers – is partly shaped by the exigencies of French aid or international co-production requirements, to talk of indigenous 'film industries' is meaningless. Even to talk of 'national cinemas' is hazardous (and a concept many filmmakers would deny). For this reason the following chapters concentrate largely either on broad developments that involve filmmakers from the whole range of countries (Chapters 5 to 8) or on the work of some of the younger directors, born after independence and chosen for the individuality of their distinctive personal styles and approaches (Chapters 9 to 14).

There are certain uniform production constraints on all filmmakers throughout the four geographical areas. Almost always, the filmmaker has to take on the triple role of producer-director-writer, and s/he will often take on another role or two as well: as editor, composer of the film score or lead actor, for example. Putting a project together is a complex activity, involving liaison with state authorities and private sector organisations, local and international funding bodies, as well as indigenous and foreign television companies. Even when – as in the nationalised film sector in Algeria up to the mid-1980s – it would seem that the state has taken on the production role, the direct responsibility has usually been put back onto the director. This is clear from Mohamed Chouikh's account of his experience working for the state film organisation ONCIC in Algeria:

> Until *Youssef*, my principal producer was the Algerian state organisation. Its function was generally limited to that of a letter-box, because you had to do everything yourself: bring together aid and financing and then hand over the management of this to the organisation, in exchange for a derisory salary. Nevertheless it had the power of life or death over the film's production.[22]

In all four areas, filmmakers have similar backgrounds, generally being members of an educated bilingual élite. Often their education in their native countries has been supplemented by university education or technical training abroad, and a surprising number have higher degrees or doctorates, in addition to formal film school qualifications. Ousmane Sembene's background as mechanic, carpenter and mason in Senegal and as factory worker, longshoreman and trade union organiser in France makes him virtually unique among African filmmakers. A more usual background is that of his Senegalese contemporary Paulin Soumanou Vieyra: boarding school in France from the age of ten, a spell studying biology at the University of Paris and then three years training at the Parisian film school IDHEC, where he graduated in 1955.

Over half of all filmmakers north and south of the Sahara have formal film school training and generally this has been been received abroad, in Europe. There are only two established training centres in Africa: the Ghanaian Film School and the Cairo Higher Institute of Cinema. No francophone filmmakers have been trained in Ghana and only two Moroccans – neither of them a major figure (Hassan Moufti and Imane Mesbahi) – are Cairo graduates. By contrast, dozens of African filmmakers are graduates of the major European film schools: the French IDHEC, CLCF and more recently FEMIS, the Belgian school INSAS,

FAMU in Prague, the Polish school at Lodz, the Moscow-based Soviet institute VGIK, and so on. There have been two unsuccessful attempts to establish a film school in francophone Africa. But the Algerian school established at Ben Aknoun in Algiers in 1964, the INC, closed after an abbreviated course with just one intake of students (though these included future feature directors Merzak Allouache, Farouk Beloufa and Sid Ali Mazif). A more ambitious attempt to set up a pan-African training institution, INAFEC, began in Burkina Faso in 1976. INAFEC received funding from UNESCO, was attached to the University of Ouagadougou and among its graduates were three of the leading Burkina Faso directors, Idrissa Ouedraogo, Dani Kouyaté and Régina Fanta Nacro, but it closed inside a decade.

It is impossible, of course, to make precise divisions between filmmakers on the basis of their date of birth, since the ages at which they make their first film vary widely. The Tunisian Ferid Boughedir was just twenty-six when he co-directed his first feature, as was Jean-Pierre Bekolo from Cameroon when he made *Quartier Mozart*. In contrast, two documentarists, the Senegalese Paulin Soumanou Vieyra and the Moroccan Abdelmajid Rchich, were fifty-six and fifty-eight respectively at their fictional feature film debuts. But certain generalisations are possible, since the age profiles of filmmakers in all four areas north and south of the Sahara are remarkably similar and it is instructive to align African filmmakers in terms of their age in relation to the date of national independence (1956 for Morocco and Tunisia, 1958 for Guinea, 1960 for the other Sub-Saharan states and 1962 for Algeria).

If we compare the statistics concerning the 153 Maghrebian and 100 Sub-Saharan filmmakers whose birth dates are known, we find that in both cases there is a small number of filmmakers (fifty-three in all, just over a fifth of the total) who were born in 1940 or before. If we take twenty to be the age of adulthood, these future filmmakers were adults at the time of independence. Among this group we find most of the key figures in the first years of African cinema: Mohamed Lakhdar Hamina and Ahmed Rachedi in Algeria, Omar Khlifi in Tunisia, Med Hondo in Mauritania, Ousmane Sembene in Senegal and Souleymane Cisse in Mali among them. Though only a few were directly involved in the liberation struggle, a concern with the anti-colonial struggle as well as the harsh contradictions of emerging post-independence societies is common in their films. Though state censorship tends to limit what they can say directly, they are often extremely critical of the ways in which African societies have developed.

Over 60 per cent of all filmmakers North and South of the Sahara (about 158 in total) were born between the early 1940s and the end of the 1950s and so were teenagers or children when independence was acquired. The characterisation of these younger Arab filmmakers of his own generation made by Nouri Bouzid (himself born in 1944, eighteen years before Tunisian independence) can also be applied to filmmakers south of the Sahara, many of whom were brought up as Muslims:

> Born in the 1940s, they grew up on Nasserite slogans. Then they tasted defeat [the 1967 Israeli war], then experienced the May 1968 student movement in Europe, then learnt about democracy and discovered international cinema. When they returned home, they were full of hopes and dreams. But the harsh reality hit them in the face: no resources, no market, no freedom of expression.[23]

Many of this generation have continued to concern themselves with social issues treated in a generally realistic manner (one thinks, for example, of the Moroccans Jillali Ferhati, Hakim Noury and Mohamed Abderrahman Tazi). But it is also to this generation that we owe the stylistic renewal and move towards both abstraction and interiority which occurred from the mid-1980s onwards. The key figures in this group – Bouzid himself and Ferid Boughedir in Tunisia, Merzak Allouache and Mohamed Chouikh in Algeria, Gaston Kabore and Idrissa Ouedraogo in Burkina Faso, Djibril Diop Mambety in Senegal and Cheikh Oumar Sissoko in Mali among them – are the filmmakers who have given us both a new sense of the individual African experience and some of the cinema's most vivid evocations of a perhaps nostalgically viewed African past from which the coloniser is absent. It is the very diverse work of these two founding generations which forms the subject matter for the following four chapters.

There are also some forty filmmakers who were born after independence, making up some 17 per cent of the overall total of francophone African filmmakers. Within this generation we have a wide variety of voices, some of which are analysed individually in the latter chapters of this study. Though few have made more than a couple of features there are major talents already apparent here: Nabil Ayouch from Morocco, Raja Amari from Tunisia, Abderrahmane Sissako from Mauritania, Mahamat Saleh Haroun from Chad, Dani Kouyaté from Burkina Faso, and Jean-Pierre Bekolo from Cameroon among them. There is an interesting contrast between these younger filmmakers and their elders, noted by Melissa Thackway.[24] After completing their film training in Europe and making their debut films from a base there, the filmmakers of the 1960s and 1970s always intended to return to settle in Africa and usually did so. The new post-independence generation, by contrast, mostly comprises filmmakers permanently based in Europe (some were indeed born there) who visit Africa largely when they are shooting their films. Given the current forces of globalisation and pressures towards cultural hybrity present in twenty-first-century world cinema, this group must struggle to avoid one of the pitfalls for the 'native intellectual' predicted by Frantz Fanon, namely that of becoming 'individuals without an anchor, without a horizon, colourless, stateless, rootless – a race of angels'.[25]

NOTES

1. Raphaël Millet, '(In)dépendance des cinémas du Sud &/vs France', Paris: *Théorème 5*, 1998, p. 163.
2. Berthin Nzélomona (ed.), *La Francophonie* (Paris: L'Harmattan/*Recherches Africaines 5*, 2001), p. 8.
3. J. Barrat, cited in N'Zelomona, *La Francophonie*, p. 10.
4. Millet, '(In)dépendance', p. 164.
5. élomona, *La Francophonie*, p. 27.
6. Millet, '(In)dépendance', p. 159.
7. Jacques Gérard, in Jacques J. Maarek (ed.), *Afrique noire: quel cinéma?* (Paris: Association du Cinéclub de l'Université de Paris X, 1983), p. 35.
8. Jean-René Debrix, interview, in Guy Hennebelle and Catherine Ruelle, *Cinéastes de l'Afrique noire* (Paris: Fespaco/*CinémAction 3/L'Afrique littéraire et artistique 49*, 1978), p. 153.
9. Millet, '(In)dépendance', p. 167
10. Andrade-Watkins, Claire, 'France's Bureau of Cinema: Financial and Technical Assistance between 1961 and 1977', *Framework* 38–9, (London: 1992), p. 28.
11. Debrix, interview, p. 154.
12. Ibid., p. 156.
13. Ibid.
14. Ibid., p. 155.
15. Jean-Michel Frodon (ed.), *Au Sud du Cinéma* (Paris: Cahiers du Cinéma/Arte Editions, 2004), pp. 200–51.
16. Teresa Hoefert de Turégano, *African Cinema and Europe: Close-up on Burkina Faso* (Florence: European Press Academic, 2005), p. 10.
17. Andrée Davanture, 'Le lâchage d'*Atria*', interview, in Samuel Lelièvre (ed.), *Cinémas africains, une oasis dans le désert?* (Paris: Corlet/Télérama/*CinémAction* 106, 2003), p. 73.
18. Millet, '(In)dépendance', p. 162.
19. Turégano, *African Cinema and Europe*, p. 119.
20. Millet, '(In)dépendance', p. 142.
21. Dominique Wallon, cited in Lelièvre, *Cinémas africains*, p. 63.
22. Mohamed Chouikh, interview, in Camille Taboulay, *Le Cinéma métaphorique de Mohamed Chouikh* (Paris: K Films Editions, 1997), p. 66.
23. Nouri Bouzid, 'New Realism in Arab Cinema: The Defeat-Conscious Cinema', in Ferial J. Ghazoul (ed.), *Arab Cinematics: Towards the New and the Alternative* (Cairo: *Alif: Journal of Comparative Poetics* 15, 1995), pp. 246–7.
24. Melissa Thackway, *Africa Shoots Back: Alternative Perspectives in Sub-Saharan Francophone African Film* (London: James Currey, 2003), p. 135.
25. Frantz Fanon, *The Wretched of the Earth* (Harmondsworth: Penguin, 1967), p. 175.

PART II

CONFRONTING REALITY

African cinema connects the past and the future of Africa . . . History and tradition in Africa, and particularly in African cinema, are the equivalent not of oak trees, but grasslands; they provide sustenance for a way of life, but they also spread across the land in a complex, interwoven pattern. This complexity allows for movement, for change.

Teshome H. Gabriel[1]

5. LIBERATION AND POSTCOLONIAL SOCIETY

Cinema plays an essential role because it is a means of education, information, awareness and at the same time an incentive to creativity.

The achievement of such objectives means a questioning of the African
movie-maker or the image he has of himself, of the nature of his function,
of his social status, and in general of his situation in society.

The Algiers Charter of African Cinema, 1974[2]

INTRODUCTION

One way of examining the issues raised by the development of African cinema
in the course of the three 'generations' defined in the previous chapter would be
to deal with them in terms of a simple realist/modernist dichotomy. There is
much to be said for such an approach, but there are difficulties in applying terms
with such distinct Western connotations to African culture, and the approach
perhaps overemphasises differences, where continuities are also equally important. The approach adopted here is to consider African filmmakers in terms of
the subject which concerns them all, that of their African cultural identity. As
Raphaël Millet points out, because of the heritage of colonisation and the
present reality of dependence 'the cinemas of the South inevitably have to
discourse about identity as much as about independence'.[3]

Stuart Hall's definitions in his article on 'Cultural Identity and Cinematic
Representation' offer an extremely useful way of approaching this question of
identity. As Hall rightly observes, 'identity is not as transparent or unproblematic

as we think'. Instead of thinking of identity 'as an already accomplished historical fact, which the new cinematic discourses then represent, we should think, instead, of identity as a "production", which is never complete, always in process, and always constituted within, not outside representation'.[4] Hall goes on to contrast two ways of thinking about cultural identity, distinguishing between those who see it as a matter of 'being' and those for whom it is a matter of 'becoming'. The first position defines cultural identity in terms of 'the idea of one, shared culture . . . which people with a shared history and identity hold in common'.[5] The second position focuses more on 'critical points of deep and significant *difference* which constitute what we really are': rather – since history has intervened – 'what we have become'.[6]

The first approach characterises the bulk of African filmmakers of all generations. On the whole, they have assumed – to quote Hall once more – that our cultural identities reflect 'the common historical experiences and shared cultural codes which provide us, as "one people", with stable, unchanging and continuous frames of reference and meaning, beneath the shifting divisions and vicissitudes of our actual history'.[7] Hence they have assumed that their task is to 'discover, excavate, bring to light and express through cinematic representation'[8] a national identity conceived as having been buried during the long years of colonial rule. The approach, combining a realist style and a tone of social criticism adopted by the first generation of African filmmakers, has provided a model for many of those who have followed them through into the 2000s, though with a steady lessening of the didacticism of early African filmmaking.

Exploring the realities that surrounded them and communicating these via the screen seemed initially the key demands made on filmmakers. Over the first two decades of African filmmaking, there is a certain continuity with the mood of the 1960s – exemplified by the writings of Frantz Fanon – which sought a new awareness of national identity in all countries emerging from colonial rule. Initially the experience of anti-imperial struggles led to a simple equation of independence and nationalism, and intellectuals of all kinds felt it their duty to speak directly to their fellow citizens about these matters. In this sense they represent the third level of Fanon's 'panorama on three levels' of the returning native intellectual, namely 'the fighting phase' when 'he turns himself into an awakener of the people; hence comes a fighting literature, a revolutionary literature, and a national literature'.[9] The realities of post-independence Africa have subsequently led many to question this equation. But for the pioneer filmmakers initially considered here, who all began their careers in the 1960s – one Senegalese, two Algerians and one Tunisian – this stance not only shaped their first films, but also continued to mark their work throughout their careers. Much the same focus on social issues characterises the wider range of filmmakers north and south of the Sahara whose careers began in the 1970s.

THE 1960S PIONEERS

What interests the founder of African cinema, the French-language novelist turned filmmaker Ousmane Sembene (born 1923 in **Senegal**), is 'exposing the problems confronting my people. I consider the cinema a means of political action'.[10] Sembene's career as a filmmaker over some forty years has been exemplary, both in following this agenda and in its productivity: nine feature films and a number of shorts, accompanied by an equally impressive output of seven novels and three books of short stories (some of which he has translated to film). Sembene began his career with an incisive short film on the problems of post-independence Senegal, *Borom Sarret* (1962), and followed it with three features, all adapted from his own published French-language stories. All adopted a similar line, focusing on the plight of the individual, depicted in his or her defining physical surroundings, but not probed psychologically.

Black Girl/La Noire de . . . (1966) is a sixty-minute film dealing with a subject widely treated in the early years of African cinema: alienation. It follows the experience of a Senegalese maid who achieves her greatest ambition when her employers take her with them to France. But France does not live up to her expectations and, though she suffers no real brutality, she feels increasingly lonely and exploited. After a quarrel with her employers, she kills herself by slitting her throat. The film ends with the husband taking her belongings back to Dakar (perhaps, as Sembene suggests, hoping to hire a new maid at the same time).[11] *Black Girl* was shot without sound (for budget reasons), in black and white, and with a documentary-style simplicity. The shaping of the narrative is similarly pared down, built around simple binary oppositions: France/Senegal, black/white, mistress/servant. It begins with the maid's arrival in France, followed by flashbacks to Dakar to explain how she got there. Thereafter the film proceeds in strictly chronological manner towards its inevitable ending, making no use of the techniques of suspense and with only a touch of visual symbolism (the mask which changes hands several times). Similarly the modernist possibilities of setting the images of the Diola-speaking maid against a voice-over of her thoughts in polished French are totally ignored. Instead Sembene uses the device as a storytelling prop, as he struggles with limited resources to create a realist text in the manner of his novels and stories.

In contrast, *The Money Order/Mandabi* (1968), shot in colour and with better resources, is a lively if somewhat uncomfortable comedy, which offers a sharply focused critique of post-independence African society. Because of the demands of the co-producer (the French CNC), the film was made in a two separate versions: French and Wolof. The latter, Sembene's preferred option, caused him considerable difficulties, since the film had a French-language source and a written French script with a tight dramatic structure which he was keen to retain. Since Wolof at the time was not a written language, the dialogue had to be largely improvised by Sembene and his bilingual actors. The plot is triggered by the arrival from his nephew in France of a money order which seems to promise wealth to Ibrahima, an pompous but uneducated man living with his two wives in difficult traditional circumstances. The fact that the minimal sum represents the savings of an exiled Parisian road sweeper adds to the irony of the situation. Trying to cash the money order leads the illiterate (and hence vulnerable) Ibrahima into alien parts of Dakar, where greedy French-speaking bureaucrats and supposed helpers cheat and humiliate him. The film allows Sembene to give an unequivocal portrait of the contradictions of postcolonial Dakar, and the film ends with a muted plea for change. The deeply conservative Ibrahima is an unlikely candidate for the role of revolu- tionary, since he prefers a traditional existence, in which 'modern' issues, like questioning polygamy and facing up to the challenges of a cash economy, can be ignored. But the film as a whole reveals Sembene's own views on these matters with striking clarity, as he depicts Dakar as a city where traditional values have no power and where literacy and a mastery of two languages is merely a path to wealth and corruption. The film was widely welcomed in France, but caused enough controversy in Senegal to prove that Sembene had touched on truly sensitive issues.[12]

Xala (1974), adapted from a novel published the same year, is a savage indict- ment of the new ruling classes in Senegal (and elsewhere in Africa) who, with independence, have refused to change society, but instead have merely taken over the role of the French colonisers. Their situation is made clear in the beautifully realised balletic opening scene, where each receives a briefcase stuffed with banknotes from the French who retain their control, though they now act from the shadows. The film's protagonist, El Hadj Abou Kader, forms part of this new élite and lives an affluent life. He celebrates by marrying a third wife, Ngone (who is younger than his daughter Rama), but on his wedding night he is afflicted with temporary sexual impotence (the 'xala' of the title), resulting from the curse of a beggar he has dispossessed. His efforts to cope with this and to find a cure, lead to financial ruin, marital break-up and expulsion from the élite, in which he is replaced by a pickpocket who has grown affluent. When a marabout does affect a cure, El Hadj's problems seem to be over, but the cheque with which he pays bounces, and the curse is restored. This time it can be lifted only by ritual humiliation, as El Hadj is forced to strip and submit to the beggars spitting on him, in full view of his family.

In addition to its use of impotence as both symbol and source of black humour, *Xala* is full of genuinely brilliant comic touches (such as El Hadj having his Mercedes washed with imported Evian water) and sharp social observation (the differentiation between the three wives is a vivid representation of the changing role of women over three generations). But above all, it is for its pitiless dissec- tion of its (unnamed) African setting that the film is remarkable. As Laura

Mulvey observes, Sembene uses the language of cinema 'to create a kind of poetics of politics', giving visibility to 'the forms, as opposed to the content, of social contradiction and then, through the forms, illuminates the content.[13]

Sembene's subsequent trio of films about the colonial past – *Emitai* (1971), *Ceddo* (1977) and *Camp de Thiaroye* (1988) – were all made from original scripts and, in a very original way, show a concern to tell history in terms of groups rather than individuals. *Emitai* depicts two assaults by French colonial troops on an Diola village community, the first to persuade one of the young men of the village, who has fled into the forest, to return and to do his military service, the second to find and confiscate the year's harvest of rice, needed by the French to feed their troops. The film does not focus on the obvious protagonist from a Western viewpoint: Badji, a young African recruit, regarded by his European superiors as the finest black NCO in the district and, by chance, a native of this particular village. Instead of focusing on Badji's personal concerns, Sembene is concerned with the depiction of social forces: the conflict between traditional culture and colonialism and the role of group solidarity in shaping political events. Hence Sembene offers us a new, non-Western, film dra-maturgy. The conflict is told almost exclusively in terms of spatial oppositions between groups. The primary opposition is, of course, between colonisers and villagers. The traditional division of labour (the women growing the rice, the men acting as warriors) is translated into spatial terms through the separation of the two groups. The women, who have hidden the rice in the forest, are held captive in the village square. The men, denied access to them, become locked in debate at the shrine of the gods who seem to have deserted them, and this gives rise to a division within their ranks (between fighters and appeasers). It is between such groups – and not between individual figures who represent them or embody their values – that the drama is acted out. The focus is unflinchingly on the central conflict of colonisers and villagers, presented without the per-sonalisation of issues which invariably colours Western treatments of the themes of repression and colonial brutality.

Ceddo shows the way in which an individualistic revolt, which in the West would be a focus of attention, can in African cinema lead not just to marginal-isation, but even to literal exclusion from the narrative. Early on, Madior Fatima Fall, the king's nephew, is a key figure, since under traditional African law he is the king's heir. When he loses this position under the newly imposed Muslim law, he flamboyantly renounces his adopted Muslim faith. But though he reverts to traditional garb, he is now excluded from any role in the community and his words at the king's council go unheeded. Though – in Western terms – he embodies in his person so many of the key aspects of the film's conflicts, his role in Sembene's film is effectively extinguished as soon as he loses his role within the community. When the imam takes over in the name of Allah, Madior Fatima Fall simply vanishes from the last forty-five minutes of the narrative, in which, as a mere individual, he now has no part to play.[14] The use of a group, rather than an individual protagonist, inevitably results in a slow and measured pace and rhythm. While an individual's life can be subject to rapid change, groups shift much more slowly over time, in response to long-term social, economic and political forces.

Set in 1944, *Camp de Thiaroye* (1988) is another group portrait, but of a more conventional kind. This time a squad of *tirailleurs* (African soldiers who fought for France) return to colonial Africa, their independent spirit symbolised by their US uniforms and boots. Initially, they are warmly welcomed at the reception camp, but step by step they are cheated and humiliated by the French who want to reduce them to 'natives'. Eventually the frustrated *tirailleurs* seize a French general and attempt to negotiate. When he gives his word of honour, they release him, but of course he cannot tolerate such a humiliation and at 3am he sends in his tanks. The film ends with a fresh group of African recruits being led off to fight France's battles in Europe. *Camp de Thiaroye* has clear thematic links with Sembene's earlier works and the same strong anti-colonial stance. But the action is predictable and, at two hours twenty minutes running time, somewhat ponderous. Though most critics have accepted the film as basically a true story and a revealing tale of French colonial rule, two US critics have drawn attention to supposed historical inaccuracies. Kenneth W. Harrow argues that the soldiers in the tanks were themselves Senegalese,[15] and Josef Gugler, while seeming to support Harrow's doubts, states categorically that 'as to the tanks, the French had none in West Africa in 1944'.[16]

Sembene's three final films, all released after he had reached the age of sixty-nine, form a loose trilogy of 'stories of everyday heroism'. They are very mixed in their themes and impact, but all are directed in the same straightforward manner (a chronological narrative interspersed with clearly marked flashbacks or dream sequences). They are essentially celebratory works, with the biting satire of Sembene's earlier studies of contemporary life largely missing, even when religion and superstition are confronted. Unlike the earlier literary adaptations, *Guelwaar* (1992) was from an original script, later turned into a novel by Sembene and published in this form in 1996, with the inscription: 'An African fable of twenty-first century Africa, dedicated to the children of the continent'. As David Murray has observed, while many in the West have become pessimistic about the possibility of finding solutions to Africa's problems, Sembene 'remains resolutely committed to his Marxist ideals and his work has continued to address, in a more or less direct manner, the political and social questions facing modern Africa'.[17] This is reflected here in his rejection of international aid programmes for Africa. *Guelwaar* traces the difficulties that arise between two communities when the body of a Christian activist, Pierre Henri Thioune (known as Guelwaar), is mistakenly buried in a Muslim cemetery. As the dispute grows, the social divisions of Senegal are revealed. So too (through a series of flashbacks) are the contradictions of Guelwaar's own life (such as his refusal of foreign aid, but willingness to live off his daughter's earnings as a prostitute). Despite his Marxist beliefs, Sembene is respectful towards the Christian community but less so towards the Muslim villagers, shown as both deluded and violent. The outcome is a very muted victory for tolerance: those who struggle for peace are all rebuked by their superiors, and the credit for success is claimed by a leading local politician, who hands out international food aid as if it were a personal present. Sembene's later style allows little scope for ambiguity or suspense, but this is a serious and committed piece of filmmaking.

Faat-Kine (2000) focuses on the status of women in contemporary Senegal. In Sembene's view, 'Without women, Africa has no future. But poverty and globalisation affect them more'.[18] The protagonist, Faat-Kine, is a woman who was born in the year of Senegal's independence and, despite many difficulties, has worked her way up to owning a petrol station. On the day her two children pass their baccalaureate, she remembers her past life and the men who have successively let her down (in clearly marked flashbacks). In the present, she copes with immediate daily challenges, giving the men from her past their meuppance, and takes herself a new husband. The film as a whole has the air of a lively, well-plotted, largely French-language television soap opera.

Moolade (2002), shot in Burkina Faso with a crew drawn from all over Africa, is a more substantial film, in which the peace of a village is disturbed by the arrival of four little girls fleeing a female excision ceremony. They are given refuge (the 'moolade' of the title) by the forceful Collé Ardo, who had preserved her own daughter, Amsatou, from mutilation years earlier. The traditionally minded village elders, however, side with the troop of seven women excisers and try to combat the new ideas, even having Collé Ardo publicly flogged by her husband. The chaos in the village is witnessed by an outsider (the ex-soldier-turned-trader Mercenaire) whose eventual intervention results in his own killing by a mob of villagers. But the village women maintain their solidarity against the traditional barbarity (practised still in thirty-eight of the fifty-four states in the African Union), and they even win a few men to their cause. The film ends with a virtual propaganda pageant, as the women defiantly dance and chant their refusal of traditional ways. In the clash of two traditions (excision and sanctuary) is is very clear where Sembene stands, in a film that echoes the explicit didacticism of his earliest work, such as *Black Girl*.

Turning to the Maghreb in the 1960s, the situation in post-independence **Algeria** was, as Réda Bensmaïa has pointed out, extremely challenging for artists and intellectuals in the aftermath of the war of liberation. On the one hand, there were 'popular masses so uprooted from their culture that the very idea of a "public" seemed to be a luxury or, at best, a difficult goal to attain'.[19] On the other, there were artists who had to decide which elements to use in the attempt to rebuild a national culture: 'The forgotten past? The ruins of popular memory? Folklore? Tradition? None of these carried within it enough force and cohesion to allow it to be a stable anchor for a national culture worthy of the name'.[20] But for the pioneer Algerian filmmakers of the 1960s the choice was comparatively simple, since several of this group of directors had close personal links with the liberation struggle. The Frenchmen René Vautier and Jacques Charby were both FLN activists, Ahmed Rachedi (born 1938) had collaborated with Vautier in the army film unit, while Mohamed Lakhdar Hamina (born 1934) had worked in the provisional government's film unit in exile in Tunis. Mohamed Slim Riad (born 1932) was even able to use his own experiences as a detainee in France as the basis for his first feature, *The Way/La Voie* (1968). These filmmakers' desire to deal with the colonial past coincided precisely with the needs and demands of the new government of Houari Boumediene, who had seized power in a military coup in 1965.

The two key films of the 1960s in Algeria are Rachedi's *Dawn of the Damned/L'Aube des damnés* (1965), a brilliantly edited compilation film which showed the often violent images of the anti-colonial struggle throughout Africa which the Algerians had been unable to see during the years of French rule, and Mohamed Lakhdar Hamina's *The Wind from the Aurès/Le Vent des Aurès* (1966), a masterly study of a family destroyed by the war. As Miloud Mimoun has observed, 'The sequence where the mother in Lakhdar Hamina's *The Wind from the Aurès* moves along the barbed-wire fence, behind which the tormented and resolute faces of the Algerian prisoners are lined up, resumes, in a single tracking shot, all the elements of a dramaturgy which History has summoned up'.[21]

In the late 1960s and the 1970s both Rachedi and Lakhdar Hamina made further significant films about the liberation, this time with big budgets. Rachedi's *Opium and the Stick/L'Opium et le bâton* (1969) was adapted from a novel by Mouloud Mammeri. The film, which begins in Algiers under French oppression, follows its doctor protagonist, Bachir Lazrak, back to a remote Kabyle village where his family is divided: his younger brother is fighting with the FLN, while his elder brother collaborates with the French. The events leading to the destruction of the village are shaped for full dramatic effect, but Rachedi has admitted to 'weaknesses and concessions to the audience'.[22] The effect is to simplify a complex novel, omitting 'the anguish, the contradictions and the lucid though desperate commitment of an Algerian intellectual to the war'.[23] The use of the Arab language for the Berber protagonists also serves the state's ideological desire to depict Algeria as a unified, totally Arab entity.

Lakhdar Hamina followed two lesser films about the the anti-colonial struggle – *Hassan terro* (1968), a comic tale of an insignificant little man caught up in the resistance by accident, and *December/Décembre* (1972), which told the story through the eyes of a French officer – with what is generally recognised as his masterpiece, *Chronicle of the Years of Embers/Chronique des années de braise* (1975). This epic film, which was the first Arab or African film to win the Palme d'or at the Cannes Film Festival, was made – at a cost estimated to be equivalent to a dozen ordinary Algerian features – to celebrate the anniversary of the beginning of the Algerian war of liberation on 1 November 1954. Shot in a 70mm format, the film is technically remarkable, but the use of a lush Hollywood-style score by Frenchman Philippe Arthuys denies it a specifically national feel. Tracing events in the years up to 1954, the narrative entwines two parallel stories: that of the wise madman (played with enormous gusto by the director himself), and that of Ahmed, a totally mythologised figure, who is successively uneducated peasant, skilled craftsman and legendary swordsman. Lakhdar Hamina describes the film as a 'personal vision'[24] – which allows awkward historical facts to be elided – and oddly for a film aimed to be an epic of the national consciousness, it ends with the parallel deaths of both protagonists, just as the struggle for liberation finally gets underway. *Chronicle of the Years of Embers* is a striking, if mystificatory, film, more a work of lyrical protest than a lucid historical study.[25]

Lakhdar Hamina was unable to capture the same impact in his subsequent work, though both his 1980s films showed the desire to find an international audience. *Sand Storm/Vent de sable* (1983) is the story of an isolated rural community torn apart by male violence and characterised by the suffering of its women. By contrast, *The Last Image/La Dernière image* (1986) is, according to Lakhdar Hamina, an autobiographical piece, an evocation of his own childhood experience. Set in an Algerian village in 1939, on the eve of the outbreak of the Second World War, it shows the disruption caused in the village by the arrival of a new teacher from the metropolis, Mademoiselle Boyer.

Rachedi's later career is perhaps more successful. He offered an insightful view of immigrant life in Paris in *Ali in Wonderland/Ali au pays des mirages* (1979). In it, the protagonist shares a tiny apartment with two friends and very strict rules: no women, no animals, no visits, no heating, no kitchen smells and no Arab music. His job is as a crane operator, and from his lofty perch he works out his own philosophy:

> Open your eyes and look at them, but don't go so far as to judge them. Your view is superficial. They've looked at us too, without trying to understand us. And that's how the gulf between us has come about. Look, but don't rush to judge them.

When Ali does attempt to intervene, in order to try to save a man he has seen suffer a heart attack, he is treated as the outsider responsible for the death – the killer – by the man's white neighbours. Five years later Rachedi satirised the FLN post-independence bureaucracy in the wonderfully acerbic *Monsieur Fabre's Mill/Le Moulin de M. Fabre* (1984), his last film to date. Set a year after independence in a remote town where the biggest problems are a cow falling down a well and the goalkeeper of the local team falling unhappily in love, the film shows the repercussions of a planned visit by a dignitary from Algiers. Life is turned upside down, the run-down old mill owned by an Algerian-born French supporter of the FLN is pointlessly nationalized, and huge disputes are provoked between locals and the officials who have been sent from Algiers to create a wholly fictive image of the town. The distance between a centralised bureaucracy wanting to apply socialist principles and a rural community yet to receive the slightest sign of progress could not be wider. The film is a savage but often very funny satire on the processes of Algerian government.

There is an echo of the Algerian approach in the work in **Tunisia** of the pioneer Omar Khlifi (born 1934), who came from the Tunisian amateur film movement without formal professional training and worked initially in a context of government indifference. Khlifi made a loose trilogy set at various stages of the Tunisian 'revolution': *The Dawn/L'Aube* (1966), was set in 1954, with an epilogue showing the return to Tunis of the nationalist leader Habib Bourguiba on 1 June 1955; *The Rebel/Le Rebelle* (1968) looked back to the internal struggle against tyranny in the 1860s; and *The Fellagas/Les Fellagas* (1970) traced stages in the liberation struggle and post-independence conflict with the French from 1951 to 1961. Unlike his more committed contemporaries, Khlifi wanted to make films which both 'revive and renew our national identity' and 'have a meaning for the Tunisian people, a connection with its history', and at the same time constitute 'entertaining spectacles'.[26] After a study of women's oppression, *Screams/Hurlements* (1972), widely considered his best film, there was a fourteen-year break before his final return to filmmaking and his old subject matter with the resistance tale, *The Challenge/Le Défi* (1986).

THE 1970s

In the 1970s the ranks of filmmakers both north and south of the Sahara were reinforced by further, often younger, recruits, who tended to turn away from the past and to explore instead the realities of contemporary post-independence society. Most were unconcerned with formal experiment. Questioning the world that confronted them was usually felt to be more important than devising innovative narrative structures (though, as we shall see in Chapter 6, a few key figures of this generation did try both approaches).

The three major figures to emerge in francophone West Africa were the Paris-based Mauritanian Med Hondo, the Malian Souleymane Cisse and the Senegalese woman director, Safi Faye. Hondo, born in **Mauritania** in 1936 but resident in Paris since 1969, began his career with the highly innovative *Soleil O* (1970). This is discussed in Chapter 7 as is his second fictional feature, *West Indies/West Indies ou les nègres marrons de la liberté* (1979). Between these two features, during the early 1970s, Hondo made a series of documentaries, beginning with a huge (two and a half hours) and somewhat undisciplined mix of fiction and documentary, *The Black Wogs, Your Neighbours/Les Bicots-nègres, vos voisins* (1973). This raises a whole range of issues about immigration, exploitation and culture (including the problems of African cinema). The collage technique of bringing together in a largely unstructured manner elements of direct address, *cinéma vérité* and acted scenes is powerful. The film ends with a roll-call of those killed in racially motivated incidents and an impassioned call for solidarity. Hondo then made two documentaries – the feature-length colour film *We Have All of Death to Sleep/Nous avons toute la mort pour dormir* (1976) and *Polisario – A People in Arms/Polisario, un peuple en armes* (1978) – about the struggle of the people of Western Sahara (the vast desert space situated between Mauritania and Morocco), first for freedom from Spanish colonial rule and then to avoid annexation by Morocco. These are unashamed propaganda pieces for the Polisario Front, allowing the freedom-fighters to put their own case and celebrating their cause with songs and dances.

Hondo's third feature is *Sarraounia* (1986). The film, which was the result of years of preparation and was eventually made thanks to support from both the French and Burkina Faso governments, is set in the 1890s and based on a novel by Abdoulaye Mamami. It has an epic dimension and was the first CinemaScope film made in Sub-Saharan Africa. The production team was multinational and the film multilingual (it uses Dioula, Peuhl, and Tamashek as well as French and the pidgin French – what Hondo wittily calls *petit blanc* – of the French's black soldiers).[27] *Sarraounia* chronicles the exemplary resistance of the pagan queen of the Aznas to a powerful and well-armed French force which rampages across the Africa, threatening all who stand in its path with killing, rape and burning. But this is not just the story of an individual queen and her prowess: rather, it charts the impact of the French invasion on a whole range of African peoples, including the Muslims led by the Emir of Sokoto (who ally themselves to the French) and the Tuaregs of the Sahara (whose lives are disrupted). Sarraounia herself is less a remarkable military leader than a legendary figure who moves in and out of the narrative, living in the songs of her griots (praise-singers) and inspiring her followers as much by her reputation as by her presence. The scenes of African ritual are treated in declamatory style as solemn tableaux, with a self-conscious frontality of setting. Rather than simply tell a single striking story, Hondo spells out dramatically the collective unity of pagan and Islamic forces against the vicious invading army, which disintegrates under the pressures wrought by the overweening personal ambition of its French commander. The director's confident handling of his resources, his masterly sense of pace and rhythm and his firm control of his epic sprawling narrative place him in the fore-front of contemporary African filmmaking.

Sarraounia is Hondo's masterpiece and if his subsequent work has had less impact, it has been characteristically eclectic: *Black Light/Lumière noire* (1994) about the French government's illegal treatment of immigrants; *Watani/Watani, un monde sans mal* (1997), a documentary collage about the impact of unemployment on white and black families in Paris; and *Fatima/Fatima, l'Algérienne de Dakar* (2004), a fictional drama about events stemming from the rape of an Algerian girl in 1957 by a Senegalese sub-lieutenant in the French forces charged with 'cleansing' a mountain area of guerrillas.

Meanwhile, in **Mali**, Souleymane Cisse (born 1940) made a succession of three ever more substantial films in the period 1975–82, all shaped by his seven years of study at the Moscow film school, VGIK. This film training and education was important, since it allowed him to bring a critical gaze shaped by Marxist concepts of class analysis to his first three feature-length studies of contemporary Mali. All three treat social issues: the problems of an unmarried mother eventually driven to suicide in *The Girl/Den muso* (1975), the intermingling of lives divided by class but bound together by kinship in *Work/Baara* (1977), and the role of students under a corrupt military regime in *The Wind/Finye* (1982). Always there is a concern to offer a broad spectrum of contrasting attitudes, based on class and generation differences, and often the narratives are extremely complex in their exploration of the contradictions of contemporary African society. The films offer richly detailed portrayals of their settings and bring to the fore the physical aspects of life, whether it is the workers toiling in the factory in *Baara* or the students smoking ganja in *Finye*. But though Cisse shows this constant determination to offer a realistic picture of African life, his realism does not preclude symbolic incidents and characters (the heroine of *Den muso* is mute: old Kansaye in *Finye* become miraculously invulnerable to bullets). Cisse's work is increasingly shot through with imaginative moments of fantasy, such as some of the later scenes of *Finye* and all of his fourth feature, *Yeelen*. But the early work, analytic but never schematic, realistic but full of vivid drama, achieves the difficult feat of being both popular with African audiences and informative about contemporary Mali and revelatory to a wider public outside Africa.

Just as his previous films were the first African films to confront directly the lives of the urban working class, so too *Finye* is the first to look seriously at the workings of power in an African society under military rule. Cisse's young student heroes live in a recognisably modern world, marked by the clash of generations, the tensions of exam-taking in a corrupt educational system, a frustrated anger when idealistic illusions are shattered, and a mix of commitment and betrayal when their solidarity is tested. For all their drug-taking and campus-rioting, they retain an essential innocence, as Cisse has created complex figures who can reflect fully the ambiguities of the time. Moreover, he is careful to put the young in a context which sets them against the traditional values and beliefs of Africa. Though the bulk of the film is shot with a close and precisely focused realism and its message is addressed to the present, Cisse does not remain at this purely observational level. His social analysis is sufficiently rich to contain purely symbolic acts, such as the emblematic images of innocence and purification at the beginning and end of the film. Similarly, his style is subtle enough to shift effortlessly into dream sequences or even moments of literal unreality. The title, *Finye*, denotes 'the wind', and the wind which blows through *Finye* is the force of change which awakens men's minds. After this international success, Cisse's career took a remarkable shift with the making of his best known film, *Yeelen* (1987), a truly innovative film which is considered in Chapter 7.

Cisse's subsequent return to a realist style is more controversial. *Waati* (1995) is one of three mid-1990s films made by francophone directors in South Africa (the others being Jean-Pierre Bekolo and Idrissa Ouedraogo). This multilingual film reflects the pan-Africanist aspirations of its origins in the epic story of the growth to maturity of the heroine Nandi, whose travels embrace South African apartheid, West African culture and Saharan starvation. But separated from his Malian roots and the Bambara language, Cisse seems oddly ill at ease with the many shifts and new directions taken by his narrative and unexpectedly naive in his political assumptions.

In **Senegal** the key event in the 1970s was the emergence of West Africa's first woman director, Safi Faye (born 1943), who had studied both ethnography and filmmaking in Paris and first became involved in cinema when she appeared in Jean Rouch's film, *Petit à Petit*. *Letter From My Village/Kaddu beykat* (1975) is explicitly couched in letter form beginning with the customary opening greeting and inviting us 'to spend a moment' with the filmmaker and her family. It ends with a dedication to her grandfather who figures in the film and died eleven days after shooting ended. *Letter From My Village* has a unique tone, at once personal and distanced, since Faye's studies in Paris allow her to set her immediate responses to the people of her village in the wider context of the issues that shape their lives. The principal of these is the taxation which draws the peasants into the cash economy, driving the young men to seek work in town and making the villagers grow groundnuts for sale to the government instead of food for themselves. In this personal portrait, Faye stresses the importance of tradition and custom, the repetitive rhythm of the passing days and the sense of community and mutual aid in the village. If the desire of two young people to get married constitutes one important (fictionalised) element in the film, a second is the daily ritual of assembly under the tree in the village, when the men debate the issues of the day. *Letter From My Village*, with its black-and-white images and sparse commentary gives a vivid picture of everyday African village life, exploring the different and complementary areas of responsibility of men and women. Faye has explained that it is a document which she sees as necessary to her own child (and her friends), so as not to deny them their African identity.

In *Fad'jal* (1979), Faye made a second feature-length study of her home village, again with assistance from the French Ministry of Cooperation but this time in colour. The film concentrates on oral tradition and allows the villagers to tell their stories and describe the problems they face in a changing world. The film illustrates Amadou Hampaté Ba's dictum that when an old man dies in Africa, it is as if a library has burned down. Beti Ellerson notes that 'returning to her Serer community as researcher, she was amazed to find that the oral historians of her village could trace back seventeen generations to tell their history'.[28] Nine further shorter documentaries followed in the next decade before Faye turned to fiction with the feature-length film, *Mossane* (1996). Though drawing on Serer mythology and social customs, all aspects of the film were imagined and staged by Faye. Made when her own daughter was fourteen, it is the story of a fourteen-year-old African girl who is beautiful, pure and innocent. As Faye has explained:

> I wanted the most beautiful woman to be an African girl . . . she looks as if she does not belong to this world – because she is so beautiful. The entire world loves her, including her brother. She is so pure and beautiful, but she cannot stay in this world because the spirits who died or departed long ago will come back to take her.[29]

Indeed Mossane's death comes when she is prevented from marrying the one man she truly loves and rejoins the ancestors. In her work Faye does not make rigid divisions between fiction and documentary, but, as Ellerson notes, one element has been constant throughout her career: 'representing the realities of Africa'.[30]

Though Safi Faye was the first francophone African woman to complete a feature film, there were two further features made by women directors within two years: *La Nouba* (1978) by the Algerian novelist Assia Djebar (which is discussed in Chapter 7), and *Fatma 75* (1978), the first feature-length film directed by a Tunisian woman, Selma Baccar (born 1945). This is a study of women in Tunisian history which, like Faye's early work, contains both documentary and enacted sequences. Baccar, who made a first fully fictional feature, *The Fire Dance/La Danse du feu*, in 1995, has said of her first work that it is addressed to women, and Tunisian women in particular': 'I hope to be able to show it to those who don't usually go to the cinema, to get out of the traditional film circuit, to present it as a starting point for discussions with women.'[31]

The 1960s filmmakers in **Algeria** made striking films about the independence struggle by choice, because the subject was of immediate concern to them. Hence the power of many of the works produced. But subsequent younger filmmakers were forced to chose the same subject matter, whether it concerned them or not. The situation is made clear by Ahmed Rachedi, who was head of the monopoly state production organization, ONCIC, from 1967 to 1973. While claiming in a 1970 interview that 'the Algerian filmmaker is king. Everyone can make the film he wants, so long as he has something to say', he added, from his administrative stance,

> The first years of our cinema have been dedicated to the illustration of our liberation struggle, which has been heroic. That allowed film makers to acquire a revolutionary conscience. It was a stage and not an end. We will make more films about the liberation struggle. One day we will begin a cycle of social films. But given the stage we are at, every Algerian film-maker must begin by making a film about the war.[32]

The first dozen or so Algerian features therefore all dealt with the war, as did the debut sketches contributed by six newcomers to two 1960s fictional feature-length compilation films about the war. Conventionally structured war stories continued to be made through the 1970s; indeed, they were still being made as late as 1993, when the film editor Rachid Benallal directed his sole feature film, *Ya ouled*.

In general Algerian critics have been harsh in their response to the majority of the 1960s and 1970s war films. Ahmed Bedjaoui's response is typical, when he argues that the Algerian film 'has practically never been able, in the course of the ten years following independence, to make a work of history or to explain, for example, who had chosen to fight and above all why'.[33] When the focus of Algerian film production shifted to the Agrarian Revolution in 1972, there was a double emphasis: on the one hand, struggles during the colonial period, with themes such as high taxation, land seizure, eviction and forcible military enlistment; on the other, studies of the contemporary situation, stressing the positive new approaches. In general the studies of the contemporary situation were muted because of production and censorship constraints (including self-censorship). But some of the studies of the colonial period were more forceful, the most significant being *Noua* (1972), the only film of Abdelaziz Tolbi (born 1937). Set in 1954, it details the oppressive impact of French colonial rule on the peasantry: high taxation and imprisonment for those too poor to pay, eviction and seizure of land, forcible enlistment in the army (to fight in Indo-China). Those directly oppressing the peasants are wealthy Algerians – the caïds or chieftains – who collaborate with the French. The film ends with their death at the hands of the anti-colonial rebels who begin to make their first appearance as the narrative unfolds. Claude Michel Cluny rightly says of *Noua* that it 'remains one of the most important films of the new Arab cinemas, one of those which demonstrate that a small crew can make an epic film, a film which shows itself moreover to be an incomparable cultural and political tool'.[34]

But in general the response of the Algerian filmmakers to their production situation was to turn to the tried-and-tested formulas of classical Hollywood narrative, with very mixed results. The dominant style of the state-run Algerian cinema is a conscious didacticism, depicting total national unity in the liberation struggle and praising as incontestable the advantages of the proposed land reforms of the 1970s. The style has inherent weaknesses: manicheanism, flawless heroes, stereotyped villains and predictable endings. In Lotfi Maherzi's eyes, however, the films did serve the ideological function of clouding the view of the present: 'The cult of heroes and epics about the liberation struggle, just like commercial cinema, turns the Algerian spectator away from the new realities of his country, judged as lacking in contradiction'.[35] It is hardly surprising that Algerian audiences 'could not recognise themselves in the deformed image of the struggle offered by Algerian cinema'.[36]

The 1970s were also, as Ratiba Hadj-Moussa has observed, the years when Algerian cinema 'started dealing with social problems such as housing shortage, unemployment, and problems which faced the youth and women' and also when 'the first images of Algerian postcolonial images were constructed'.[37] Few of these films had much impact on national or international audiences, but one film which can be taken as representative is *Leila and the Others/Leïla et les autres* (1978), directed by Sid Ali Mazif (born 1943). The film parallels the lives of two women, the factory worker Leïla and the school girl Meriem, who live in the same apartment block. The film does not minimise the male prejudice which they experience in their everyday lives, but both emerge with their personal status enhanced, Leïla being a leading figure in a strike at the factory where she works and Meriem refusing the marriage which her family wishes to impose on her. The difficulties faced by women in Algerian society are vividly displayed, but the film is in no way a critique of Algerian 'socialist' society: the offending factory is a privately owned concern forced to face up to government regulations on behalf of the workers. *Leila and the Others* is a social statement perhaps, but in no way a social critique.

Tentative steps towards a socially committed cinema exploring contemporary issues were also made at the beginning of the 1970s in both **Morocco** and **Tunisia**. A number of filmmakers (most of them with formal film school qualifications), whose later careers would go in different directions, were united in the 1970s by the need to show a Maghrebian view of Maghrebian society. The first significant film is IDHEC graduate Abdellatif Ben Ammar's first feature, *Such a Simple Story/Une si simple histoire* (1970), which anticipates the approach of many 1970s directors. Ben Ammar commented that he wanted to 'reflect on our civilisation, which we have often looked at through the gaze of the other: the West'.[38] In his second film, *Sejnane* (1974), Ben Ammar set out to ask one of the questions largely ignored by Algerian filmmakers: why does a militant become a militant and not something else? *Sejnane*, set in 1952 at the height of the opposition to the French, traces a double story of defeat. Kemal, radicalised when he reads his murdered father's diary, is killed fighting on behalf of striking miners, while Anissa, the woman he loves, submits to a forced marriage to an older, richer man. The intercut sequences of their matched fates give the film its powerful climax.

Subsequently a sequence of films was produced in Tunisia and Morocco, each of which looked with real passion at one specific aspect of post-independence Maghrebian society. In *And Tomorrow?/Et demain?* (1972), directed by another Tunisian IDHEC graduate Brahim Babaï (born 1936), the focus was on drought and the resultant rural exodus. The film, which as its title indicates offers no solution for its uprooted protagonist, is intended as a warning to politicians and those in authority about problems in Tunisian society. The film was widely shown and acclaimed, but Babaï had to wait almost twenty years before he was able to complete a second, *The Night of the Decade/La Nuit de la décennie* (1991). *A Thousand and One Hands/Mille et une mains* (1972), the debut film of the Moroccan Souheil Benbarka (born 1942), who had studied in Italy (at the Centro sperimentale) and worked as assistant to Pier Paolo Pasolini, attacked the Western exploitation of those who weave the Moroccan carpets so prized by foreign buyers. His second feature, *The Oil War Will Not Take Place/La Guerre du pétrole n'aura pas lieu* (1974), was also a political film, this time in the contemporary manner of Yves Boisset and Costa-Gavras, a comparison strengthened by Benbarka's use of European actors. His third feature, *Blood Wedding/Noces de sang* (1977), an adaptation of the Garcia Lorca play starring Irene Papas and Laurent Terzieff, marked the beginning of the director's transition from being a committed national advocate to a maker of films for the international market. *Amok* (1982), for example, is a loose and uncredited version of Alan Paton's *Cry the Beloved Country*, which looks at apartheid in South Africa. Subsequently Benbarka has sought a world audience for his films, while at the same time becoming the dominant figure at home in Morocco, serving as head of the state organisation, the CCM, for some twenty-five years and owning his own production, distribution and exhibition company. Benbarka has of late made huge historical spectacles – *Drums of Fire/Tambours de feu* (1991), *Shadow of the Pharaoh/L'Ombre du pharaon* (1996), and *The Lovers of Moghador/Les Amants de Moghador* (2002) – enjoying budgets other Moroccan directors can only dream of, but achieving little international success.

A further extremely original 1970s political film, focusing this time on the life of emigrant workers in France, is *The Ambassadors/Les Ambassadeurs* (1975), by the Tunisian Naceur Ktari (born 1943). It takes on board the problems and challenges of solidarity against racism and a forceful and committed study of the lives of emigrant workers in France. The ironic title derives from the words of a politician who addresses the workers as they leave for Europe and in no way reflects their actual status there. The film's strong narrative line traces the group's shift from individual concerns to real friendship and, after two racist killings, the move to political action. But despite the evident qualities of this first feature, Ktari had to wait twenty-five years to make his second.

Another 1970s film with real denunciatory power is *Hyena's Sun/Soleil d'hyènes* (1977), the debut feature of the Tunisian Ridha Behi (born 1947). This attack on the impact of the tourist industry on Tunisian rural society had to be shot in Morocco (near Agadir) and was largely funded by Dutch co-producing companies. It shows the totally unequal battle between the modernising ambitions of foreign (German) capital, supported by the Tunisian government, and the local fishermen keen to keep their traditional way of life. Thieves and profiteers prosper, while the honest poor are forced into virtual prostitution in the face of the foreign impact. The last word is appropriately left to that recurrent figure in Arab literature and film, the 'fool' who turns out to embody real insight. Subsequently, Behi sought, with limited success, to reach international audiences, making *Angels/Les Anges* (1984) in Egyptian Arabic and then choosing French actors for the leads in *Bitter Champagne/Champagne amer* (1988) and *Swallows Don't Die in Jerusalem/Le Hirondelles ne meurent pas à Jérusalem* (1994). His most recent film, by contrast, is a largely autobiographical piece about a child's discovery of cinema, *The Magic Box/La Boîte magique* (2002).

The Moroccan Ahmed El Maânouni's, first feature, *The Days, The Days/O les jours* (1978), adopts a more documentary-style approach, reflecting perhaps the director's studies of economics. It is a study of a young peasant, who wishes to achieve his independence and sees only one way of doing it: emigration to Europe. It was based on three months' research and shot with a crew from INSAS, the Belgian film school where El Maânouni had studied. His aim was to make 'a portrait from "inside" as it were' and 'to allow the peasant world to represent itself'.[39] The film achieves its poetic force from the director's willingness to reflect the rhythm of the lived peasant experience. Subsequently El Maânouni completed a documentary, *Trances/Transes* (1981), about the popular musical group Nass el-Ghiwane, but he has made no further fictional features.

Perhaps the culmination of this 1970s Maghrebian strand of realism is Abdellatif Ben Ammar's *Aziza*, which focuses on the situation of women and was actually released in 1980. Looking directly at contemporary Tunis, the film deals with a family which moves out of the medina into the new suburbs. The results are varied: the father's health declines, the son fails in business, but for the niece, Aziza, who has lived with the family since the death of her father, the new world offers a challenge of independence which she willingly takes up. Ben Ammar's strength lies in the detailed shaping of scenes, such as that in which the father and Aziza's new friend, the television actress Aïcha, sing an old 1920s song by Habiba Messika, or when Aziza and the drunken, defeated son share a moment of tenderness. In all, the director offers a lively and sensitive picture of the tensions within the family and among their new neighbours. Aïcha goes off to seek a dubious happiness in the Gulf with a passing 'emir', but Aziza stays behind in the Tunisian suburbs, vulnerable but resolute.

NOTES

1. Teshome H. Gabriel, Foreword to Nwachukwu Frank Ukadike, *Questioning African Cinema: Conversations with Filmmakers* (Minneapolis: University of Minnesota Press, 2002), pp. ix–x.
2. Reprinted in Ibrahim M. Awed, Dr Hussein M. Adam and Lionel Ngakane (eds), *First Modadishu Pan African Film Symposium* (Mogadishu: Mogpafis Management Committee, 1983), pp. 109–10.
3. Raphaël Millet, '(In)dépendance des cinémas du Sud &/vs France', *Théorème 5*, Paris, 1998, p. 174.
4. Stuart Hall, 'Cultural Identity and Cinematic Representations', *Framework 36*, London, 1989, p. 69.
5. Ibid.
6. Ibid., p. 70.
7. Ibid.
8. Ibid.
9. Frantz Fanon, *The Wretched of the Earth* (Harmondsworth: Penguin, 1967), pp. 178–9.
10. Françoise Pfaff, *25 Black African Filmmakers* (New York: Greenwood Press, 1988), p. 243.
11. Ousmane Sembene, quoted in Françoise Pfaff, *The Cinema of Ousmane Sembene* (Westport: Greenwood Press, 1984), p. 123.
12. For reaction to the film, see David Murphy, *Sembene: Imagining Alternatives in Film and Fiction*, (Oxford: James Currey and Trenton, NJ: Africa World Press, 2000), pp. 75–9.
13. Laura Mulvey, 'The Carapace that Failed: Ousmane Sembene's *Xala*', in *Fetishism and Curiosity* (London: BFI & Bloomington: Indiana University Press, 1996), p. 120.
14. For a fuller discussion of *Ceddo*, see the chapter 'The Group as Protagonist: *Ceddo*', in Roy Armes, *Action and Image: Dramatic Structure in Cinema* (Manchester: Manchester University Press, 1994), pp. 155–70.
15. Kenneth W. Harrow, '*Camp de Thiaroye*: Who's That Hiding in Those Tanks, and How Come We Can't See Their Faces', *Iris* 18, Iowa, 1995, pp. 147–52.
16. Josef Gugler, 'Fact, Fiction, and the Critic's Responsibility', in Françoise Pfaff (ed.), *Focus on African Films* (Bloomington: Indiana University Press, 2004), p. 73.
17. Murphy, *Sembene*, p. 187.
18. Ousmane Sembene, internet interview , www.africultures, 30 April 2003.
19. Réda Bensmaïa, *Experimental Nations:, Or, the Invention of the Maghreb* (Princeton: Princeton University Press, 2003), p. 12.
20. Ibid., p. 11
21. Mouloud Mimoun, 'Pour une fusion des regards', in Mouloud Mimoun (ed.), *France-Algérie: Images d'une guerre* (Paris: Institut du Monde Arabe, 1992), p. 26.
22. Ahmed Rachedi, interview in Mouny Berrah, Victor Bachy, Mohand Ben Salama and Ferid Boughedir (eds), *Cinémas du Maghreb*, Paris: *CinémAction* 14, 1981, p. 72.
23. Denise Brahimi, 'A propos de Tala ou *L'Opium et le bâton* du roman au film', Paris: *Awal* 15, 1997, p. 66.
24. Mohamed Lakhdar Hamina, interview in Berrah et al., *Cinémas du Maghreb*, p. 70.

25. For a detailed analysis of this film, see Roy Armes, 'History or Myth: *Chronique des années de braise*', in Ida Kummer (ed.), *Cinéma Maghrébin*, special issue of *Celaan* 1: 1–2, 2002, pp. 7–17.
26. Omar Khlifi, interview, in Berrah et al., *Cinémas du Maghreb*, p. 171.
27. Med Hondo, interview, in *Monthly Film Bulletin 55*: 648, London, January 1988, p. 10.
28. Beti Ellerson, 'Africa through a Woman's Eyes: Safi Faye's Cinema', in Françoise Pfaff (ed.), *Focus on African Films* (Bloomington: Indiana University Press, 2004), p. 192.
29. Safi Faye, in Nwachukwu Frank Ukadike (ed.), *Questioning African Cinema* (Minneapolis: University of Minnesota Press, 2002), p. 34.
30. Ellerson, 'Africa through a Woman's Eyes', p. 191.
31. Selma Baccar, in Touti Moumen, *Films tunisiens: Longs métrages 1967–98*, (Tunis: Touti Moumen, 1998), p. 72.
32. Ahmed Rachedi, cited in Guy Hennebelle (ed.), *Les Cinémas africains en 1972* (Paris: Société Africaine d'Edition, 1972), p. 115.
33. Ahmed Bedjaoui, 'Silences et balbutiements', in Mouloud Mimoun (ed.), *France-Algérie: Images d'une guerre* (Paris: Institut du Monde Arabe, 1992), p. 35.
34. Claude Michel Cluny, *Dictionnaire des nouveaux cinémas arabes* (Paris: Sindbad, 1978), p. 320.
35. Lotfi Maherzi, *Le cinéma algérien: Institutions, imaginaire, idéologie* (Algiers: SNED, 1980), p. 279.
36. Ibid., p. 278.
37. Ratiba Haj-Moussa, 'The Locus of Tension: Gender in Algerian Cinema', in Kenneth W. Harrow (ed.), *With Open Eyes: Women and African Cinema*, (*Matutu*, 19) (Amsterdam and Atlanta, GA: Rodopi, 1997), p. 50.
38. Abdellatif Ben Ammar, interview, in Berrah et al., *Cinémas du Maghreb*, p. 182.
39. Ahmed al-Maânouni, interview, in Berrah et al., *Cinémas du Maghreb*, pp. 228–9.

6. INDIVIDUAL STRUGGLE

The 1960s were the years of construction, of putting things in place . . .
The gaze becomes clearly more critical in the 1970s, with the accent put
on the social problems of the period; at the same time, cinema acquires
greater technical maturity. In the course of the 1980s, the individual takes
the upper hand.

Tahar Chikhaoui[1]

INTRODUCTION

It is understandable that African filmmakers of the 1960s and early 1970s were
largely concerned – after the long period of colonisation – to show Africa from
an African perspective, to make their audiences see things anew by projecting
the everyday realities around them onto the screen. In doing so, they were
calling upon audiences to recognise their own social and historical situation. As
the initial didacticism faded, the style of realism they adopted was close to that
of the Italian neorealists, showing poverty in order to expose and create sympathy, rather than to incite action. In so far as there was a focus on the individual, it was largely in terms of a failure to adapt to the challenges posed by
the wider clash of tradition and modernity. What is perhaps surprising is that
this same stance persists largely unchanged into the present for the majority of
African filmmakers. What the 1980s and 1990s brought were ways of deepen-
ing this basic realist approach by showing greater concern for the individual
character and a more questioning stance, aware of political as well as social

issues. As Tahar Chikhaoui has noted in an overview of Maghrebian cinema, which also has relevance for cinema south of the Sahara,

> We had to wait till the 1980s for the development to take a personal dimension accompanied by greater political and ideological disenchantment. From this comes a more interior inspiration, a greater investment in subjectivity. From the national epic and, from the 1970s onwards, from the critical representation of social reality, we move to a more disenchanted representation, more conscious of defeat.[2]

South of the Sahara the pioneers may continue with their epic portrayals, Med Hondo with *Sarraounia* (1983) and Ousmane Sembene with *Camp de Thiaroye* (1988), for example, but a new tone of intimism, combined with a sharper, if still nuanced, socio-political critique, is very apparent in the work of newcomers such as Ivoirian Kramo Lanciné Fadika with *Djeli* (1981) and the Malian Cheikh Oumar Sissoko with *Nyamanton* (1986).

THE 1980S

Nowhere is this shift away from the national epic more apparent than in **Algeria**, where the epic approach of the pioneers (Ahmed Rachedi's *Opium and the Stick* and, especially, Mohamed Lakhdar Hamina's *Chronicle of the Years of Embers*), gives way to the totally intimate tone of Brahim Tsaki, who won the top prize (the Étalon de Yennenga) at the FESPACO festival in 1985, almost ten years after Lakhdar Hamina won his Palme d'or at Cannes. Tsaki (born 1946) made his first feature, *Children of the Wind/Les Enfants du vent* (1981), in the context of the newsreel section of ONCIC, which he had joined after completing his studies at INSAS in Belgium. With a team of colleagues and very little money, he put together a film with three separate twenty-six-minute stories, linked by the subject matter (the experiences of children), by the use of the same young actor (the director's nephew) in all three stories, and by the recurrence of the same musical accompaniment. The themes of the various stories are very varied – personal disillusionment, a struggle to understand television images of a very different world, children's creativity with bits of wire and scraps – but there is a unifying, very personal vision of childhood. The film also sets the stylistic tone for all Tsaki's work by using virtually no dialogue and eschewing voice-over comment.

The director took this concern with silence a stage further in his second and best feature, *Story of a Meeting/Histoire d'une rencontre* (1983), a more conventionally funded ONCIC feature. The protagonists, two fourteen-year-old deaf mutes, come from very different backgrounds (he is the son of an Algerian peasant, while she is the daughter of an American oil engineer), but they are drawn together by their shared handicap and develop real communication, using signs and showing acts of mutual generosity. This is a unique moment for them both, which ends abruptly when the girl's father is assigned to another oil-field. Essentially a study of individuals who succeed in conversing without words, *Story of a Meeting* is also, for the director, a comment on modern society: 'the more new technology facilitates exchange, whether it is air travel or the transmission of an image that can be seen simultaneously in Montpellier and Algiers, the more I have the impression that it separates us'.[3] Tsaki completed his informal trilogy with *The Neon Children/Les Enfants des néons* (1990), the story of loves and jealousies – and eventual violence – between a group of young *beurs*, one of whom is a deaf-mute. Produced by the CNC and using (sparse) French dialogue, this is essentially, as Tsaki admits, a French film.[4] It seems to have received little or no distribution and proved to be his last film.

A very different trajectory was followed by Mohamed Rachid Benhadj (born 1949), who studied both architecture and filmmaking in Paris and currently lives in Italy. Benhadj began in a low-key style, akin to that of Tsaki, with *Louss/Rose des sables* (1989), the story of a crippled young man who lives with his beautiful sister Zeinab in a remote oasis situated in the timeless desert hundreds of kilometres from Algiers. Despite having no arms, Moussa lives a full life, accepted unconditionally by the few neighbours he encounters. But the balance is precarious, and with the departure of Zeinab and the loss of his beloved Meriem, he succumbs to despair. Despite the ending, most of the film has a touchingly poetic sense of innocence, and the delicacy with which Benhadj handles his players, the precision of his camerawork and the beauty of his visual style made the film a success with a wide range of audiences. Though co-produced by the state organisation, CAAIC, *Louss*'s focus on a lone protagonist living outside the social forces of modernity captures one of the key aspects of the new 1980s mood, far removed from the state propagandising of the 1970s.

Benhadj's second film, *Touchia* (1992), tackles the other key aspect of 1980s filming, revealing a new political awareness in the depiction of the rising Islamist threat of the early 1990s. As so often in Maghrebian cinema, the protagonist is a woman and the film is essentially a tale of her suffering. Here Fella, a woman in her forties, is trapped in her apartment by Islamist demonstrators on the streets, and the stress brings her to remember her childhood humiliations and in particular the day of national independence, which culminated in her rape and the murder of her best friend. The film ends with her breakdown. *Touchia* is careful plotted and the transitions between time levels are skilfully handled, but it is a more conventional film than its predecessor, showing clearly the direction in which Benhadj's career would develop. After two Italian films, Benhadj made an unashamedly commercial movie, the international block-buster *Mirka* (2000), in which the talents of Vanessa Redgrave and Gérard

Depardieu and the cinematographic skills of Vittorio Storaro are expended on a rather slight if well-meaning tale of a small boy bullied because he is the outcome of a brutal rape during ethnic cleansing in the Balkans.

In **Morocco** too there is a new concentration on the individual, sometimes on the defeat of inarticulate males, but more often on the suffering of young women, in a rigid Muslim culture. The central core of cinema in Morocco during the 1980s is a series of socially realist films directed by Jillali Ferhati and Mohamed Abderrahman Tazi, supplemented by *The Barber of the Poor Quarter/Le Coiffeur du quartier des pauvres* (1982) directed by the legendary Mohamed Reggab (1942–90).[5] Ferhati (born 1948) studied sociology and drama in Paris for ten years, before returning to Morocco where he worked extensively as an actor on stage and screen. After a couple of shorts and a first, little-shown feature, *A Hole in the Wall/Une brèche dans le mur* (1977), he made four further films spread at long intervals over twenty years. Three of the films have simple narrative lines and focus on a female victim. Aïcha in *Reed Dolls/Poupées de roseau* (1982) is a very young widow, forced to work to support her three children, who is abandoned by her lover when she gets pregnant and consequently has her children taken from her. Mina in *The Beach of Lost Children/La Plage aux enfants perdus* (1991) is hidden away by her father when she gets pregnant and inadvertently kills her violent lover, but eventually the truth emerges and she is left isolated. Saïda, in *Braids/Tresses* (2000), is struck dumb after being raped by the son of a powerful lawyer-politician and, even when he dies, the family cannot be put together again as it was before. Ferhati's other feature, *Make-Believe Horses/Chevaux de fortune* (1995), has a wider focus, chronicling the stories of a disparate group of Moroccans in Tangiers, all of whom – for various reasons – want desperately to make the crossing to Europe. Though Spain is so near, their dreams are blocked and the film ends in death for the two leading characters.

All Ferhati's films are the fruit of intense and careful preparation. Realism is integral to his work, as for him 'the imaginary isn't something fabulous. It is based on the real'.[6] The movement of the deliberately paced narrative is always well organised, with great attention given to lighting and composition. For Ferhati, the cinema entails conveying meaning visually, so that dialogue in his work is sparse. For him 'good cinema is the image and therefore silence' and the spectator is 'to be invited to uncover the meaning, to work at the reading of the film'.[7] Ferhati shows great sympathy for his powerless and tormented heroines who, like the obsessed gambler Mohamed in *Make-Believe Horses*, are, as it were, sleepwalking to death, disaster or isolation, their dreams unanswered and their efforts to escape brushed aside by a hostile environment.

Mohamed Abderrahman Tazi (born 1942), who studied film in Paris and New York, made several documentaries before his first feature *The Big Trip/Le Grand voyage* (1982). Scripted by Nour Eddine Saïl, this low-budget production is essentially a road movie, following a truck driver's journey along the coast road from Agadir in the south to Tangier in the north and taking in the cities of Essouira, Casablanca and Rabat. The taciturn Omar is essentially a good man, eager to help others he meets, but he is also an innocent, robbed and cheated all the way. Persuaded to sell his truck and to emigrate, he finds he has been duped again, cut loose in a rowing boat in the middle of the ocean. The film, which ends with a freeze-frame of him waving in despair, is a bleak tale of defeat.

Badis (1998), again scripted by Saïl but this time in collaboration with the writer-director Farida Benlyazid, is, if anything, bleaker still, despite (or perhaps because of) the beauty of the setting and the vivacity of the central characters. The island on which the village of Badis is situated is a Spanish enclave, left over from the colonial period. Two oppressed women, who are drawn together in real friendship, plan to run away to freedom, but their every move has been spied on by the villagers and they are quickly caught and – horrifyingly – stoned to death. It is another woman who throws the first stone. This ending was chosen by Tazi against the wishes of his co-scriptwriters and has been much criticised for its total negativism, with feminists such as the Moroccan sociologist Fatima Mernissi arguing that the film 'shouldn't have ended in that defeatist, pessimistic manner, because the film was made at a time when Moroccan women were starting to take their lives into their own hands'.[8]

In **Tunisia**, the director who most clearly combines the decade's themes of intimacy and sharp political critique is Nouri Bouzid (born 1945). With five feature films directed in sixteen years from 1986 and contributions to the scripts of six others, Bouzid emerged as a major figure in Maghrebian cinema. Bouzid has a complex past – he trained at INSAS in Belgium and worked extensively as assistant on foreign features shot in Tunisia, but he was also imprisoned for five years for left-wing political activities. His first features have an autobiographical style rare in Arab cinema, but are also examples of what he promoted as a 'new Arab realism', coloured by the 1967 Arab defeat in the war against Israel. The aim of the new filmmakers was, in Bouzid's view, 'to subvert norms, refuse prohibitions and unveil sensitive areas such as religion, sex, the authorities, the "father figure" '.[9] Bouzid's own first three films – all produced by the innovative producer Ahmed Attia – feature damaged male figures who are defeated by experiences rarely mentioned in Arab or African cinema. In *Man of Ashes/L'Homme de cendres* (1986) Hachmi, a young carpenter, celebrates his last bachelor night with his friends, but his mind is flooded with memories of childhood abuse: male rape when he was just twelve years old. In *Golden Horseshoes/Les Sabots en or* (1988) the hero Youssef is a former political prisoner who emerges from prison but is unable to cope with the failure of his own ideals and the changed society which confronts him. Roufa, in *Beznes* (1992), tries vainly to reconcile his love of his own country with his urgent desire to emigrate, and his macho urge to dominate the lives of his sister and girlfriend with his personal role as a prostitute selling himself to wealthy male and female tourists.

In breaking taboos in this way Bouzid gave realist cinema in Tunisia an unprecedented edge and bite, and the emotional involvement with the tormented male figures is intense. The unfolding present is always shot through with painful memories of the past which intrude into the characters' immediate lives and fragment the flow of the film narrative. Bouzid's subsequent features from the late 1990s, focusing on female protagonists, are also impressive, but lack the unique force of these three initial films. *Bent familia/Tunisiennes* (1997) was a study of three women who come together in their shared efforts to find space for themselves in a male-dominated world. But the film ends inconclusively, as the women are driven apart by factors outside their control. Bouzid's most recent film, *Clay Dolls/Poupées d'argile* (2002), focuses on young girls from outlying villages sold into domestic service in Tunis. The view of Tunisian society is so bleak that no favourable outcome is remotely possible.

South of the Sahara too there is a strong concern not just with social problems but with the individual response to them. In the **Ivory Coast** Kramo-Lancine Fadika (born 1948) made *Djeli* (1981), a sensitive and thoughtful study of the caste barriers still existing in the country (the origins of which are shown in a sepia insert in the early part of the film). Fanta and Karamoko's romance was acceptable in the modern, French-language environment of Abidjan University, but it causes real concern at their rural home. Ironically, it is her traditionally-clad older uncle who urges her father's acceptance of changed times, and the film ends with a freeze-frame as the father is about to take Karamoko's hand at Fanta's hospital bedside. Despite the success of his first feature, Fadika had to wait thirteen years before he could complete a second, *Wariko, le gros lot* (1994), which dealt with a policeman and his family whose peaceful and industrious life is shattered when the wife buys a winning lottery ticket which cannot be found when it is time to claim the prize.

The year 1986 saw the emergence of the second major director (after Souleymane Cisse) in **Mali**, Cheikh Oumar Sissoko (born 1945), who had studied both filmmaking and African history and sociology in Paris. His first feature, *Nyamanton* (1986), was an engaging study of street children in Bamako and shows perfectly his political engagement and his 'commitment to film as the medium of expressing the realities of our societies'.[10] Two children are excluded from school because their family cannot afford the necessary expenses and are sent out to work: the boy picking through the garbage and the girl selling oranges. Their liveliness and good humour serve only to strengthen Sissoko's attack on official indifference. Despite being shot on a tiny budget and in a virtually documentary style, *Nyamanton* became one of the most popular of all films in Mali: 'People recognised the deteriorated condition they lived in, realising the grave consequences'.[11]

Sissoko's second film, *Finzan* (1989), looked at women's problems in society and their attempts at rebellion. On the death of her husband, Nanyuma refuses the traditional demand to marry his younger brother Bala, the village idiot, who already has two wives. She is harshly treated by the community, but the fate of her friend Fili, who is forcibly excised by an irate group of older women, is worse. The film ends with Nanyuma's lament, 'Women are like birds that have nowhere to perch. There is no hope. We must stand up and fight for ourselves, because without emancipation, our country will never develop'. Sissoko's view of tradition is harsh, and he openly mocks old superstitions. Though the film comes close at times to a political tract in its treatment of women's issues, there is plenty of (often crude) humour in the handling of Bala and some wonderful scenes involving the little boys who torment him imaginatively. After completing these two essentially realistic studies of contemporary life, which show clearly and directly his social commitment, Sissoko followed his compatriot Souleymane Cisse's example and turned to using history and myth as ways of conveying his message about the need for change. His masterly 1990s films are considered in Chapter 8.

In **Burkina Faso** 1987 saw another major debut, that of S. Pierre Yaméogo (born 1955), who, with Kabore and Ouedraogo, is one of the trio of filmmakers who dominate the country's film output, and a filmmaker with a distinctive voice. Yaméogo has stated that he is inspired by reality, that he considers cinema to be above all information, and that many things in Africa deserve to be revealed and underlined.[12] The short feature *Dunia* (meaning 'the world') set the pattern in 1967, being a simple report on women's lives in Burkina Faso, treating issues such as sterility, isolation and teenage pregnancy, as seen through the eyes of a little girl, Nongma. *Laafi* (1990) looks at an older age group: students who have just completed their 'bac' and are looking for university placements. The early part of the film looks at both the good reasons for so few students to be sent abroad (too few ever return) and at the bad ones (the corruption of local officials). The latter part of the film focuses more on the students' emotional lives with partners and parents, setting their lifestyles against that of the self-styled 'man of the people' who serves them their coffee and sandwiches in the street. The anti-corruption stance is weakened at the end of the film, when, out of the blue, the hero Joe gets his longed-for Parisian placement, but it gives a vivid picture of the moped-riding young people who crowd the streets of contemporary Ouagadougou.

In his subsequent features, Yaméogo kept up his keen gaze at social issues. *Wendemi* (1992) took as its protagonist a young man whose name, Wendemi ('child of the good Lord'), indicates his status as the abandoned child of an unmarried mother driven from her community. Grown to adulthood, Wendemi finds that his lack of knowledge of his parents frustrates his attempts to build himself a life. But his attempts to find out his origins plunge him into the murky side of African city life (the prostitution of very young girls) and lead him to a dark discovery. *Silmandé* (1998) is perhaps Yaméogo's most outspoken attack on corruption. It points unflinchingly at the involvement of both Lebanese businessmen and African politicians in shady and self-serving deals and aroused real anger in Ouagadougou's expatriate Lebanese community (which runs many of the local cinemas). Never content just to document a situation, Yaméogo makes a powerful plea for social change. *Me and My White Guy/Moi et mon blanc* (2002) uses a thriller structure, showing two men – one French, the other an African student – on the run from drug dealers they have double-crossed. The aim is to lay bare both unthinking Western prejudices and African corruption. *Delwende* (2005) is a powerful denunciation of superstition and blind adherence to tradition in the rural community. Napoko, already troubled when her daughter Pougbilia is raped and will not name the aggressor, is devastated when the sixteen-year-old Pougbilia is married off by her father Diarrha to her fiancé in the next village and when she herself is designated a witch and driven into exile at the 'siongho' ceremony organised by the men of the community, who are troubled by the unexplained deaths of children (in fact it is an outbreak of meningitis). Eventually she is located by her single-minded daughter Pougbilia in an old women's refuge in Ouagadougou. Together the two return to the village to confront the cause of all their troubles: Diarrha. While the story is slight, the images of Pougbilia searching for her mother in a women's refuge, filled with literally hundreds of elderly women, all driven from their villages as witches, is enormously powerful. Yaméogo's work is always lively and committed and raises fundamental questions about contemporary African society.

THE 1990S

The realist tendency of African filmmaking continued unabated in the new decade. Characterising Algerian cinema as 'political', Moroccan cinema as 'cultural' and Tunisian cinema as 'social', Tahar Chikhaoui has argued that in the 1990s all three shared a common aim: 'a will to move people's consciences and to play a part in mental development'.[13] From his Tunisian perspective, he notes that the greatest debates have been provoked by the way in which woman is represented and, in particular, 'the liberty with which the female body is filmed'.[14] His prime example is *Silences of the Palace/Les Silences du palais* (1994), the debut film of Moufida Tlatli (born 1947) whose work is a fine example of the new impetus given to cinema in **Tunisia** by Nouri Bouzid (who co-scripted the film).

Tlatli is perhaps the most talented of a number of African female directors who – following Safi Faye, Assia Djebar, Neija Ben Mabrouk and Selma Baccar – made their debuts in the 1980s and 1990s. In Tunisia, Tlatli's breakthrough was followed by that of her contemporary, Kaltoum Bornaz (born 1945), with *Keswa*

(1997) and the much younger Raja Amari (born 1971), whose *Satin Rouge* (2002) is discussed in Chapter 12. In Morocco, Farida Bourquia (born 1948), who has worked largely in television, made her sole feature, *The Embers/La Braise* in 1982. She was followed by Farida Benlyazid (born 1948), who had begun as a scriptwriter for Ferhati and Tazi and directed three notable feature films, *Gateway to Heaven/La Porte au ciel* (1987), *Women's Wiles/Keid Ensa* (1999) and *Casablanca Casablanca* (2003). Again there was a renewal in 2002 with the appearance of Narjiss Nejjar (born 1971) with her first feature, *Cry No More/Les Yeux secs* (2002), and of Yasmine Kassari (born 1968). In Algeria the novelist Hafsa Zinaï-Koudil (born 1951) directed the 16mm feature *The Female Demon/Le Démon au féminin* (1993) for Algerian television (RTA). Then there was a wait until 2002 before Yamina Bachir-Chouikh (born 1954) completed the first Algerian 35mm feature to be made by a woman, *Rachida* (2002). Developments were slower south of the Sahara and it was not until 2004 that Safi Faye found two Burkinabè successors in Régina Fanta Nacro (born 1962), with *The Night of Truth/La Nuit de la vérité*, and Apolline Traoré, with *Under the Moonlight/Sous la clarté de la lune*. These female directors largely gave a feminine slant on a subject frequently treated by male directors, the problems of women in Arab and African society. But in general they are more positive in seeing opportunities as well as difficulties for women in Islamic society. The work of the younger women filmmakers is discussed in Chapter 9.[15]

Tlatli's *Silences of the Palace/Les Silences du palais* is a reflection on relations within a family, the director's own thoughts about her mother and her concerns for her teenage daughter. The narrative, which traces the return of a young singer, Alia, to the beys' palace where she was born and where her mother was a servant, has a deliberately melodramatic structure. Tlatli worked for twenty years as an editor on many major Arab features and her own first film is full of striking juxtapositions and brings together at its climax the death of the mother and (partial) liberation of the daughter. It is a film of opposing spaces, with the warm solidarity of the women working in the kitchen contrasted with the cold and the ruthless exercise of male power by the beys in their upstairs apartment. This is a world of total patriarchy where women servants are totally at the sexual call of their masters and a teenage servant's virginity is always at risk. Tlatli's use of women performers – the mother exhibited as mistress-dancer by one of the beys and the daughter struggling to find an individual identity ten years later as a singer – gives particular force to the film's examination of women's subjugation and the (tentative) beginnings of a female revolt. As Zahia Smail Salhi notes, the film is an invitation for women of her generation 'to take the achievements of yesterday's revolution towards new horizons through a new social revolution'.[16]

The Men's Season/La Saison des hommes (2000), Tlatli's second feature, has an even more complex twenty-year time scale, but was less successful, perhaps because the lead actors were required to play themselves both as newly-weds and as adult parents one and two decades later. The focus is characteristic of Tlatli, with a group of women of varying ages on the island of Djerba joined in unity, their mutual friendships compensating at least in part for the absence of their menfolk who spend much of the year living and working in Tunis. A key figure is the autistic son whose situation is totally ambiguous, in that he both liberates his mother (through his gender) and imprisons her (through his disability). The film is full of beautifully realised scenes reflecting both the difficulties caused by lives lived largely apart (the men return for just one season a year) and the surprises for the women who find an unexpected independence and self-realisation in this lifestyle. The film is audaciously edited and ends with a typical Tlatli multiple climax (here bringing together childbirth, seduction and marital reconciliation). A tribute to women's survival of years of lack and longing, the film confirms Tlatli as a major figure in Maghrebian cinema.

In **Morocco** in the 1990s a new and more challenging political tone was adopted by Abdelkader Lagtaâ (born 1948), who trained at the Lodz film school in Poland and describes himself as more influenced 'by Polish cinema or, more generally, by the cinemas of Eastern Europe, than by Western cinema or, for that matter, by Egyptian cinema'.[17] One Moroccan critic, keen to distinguish his work from the dominant 1980s group, has dubbed his approach 'socio-political', because of the filmmaker's willingness to 'unveil the unspoken and to confront taboos'.[18] Indeed Lagtaâ is quite explicit about his intentions: 'I see my role as questioning society, questioning social practices, questioning how people behave and the kinds of relationships they have with each other'.[19] In addition, Lagtaâ was one of the first Moroccan directors to reach a mass audience with his first feature, *A Love Affair in Casablanca/Un amour à Casablanca*, which both shocked and delighted its viewers when released in 1991. The film has a complicated plot which depicts a father who discovers that he and his son are both involved in sexual relationships with the same eighteen-year-old schoolgirl. The film ends with the boy's suicide. *The Closed Door/La Porte close*, Lagtaâ's second feature, was shot in 1993 but not released until 2000 because of the bankruptcy of the French co-producer and censorship problems in Morocco. It deals with a young man who has an excessive relationship with his dominating young stepmother and develops a real friendship with a homosexual colleague, whose suicide forms the film's climax. Both films give a very striking image of modern life in an Arab society where alcohol, drugs, prostitution and casual sex abound.

In *The Casablancans/Les Casablancais* (1998) the focus is wider, with three linked contemporary urban tales: a bookseller is terrified when he (mistakenly) receives a police summons, a beautiful young school teacher is harassed when she applies for a visa to visit France, and a young schoolboy is corrupted by his Islamist tutor and driven to despair. Though the film is shaped as a comedy, it too gives a tense and disturbing picture of contemporary Morocco: arbitrary police power, censorship, male sexual obsession and creeping fundamentalism. Throughout the film, the authorities are scorned and derided, while corruption is exposed as commonplace.

A more commercial approach is that of Hakim Noury (born 1952), who worked as assistant to Souheil Benbarka. He made a first feature, *The Postman/Le Facteur*, in 1980, but then had to wait ten years before he could complete his second, *The Hammer and the Anvil/Le Marteau et l'enclume* (1990), the unhappy tale of an office worker forced into early retirement. He followed this with four further features in quick succession, to become the most prolific Moroccan director of the decade. His best qualities are seen in *Stolen Childhood/L'Enfance volée* (1993), a film in two distinct parts, viewing the protagonist Rkia at age ten and again at eighteen. As a child she is hired out from her village to work for a rich family in Casablanca. Later, as a naive girl, she is seduced, made pregnant and abandoned to become a whore in the big city. The film ends with a dealer returning to Rkia's village to fetch her younger sister. Noury subsequently turned to comedy to achieve enormous box-office success with *She is Diabetic and Hypertensive and She Refuses to Die/Elle est diabétique et hypertendue et elle refuse de crever* (2000).[20]

In **Algeria**, Merzak Allouache, who had begun with one of the most innovative of Maghrebian comedies, *Omar Gatlato* (discussed in Chapter 7), continued in the 1980s with a curious but affecting tale of a man's plunge into madness and murder, *The Man Who Looked at Windows/L'Homme qui regardait les fenêtres* (1982), and a minor film shot in France, *A Parisian Love Story/Un amour à Paris* (1987). His first 1990s film was *Bab el Oued City* (1994), perhaps the finest of all studies of the rise of Islamist violence. The film begins, as it will end, in typical Arab fashion, with the sufferings of a woman, in this case Yamina, who has waited three years for news from Boualem, the man she loves. The main inset story explains his absence. Driven crazy by the mosque loudspeaker situated on his balcony, Boualem tears it down and throws it into the sea. He immediately regrets his action, which serves as a pretext for Yamina's brother Saïd (a hero of the October 1988 uprisings) to bring 'order' to the neighbourhood through a reign of violence, with the claim that Boualem's act is 'muffling the voice of God'.

Mixing humour with serious social insights and making good use of popular music, *Bab el Oued City* paints a vivid picture of the inhabitants of the neighbourhood: Saïd who puts on mascara before strutting out to bring his version of justice to the people; Marbrouk, Boualem's colleague at the bakery, who dabbles in smuggled goods; Ouardya, a French-speaking former left-wing activist, who now drinks heavily and is attracted to Boualem; Mess, who claims to be French and finally and unexpectedly gets his passport. In the background are young women (including Yamina) seeking romance from novels and television, young men dabbling (in one case fatally) in drugs; and Paolo, a former settler, who is taking his blind aunt on a tour of Algiers, pretending that nothing has changed since colonial days. Behind Saïd, and seemingly controlling him, are shadowy, unnamed figures who make half a dozen enigmatic appearances and who are presumably responsible for his death when he has served their purpose. The mood gradually darkens as the film proceeds, with Saïd and his small band of bearded, black-jacketed supporters bringing increased violence and intimidation, and the moderate imam resigning in despair. When Boualem is beaten up by the gang, he decides to emigrate, leaving Yamina, after one stolen kiss, to mourn his exile as a kind of death.

Subsequently based in Paris, Allouache has achieved considerable success by alternating comedies of immigrant life there – *Hello Cousin!/Salut Cousin!* (1996) and *Chouchou* (2003) – with tales of Algerian 'returnees' – *Algiers-Beirut: In Remembrance/Alger-Beyrouth, pour mémoire* (1998) and *The Other World/L'Autre monde* (2001). But he has never recovered the level of his best early work and has become, in effect, a French filmmaker. *Bab el Web* (2004), a slight, French-language comedy, is very much an outsider's view of Bab el Oued twenty-eight years after *Omar Gatlato*. Allouache has moved far from his roots, but his output of ten features in under thirty years makes him the most prolific filmmaker to stem from the Maghreb.

A key feature of mid-1990s Algerian filmmaking – and a political event in its own right – was the making of a trio of films not only set in the Altas mountains, but using the Berber language, Tamazight. Until the 1990s this had been expressly forbidden by the government, which – despite the existence of 5 million Algerians who speak only that language[21] – had wanted to proclaim Algeria as one nation with one language and one religion. But in the 1990s, faced with political upheaval and with the state system in crisis, CAAIC could no longer ban the making of such films, even if it contributed very little financial or other support (it was itself dissolved in 1997). The three directors, Abderrahmane Bouguermouh (born 1938), Belkacem Hadjadj (born 1950) and Azzedine Meddour (born 1947), had much in common. All three had trained aboard (at IDHEC, INSAS and VGIK, respectively) and each had already made a name for himself: Bouguermouh with television dramas and an initial feature for cinema release in 1986, Hadjadj with a series of ten fictional shorts, and Meddour as a documentarist. All three had tiny budgets (in Bouguermouh's case the film was only able to go ahead because of public subscription) and, for all three, shooting was dangerous, since this was still a time of civil unrest and ruthless violence by Muslim fundamentalists.

Bouguermouh had wanted to adapt Mouloud Mammeri's celebrated 1952 French-language novel *The Forgotten Hillside/La Colline oubliée* for some twenty years and had discussed his adaptation with the author. He was the first to get under way in 1994, though various production and post-production delays (especially with the sound track) meant that the film was not released until 1996. Set in 1939 against a background of French colonisation, the film focuses squarely on the love stories of two young friends, who have abandoned their studies in France. Since their return, they have been uncertain of their roles in a community in crisis, still ruled by the older generation which sees no way forward. The film does not seek to dramatise events, capturing instead the villagers' sparse daily routines as they confront the realities of poverty and claustrophobia. An important feature is the use of songs by the Berber poet Taos Amrouche.

Hadjadj and Meddour set up a joint production company, Imago Film, to aid their efforts, and Hadjadj's *Once Upon a Time/Machaho* was released in 1995. Set in an unspecified past, the film avoids political issues and concentrates instead on a rural drama concerning a peasant who avenges the seduction of his daughter, only to discover too late that the lover had returned to marry her. The film, in which Hadjadj plays the leading role, has a clear dramatic line and a simple dramatic irony. Despite the circumstances of its making, *Machaho* has a striking air of tranquillity. Though on one level a critique of traditional values, it approaches the Berber lifestyle with great respect, lovingly showing its costumes and rituals. Hadjadj's only other feature, *El manara* (2004), has a more precise location in time, dealing with the upheavals in the lives of a trio of young people caused by the uprisings of October 1988.

Azzedine Meddour, whose mother tongue is Tamazight, was confronted by even greater difficulties when he shot *Baya's Mountain/La Montagne de Baya* (1997), since an unexplained explosion killed thirteen members of the crew. As Meddour has said, 'We began to live what Baya lived. She fought for the survival of certain values. So did we'.[22] The film, which again has a strong individual storyline, celebrates traditional values. Set in the Kabyle mountains at the beginning of the twentieth century, it is an epic tale of Berber villagers driven into the mountains when their land is confiscated by the French and their upper-class Arab allies. Baya, the daughter of the tribe's spiritual leader, receives blood-money ('diya') for the murder of her husband. But despite the tribe's sufferings, she refuses to use this money to help them or to admit her own love for Djendel, the tribe's revered bandit-cum-poet, until her husband has been avenged. For Baya, only blood can answer blood, but her personal heroism and sense of traditional values are submerged in the wider drama of the community, as a new and even bloodier assault is made on the tribe's new fields and dwellings. This two-hour epic – enlivened by traditional costumes, songs and rituals – was Meddour's only feature film, as he died of cancer three years after the film's release.

South of the Sahara, **Cameroon** led the way in the early 1990s with the work of three new and talented directors, working during what Ekema Agbaw has described as 'the climax of what can be described in Cameroonian terms as a social revolution'.[23] The uniquely experimental work of Jean-Pierre Bekolo is discussed in Chapter 9, but the other two filmmakers follow the direct, socially committed pattern which concerns us here. The writer and filmmaker Bassek Ba Kobhio (born 1957) drew on his own experiences to make his first feature, *The Village Teacher/Sango Malo* (1991), dealing with the experiences of a newly appointed school teacher who disrupts the traditional life of the village. There is a clash of values with a school's headmaster when Malo introduces modern teaching methods and a curriculum relevant to the children's needs and talks about politics and sex . Imbued with his new ideas, the children ransack the village store when a child is beaten by its owner, provoking the latter to turn to new economic methods (importing prostitutes from the city). Malo shows disrespect for traditional authority (the village chief) and encourages the villagers to set up a farm cooperative. But his contempt for tradition is excessive. When he marries a village girl but refuses to pay her dowry, he provokes her father's suicide. When he proposes cutting down the sacred forest, he has taken a step too far and is arrested. But the collective continues. The film not only allows clear insights into the social organisation of a contemporary village, but also offers a lively picture of the different attitudes (strengths and weaknesses) of a new generation born since independence.

Whereas his first film looked at the political needs of contemporary Cameroon, Bassek Ba Kobhio's second, *The Great White Man of Lambaréné/ Le Grand blanc de Lambaréné* (1995), looks back at the colonial era. The film, which covers a vast sweep of some twenty years up to Albert Schweitzer's death in 1965, is full of ambiguities, not least because of the failure of some characters (including Schweizer himself) to age visibly. As French Equatorial Africa moves from French colony to a group of independent states (including present-day Gabon, where the film was shot), we see a succession of juxtaposed scenes revealing the complexity of Schweitzer's relationship with Africa and his abiding certainties, which are challenged as much by returning ex-soldiers in 1944 as by independence in 1960. Bassek Ba Kobhio has clearly felt the need to include all aspects of his protagonist's character: his refusal to recognise that an African could ever be a doctor, his contradictory approaches to African tradition and African women, as well as his evident commitment to his missionary role. It includes European criticisms of his medical methods, as well as the more telling African complaint that he failed to love Africans and that he was in Africa to save his own soul, not to help Africa to develop.

Though the subjects treated in Bassek Ba Kobhio's two features are very different, both offer vivid portraits of flawed idealists who wish to do good, but are authoritarian, puritanical, at odds with their surroundings and neglectful towards their womenfolk. In 2004, after a number of short films, Bassek Ba Kobhio co-directed, with Didier Ouenangare, the first film to be made in the Republic of Central Africa, *The Silence of the Forest/Le Silence de la forêt.*

The second major Cameroonian filmmaker in this tradition is Jean-Marie Teno (born 1954), who trained in Paris, where he now lives, and has worked largely in documentary since 1984. Among the dozen or so documentaries he has made in twenty years are several powerful feature-length works which have been widely distributed and fully reflect his aim of 'uttering a great cry of rage against injustice in Cameroon and showing elements which allow the under-standing and eventual untangling of the complex threads of oppression in Africa'.[24] *Africa, I Will Fleece You/Afrique, je te plumerai* (1992) examines the cultural history of Cameroon, beginning in the present and moving back through time to uncover the roots of the present dire situation in the practices instituted during the colonial era. *Chief!/Chef!* (1999), provoked by a chance encounter with a boy of sixteen about to be lynched by a mob for stealing some chickens, examines the role of authority in Cameroon – not only the position of the dictator, who is all-powerful, but also the situation of every Cameroonian husband, who has absolute power over his wife. In *Holiday Back Home/ Vacances au pays* (2000) Teno uses a trip back to places he knew before, to explore education, local administration and village democracy.

Clando (1996), Teno's first fictional film, is a study of exile. But the opening scenes in Douala and the flashbacks from abroad show the same world as that depicted in the documentaries. As he says in *Chef!*, poverty, violence and cor-ruption live in a *ménage à trois* and a whole black economy exists to provide what the state fails to supply. In this broken-down society there are a few pos-itive points: family, self-help groups, friendship. But arrest and torture by the political police for some minimal political activity almost break the protago-nist, Sobgui. His attempt to rebuild his life by becoming a clandestine taxi driver (the 'clando' of the title) exposes him to another facet of Cameroonian society, namely the murderous violence that the poor (in this case, the licensed taxi drivers) mete out to the poor (the 'clandos'). In exile, in Cologne, Sobgui's affair with a German activist makes him rethink his position, as does the meeting with an old friend and mentor now destroyed by exile. At the end it is by no means clear what he will actually do when he returns, with his friend, to Cameroon. Like all Teno's work, *Clando* gives a vivid image of Cameroon and its multiple problems. Like his documentaries, it works by juxtaposing scenes and situations, rather than by establishing a strong narrative line. As always the ending is tentative, a call for reflection rather than direct action. Together, this 1990s work establishes Teno as a major voice in contemporary African cinema. The filmmaker's latest film, *The Colonial Misunderstanding/Le Malentendu colonial* (2004), typically takes as its theme Desmond Tutu's celebrated dictum (which it cites): 'When the first missionaries reached Africa, they had the bible and we had the land. They asked us to pray. So we closed our eyes to pray. When we opened them again, the situation was reversed. We had the bible and they had the land'.

In **Burkina Faso** after the huge success of his first three films, *Yam daabo*, *Yaaba* and *Tilaï* (which are discussed in Chapter 8), Idrissa Ouedraogo continued to work prolifically throughout the 1990s and into the 2000s, making four further features, shorter fictional pieces for television, numerous documentaries and a twelve-part television series shot on video. But though he has repeatedly varied his approach in a constant effort at renewal, he has frustratingly never regained in this more realistic work the international success that greeted his early features. The first of his 1990s features, *Karim and Sala* (1991), which was made for French regional television and featured the two young players from his second feature, *Yaaba*, was a further village film depicting the romance of two twelve-year-olds. It received limited cinema screening.

Responding to criticism that he was ignoring Burkina Faso's real social problems and merely giving back to the West its own fantasised image of Africa, he next made *Samba Traoré* (1992), a thriller intended as 'an act of rebellion against the ghetto in which they are trying to put us'.[25] The film follows its protagonist, involved in a robbery and killing in Ouagadougou, as he flees back to his native village and tries to recreate his life there. At first he seems to succeed, but in classic thriller style his past catches up with him. Ouedraogo directs with fluent assurance, the action is lively, full of humour and telling detail, and the playing is assured. One of Ouedraogo's strengths as a filmmaker is the directness of his storytelling, and here the problem that Samba's (stolen) wealth causes the villagers helps to maintain the narrative flow. The drama comes to a satisfying conclusion when he is arrested at the very moment he has resolved his family problems. Perhaps the film's greatest strength is the way it makes us sympathise with Samba though we know he is a thief on the run. As always in Ouedraogo's work, everyone has their reasons.

In a further attempt at renewal, Ouedraogo made *Le Cri du Cœur* (1994), which is, by any measure (funding, language, crew, writers) a French film. The eleven-year-old Moctar, brought from Africa by his mother to rejoin the father he has not seen for five years, feels increasingly isolated and is haunted by recurrent visions of a hyena. These fears are eventually resolved – partly through his friendship with Paolo, a socially marginal figure played by the French star Richard Bohringer – when the hyena is identified with Moctar's beloved grandfather who, it later emerges, was dying at the time. Though it contains many familiar features of Ouedraogo's style (the visual polish, the central figure of a child, the stress on father-son relationships), the film is strangely unaffecting, as certain key elements of the plot are totally unconvincing – in particular the unmotivated relationship with Paolo. The ritual magic at the end, exorcising the hyena, lacks conviction. The critical reception of the film was disastrous, with African critics accusing Ouedraogo of wanting to become French (he lives in Paris) and French critics telling him, in effect, to go back to Africa.[26]

Given his constant concern to adopt new approaches to film, it was perhaps inevitable that Ouedraogo would be one of three francophone filmmakers (alongside Cisse and Jean-Pierre Bekolo) to explore English-language production, in Zimbabwe and South Africa after the fall of apartheid. Though critical reaction to the film was mixed, Ouedraogo has described the resulting film, *Kini & Adams*, as 'the great work of my cinematic career, with an alternative vision and curiosity for the world'.[27] The film is the story of a lifelong friendship, that of Kini and Adams, who start with a dream that they gradually begin to fulfil, only for differences to emerge. Adams, a lone dreamer, who becomes increasingly jealous of Kini's success, eventually succumbs to despair. Here we have characters both drawn to and repulsed by the Western concept of individualism, and Olivier Barlet rightly draws attention to 'the way they hesitantly and painfully weave this fabric of the "revolt of the self " . . . in a manner which is quite different from the Western model'.[28] Though he admits his command of English is limited, Ouedraogo handles the dialogue well and gets good performances from his two key players, Vusi Kunene and David Mohloki, who both come from South African popular theatre.

Another Burkina Faso director of the 1990s whose work demands consideration is the self-taught filmmaker Drissa Touré (born 1952). The first of his two features, *Laada* (1990), is a rural fable about the false lure of city life which offers an idyllic portrayal of Bambara village life and traditional culture. In contrast, *Haramuya* (1993) offers a powerfully realistic image of life in an ugly shanty town on the outskirts of Ouagadougou. In the bars, cafés, and above all on the streets, prostitution, drugs, cheating, robbery and corruption abound. Greed, deceit, lust and addiction are commonplace among the dirt, junk and poverty, and the police are omnipresent. The film does not have a strong narrative line but instead offers a a collage of scenes following, in an intermittent fashion, the lives of a dozen or more characters of all types and ages. This is a world of shifting interactions and relations, where traditional values are questioned by the young and the simple certainties of patriarchal Islam lead to gross distortions. The portrait of a 1990s African city that emerges is vivid and engrossing.

In **Mali** Abdoulaye Ascofaré (born 1949), who trained like so many Malian directors at the VGIK in Moscow, made *Faraw! Mother of the Dunes/Faraw! Une mère des sables* (1996). This is the story of a courageous woman, for whom everything is a struggle: there is no money, her husband is mentally disabled and her three children all cause problems. The action is compressed into a single day and largely expressed physically, but the story is always seen from the protagonist Zamiatou's perspective and her memories and dreams are included. Zamiatou is totally fatalistic in her submission to what she conceives as God's will, but eventually she solves her problems by obtaining a donkey from the man she should have married twenty years earlier and becoming a water-seller. Next morning she can face the dawn with a smile. Just as the action is totally focused and the time-scale pared down, so too the visual style is very composed, comprising largely static, long-held shots. What is remarkable is the physical intensity which Ascofaré brings to the playing and the brutal clarity with which the key themes – grinding poverty, family tensions, the sexual demands of the French workers – are expressed. One understands Tahar Chikhaoui's view that *Faraw!* is 'one of the important African films of recent years'.[29] Though Zamiatou's sons have picked up new ideas from school, the daughter is totally repressed, forbidden even to ask questions, and there is little hope for change (the title 'faraw' means total deadlock or standstill).

As we shall see in Chapter 9, African filmmakers' forty-year concern to probe the realities of African life after independence continues to form an essential part of the work of many of the younger filmmakers born after independence, in the 1960s and 1970s.

NOTES

1. Tahar Chikhaoui, 'Le cinéma tunisien de la maladroite euphorie au juste désarroi', in Abdelmajid Cherfi et al. (eds), *Aspects de la civilisation tunisienne* (Tunis: Faculté de Lettres de Manouba, 1998).
2. Tahar Chikhaoui, 'Maghreb: De l'épopée au regard intime', in Jean-Michel Frodon (ed.), *Au Sud du Cinéma* (Paris: Cahiers du Cinéma/Arte Editions, 2004), p. 26.
3. Brahim Tsaki, interview in *Actes des Septièmes Rencontres de Montpellier* (Montpellier: Fédération des Oeuvres Laïques de l'Hérault, 1986), p. 68.
4. Brahim Tsaki, interview in *El Watan*, Algiers, 17 January 1997, p. 14.
5. '*The Barber of the Poor Quarter*, a unique and mythical film by the no less mythical Mohamed Reggab, the title says it all', according to Ahmed Fertat, 'Le Cinéma marocain aujourd'hui', in Michel Serceau (ed.), *Cinémas du Maghreb* (Paris: Corlet/Télérama/*CinémAction* 111, 2004), p. 55.
6. Jillali Ferhati, interview, in Serceau, *Cinémas du Maghreb*, p. 175.
7. Ibid.
8. Kevin Dwyer, *Beyond Casablanca: M. A. Tazi and the Adventure of Moroccan Cinema* (Bloomington: Indiana University Press, 2004), p. 230.
9. Nouri Bouzid, 'New Realism in Arab Cinema: The Defeat-Conscious Cinema', in Ferial J. Ghazoul (ed.), *Arab Cinematics: Towards the New and the Alternative* (Cairo: *Alif* 15, 1995), p. 243.
10. Cheick Oumar Sissoko, interview, in Nwachukwu Frank Ukadike (ed.), *Questioning African Cinema: Conversations with Filmmakers* (Minneapolis: University of Minnesota Press, 2002), p. 183.
11. Ibid., p. 184.
12. Pierre Yaméogo, interview with Olivier Barlet, www.africultures, 19 July 2002.
13. Tahar Chikaoui, 'Le Cinéma tunisien des années 90: permanences et spécifités', *Horizons Maghrébins* 46, Toulouse, 2002, pp. 114–15.
14. Ibid., p. 115.
15. For a fuller discussion of aspects of women's filmmaking, see two volumes edited by Kenneth W. Harrow: *With Open Eyes: Women and African Cinema* (Amsterdam and Atlanta, GA: Rodopi/*Matutu* 19, 1997) and *African Cinema: Postcolonial and Feminist Readings* (Trenton, NJ and Asmara, Eritrea: Africa World Press, 1999). Also Abdelkrim Gabous, *Silence, elles tournent!: Les femmes et le cinéma en Tunisie* (Tunis: Cérès Editions/CREDIF, 1998).

16. Zahia Smail Salhi, 'Maghrebi Women Film-makers and the Challenge of Modernity: Breaking Women's Silence', in Naomi Sakr (ed.), *Women and Media in the Middle East: Power Through Self-Expression* (London and New York: I. B. Tauris, 2004), p. 71.

17. Abdelkaader Lagtaâ, cited in Kevin Dwyer, '"Hidden, Unsaid, Taboo" in Moroccan Cinema: Abdelkader Lagtaâ's Challenge to Authority', *Framework* 43: 2, Detroit, 2002, pp. 117–33.

18. Ahmed Ferhat, 'Le Cinéma marocain aujourd'hui: les atouts et les contraintes d'une émergence annoncée', in Serceau, *Cinémas du Maghreb*, p. 52.

19. Fatima Mernissi, cited in Dwyer, *Beyond Casablanca*, p. 190,

20. For a discusion of this and Tazi's comedy hit, see Kevin Dwyer, 'Un pays, une décennie, deux comédies', in Serceau, *Cinémas du Maghreb*, pp. 86–91.

21. Saïd Bakiri, interview, in Samuel Lelièvre (ed.), *Cinémas africains, Une oasis dans le désert?* (Paris: Corlet/Télérama/CinémAction 106, 2003), p. 211.

22. Azzedine Meddour, interview, Serceau, *Cinémas du Maghreb*, p. 214.

23. Ekema Agbaw, 'The Cameroonian Film as Instrument of Social and Political Change: 1991–1992', in Maureen N. Eke, Kenneth W. Harrow and Emmanuel Yewah (eds), *African Images: Recent Studies and Text In Cinema* (Trenton, NJ and Asmara, Eritrea: Africa World Press, 2000), p. 91.

24. Jean-Marie Teno, cited in '*Afrique je te plumerai!*', www.africultures, 13 November 2002.

25. Idrissa Ouegraogo, cited in Lelièvre, *Cinémas africains*, p. 128.

26. See Olivier Barlet, *African Cinemas: Decolonizing the Gaze* (London: Zed Books, 2000), p. 211.

27. Idrissa Ouedraogo, interview in Nwachukwu Frank Ukadike (ed.), *Questioning African Cinema: Conversations with Filmmakers* (Minneapolis: University of Minnesota Press, 2002), p. 152.

28. Barlet, *African Cinemas*, p. 42.

29. Tahar Chikhaoui, 'Juste courageuse, la mère', *Cinécrits* 17, Tunis, 1999, p. 25.

PART III

NEW IDENTITIES

The past continues to speak to us. But this is no longer a simple, 'factual' past, since our relation to it is, like the child's relation to the mother, always-already 'after the break'. It is always constructed though memory, fantasy, narrative and myth. Cultural identities are the points of identification or suture, which are made, within the discourses of history and culture.

Stuart Hall[1]

7. EXPERIMENTAL NARRATIVES

Although the pioneering films tell important stories, their points of view and their originality in general are what makes them uniquely African. The points of view taken by the younger directors break the mould of traditional paradigms and allow new 'revolutionary' forms of expression and interrogative models of narrative patterns and aesthetic orientations to proliferate, thus challenging entrenched notions of cinematic orthodoxy.

Nwachukwu Frank Ukadike[2]

INTRODUCTION

The situation facing the new African filmmakers is very much akin to the predicament which Réda Bensmaïa, from a Maghrebian perspective, attributes to contemporary Algerian writers: 'Under today's postmodern conditions, it is not geographical or even political boundaries that determine identities, but rather a plane of consistency that goes beyond the traditional idea of nation and determines its new transcendental configuration'.[3] To help define this new relationship between artists and their national context, Bensmaïa coins the term 'experimental nations', so named because 'they are above all nations that writers have had to imagine and explore as if they were territories to rediscover and stake out, step by step, countries to invent and to draw while creating one's language'.[4]

For those African filmmakers who experienced independence as adults, the question of national cultural identity was naturally an on-going concern in subsequent years. Many, like Ousmane Sembene, keep to the views they had at the time, and this is reflected in their post-independence work. But most of the next generation, those who had been children or adolescents at independence – and the bulk (over 60 per cent) of all Maghrebian and Sub-Saharan filmmakers fall into this category – could not approach notions of national and cultural identity in the same unself-conscious way. Instead of simply capturing or reproducing a reality which was deemed simply 'to be there', a number of them were more concerned with recreating imaginary or mythical worlds of the past – that of the African village community or the Tunisian medina, for example – or searching their own personal histories for exemplary tales from the world of childhood. This placing of the past above the present, the personal above the social, was, however, not necessarily a withdrawal from social commitment. In choosing this path, the filmmakers were not ignoring current social or political problems, but rather finding – by distancing themselves from all-too-present immediate concerns – new ways of confronting them.

Indeed it could be argued that African filmmakers are in fact too serious in their approach, as has been conceded by the Ivoirian filmmaker Kramo-Lanciné Fadika who asks, 'Why must we just be intellectual when Louis de Funès gets laughs in African cinemas?'[5] Very few African filmmakers have produced out-and-out comedies, and comedy can in no way be regarded as one of the 'traditions' of African cinema. Yet those comedies which have been made have often found huge audiences. In an article on Moroccan film comedy, Kevin Dwyer notes that though Moroccan cinema has barely half a dozen comic films, the two most popular Moroccan films of all times – Mohamed Abderrahman Tazi's *Looking for my Wife's Husband/A la recherche du mari de ma femme* (1993) and Hakim Noury's *She is Diabetic and Hypertensive and She Refuses to Die/Elle est diabétique et hypertendue et elle refuse de crever* (2000) – are both comedies. Since Dwyer wrote his article, another comedy, Saïd Naciri's *Crooks/Les Bandits* (2004), has surpassed even these two films in popularity. Dwyer can offer no reason for the avoidance of humour: 'Humour serves as an outlet which could please Moroccan filmmakers seeking to stigmatise the problems of their society'.[6] Similarly, the most popular film in Tunisian film history is Ferid Boughedir's comedy of a little boy's discovery of sex, *Halfaouine* (1990). South of the Sahara the list is also limited, with only Daniel Kamwa from Cameroon – especially with *Pousse-Pousse* (1975) and *Our Daughter/Notre fille* (1980) – and Henri Duparc from Ivory Coast – with a succession of six features culminating in *Rue Princesse* (1994) and *Coffee-Coloured/Une couleur café* (1997) – emerging as specialists. Yet, as Olivier Barlet notes, comedy can serve a serious function, as well as merely stimulating laughter: 'Rather than promoting the projection of their own difficulties on to other peoples or social groups, black styles of humour guide human beings in unravelling the inextricably tangled threads of their destiny'.[7]

The approach of the majority of African filmmakers seeking a serious alternative to social realism is captured with great clarity in the second part of Stuart Hall's two-part definition of cultural identity:

> Cultural identity in this second sense, is a matter of 'becoming' as well as of 'being'. It belongs to the future as much as to the past. It is not something which already exists, transcending place, time, history and culture. Cultural identities come from somewhere, have histories. But, like everything which is historical, they undergo constant transformation . . . Identities are the names we give to the different ways we are positioned by, and position ourselves within, the narratives of the past.[8]

Faced with the inherent social, political, economic and cultural contradictions of postcolonial Africa, some filmmakers felt the need to escape the everyday and find a new starting point for their work. From the beginning of the 1970s too, a number of filmmakers argued that new formal structures, owing far less to the conventions of mainstream Western cinema, were needed if African cinemas were to reflect the reality of postcolonial rule from a truly African perspective. The Moroccan director Moumen Smihi, for example, talked of 'forms which would function precisely to translate another way of living and thinking, another culture, other social options than those put forward up to now by the West'.[9]

As we have seen in Chapters 5 and 6, there has been a constant, dominant stream, over the past forty years, of socially realist films which accept identity as a given and are based on a sense of common historical experiences and shared cultural codes. Alternative or experimental films which call into question that approach have been sporadic, though none the less valuable for that. Most often these have been isolated, individual works within the overall output of a filmmaker who has earlier worked in, or subsequently reverts to, the realist mainstream (as with Smihi, Med Hondo, Souleymane Cisse or Merzak Allouache). On occasion these questioning works are virtually the sole output of a filmmaker denied further funding for decades (Djibril Diop Mambety or Hamid Benani), and indeed sometimes they represent the filmmaker's only occasion to realise a full feature-length work (Ahmed Bouanani, Farouk Beloufa, Assia Djebar or Moncef Dhouib). Such a non-realistic approach often demands a complex response from the spectator if its social or political commitment is to be understood. As Olivier Barlet has said of the Paris screening of Souleymane Cisse's *Yeelen*, the French audience saw only the magic, 'while the film is nothing but a tool serving a political message against the appropriation of the power of knowledge by the fathers'.[10]

THE 1970S

In Sub-Saharan Africa, two isolated examples of an alternative approach are the debut films of two major figures in African cinema, both of whom are self-taught: Med Hondo (born 1936) – born in **Mauritania** but based in Paris – and the Senegalese Djibril Diop Mambety (1945–98). Both later continued to work in alternative forms, Hondo with a musical spectacle and Diop Mambety with a formalised literary adaptation.

Hondo's debut film *Soleil O* (1970) reflects his earlier work in theatre, particularly in the opening sketches of Christian baptism and colonial army recruitment performed by a small team of actors switching roles. But as the film proceeds, its stylistic means broaden to take in documentary footage, interviews and naturalistically played re-enactments, and there is a constant interplay (and frequent juxtaposition) of voice and image. The film opens with a ringing affirmation of African identity: 'We had our own civilisation. We forged our own iron. We had our own songs and dances . . . We had our own literature, our own religion, our own science, our own methods of education'. But it ends in a scene of alienation and anguish, with the protagonist's screams and the burning of portraits of the great 1960s revolutionary heroes, Malcolm X, Che Guevara and Patrice Lumumba among them. The film's central portion follows the experience of an African immigrant from his arrival in Paris through a series of encounters which allow Hondo to explore a wide range of issues: housing, work and sexuality, as well as inner doubts and illusions. Both dialogue and voice-over point out the mixture of gullibility and hypocrisy, passivity and inner violence that characterise the interactions of black and white Parisian residents. Even after thirty-five years *Soleil O* retains its power, remarkable for its certainty, its richness and its balanced tone. As Ibrahima Signaté wrote in 2002, it is 'the founding film. The one from which everything flows. Hence its importance. It announces, in one way or another, all the others. As much from the thematic point of view as on the level of film technique'.[11]

After making documentary films supporting the Polisario Front, Hondo turned to overtly stylised fiction with *West Indies/West Indies, ou les nègres marrons de la liberté* (1979), made with part-funding from Algeria and Mauritania. The result is a piece combining music, sound effects, dance, declamation and song, entirely shot on the huge set of a slave ship built in a disused Parisian railway station. *West Indies* is a colourful musical spectacle, ranging back and forth between the present and the origins of the slave trade between France and the Antilles. The staging – like the opening of *Soleil O* – reflects Hondo's theatrical background in the frontality of the positioning of the actors, but the whole is lively, vivid and vigorous. The freedom from a narrative based on individual, personal stories allows Hondo to raise a whole number of the contradictions thrown up by slavery and its impact on West Indian society, as well to confront European hypocrisy. The film does not, however, give a fully alternative history, since all the dates and names are those of the coloniser, while the Antillean people remain anonymous, their struggle abstracted into dance. The ending, for example, is a vivid communal dance heralding a new dawn of liberation which dissolves into a blur of whirling colours and shapes. As always, Hondo's work stands out from the mainstream of African production – a perfect example of a work restoring imaginary fullness – in Stuart Hall's sense – and offers resources of resistance and identity.

In **Senegal** Djibril Diop Mambety directed just two features – *Touki Bouki* (1973) and *Hyenas/Hyènes*, which was shot nineteen years later – together with five shorter works, in a thirty-year career as a filmmaker, but the importance of his work for African cinema and the personal affection with which he is regarded is illustrated by the appearance of three books about him and his work since his death in 1998. Nar Sene stresses the personal aspects of Diop Mambety's work, which he sees as a single whole: 'The characters in his films just accompany him, reply to him, do not exist on their own, but to give him existence as the focus of looks and attention, waiting for answers slow to come, on the part of the person who is looked at: Himself'.[12] Sada Niang places his emphasis on the narrative structure: '*Touki Bouki* is an assembly of facts and characters, guided by a barely sketched-in drama, clarified gradually as the action unfolds. The film demands of its spectators a "synthetic" approach'.[13] For Anny Wynchank, the key to *Touki Bouki* is oral story-telling: 'Despite the modern techniques used and the immediacy of the subject it presents, this film is profoundly anchored in traditional African culture . . . Numerous motifs, like the formulas of oral tales, recur in the film. A didactic, Mambety warns his fellow citizens against the illusion of escape'.[14]

In a very real sense they are all correct, since Diop Mambety's work – typified by *Touki Bouki* – is a very personal mixture of contradictions: both modern and traditional in its narrative styles, didactic and free-flowing, humorous and yet with a very strong social commitment. Basically the film is the story of two young people from Dakar, Anta and Mory, who fall in love. Both are outsiders – she dresses as a boy and he spends his time endlessly circling on a motorbike ornamented with the horns of the cattle he used to herd as a child in rural Senegal – so it is hardly surprising that they decide to emigrate to France. In this they are following, it seems, the director's own unsuccessful attempt to stow away on board a boat bound for France.

Everything in the film is related to this story, but in a very real sense it is little more than a thread on which to hang, bead-like, a series of always vivid but often very differently shaped stories. In a way that some critics have compared to the filmmakers of the French New Wave, to which he had some access through the French cultural centre in Dakar,[15] Diop Mambety follows the couple's progress in zigzag and fragmentary fashion, as they travel, make love, steal, hide from the police and, eventually, reach their goal, the harbour. He uses their enthusiasm and energy to hold the spectator's attention, as he constantly plays games with space and time, showing scenes out of order and including flashbacks and flashes forward to other parts of the narrative. One particularly successful technique as they travel in and around Dakar is to stay behind when they have passed through a space (to watch the slaughter of the cattle in the opening scene, to follow a fat policeman's plodding progress, to show two women fighting, and so on). Scenes of direct interaction mingle with memory images and dreamlike encounters (such as Anta's vision of the savage in the tree who steals Mory's motorbike). Throughout its length *Touki Bouki* includes purely symbolic images of blood and water, sea and sacrifice. Since the film begins and ends with the young Mory riding across the savannah with a herd of oxen, the whole film could be a little boy's dream. It certainly has the necessary liveliness and intense sense of longing, as well as overflowing wit and imagination.

Diop Mambety's second feature, *Hyenas/Hyènes* (1992), has a much stronger dramatic storyline and fewer digressions, no doubt because it is a fairly faithful version of Friedrich Dürrenmatt's Swiss play *The Visit/Der Besuch der Alten Dame*. Here an impoverished African village greets the return of its richest ex-citizen, Lingère Ramatou, who offers them all great wealth, but only if they kill the lover who betrayed her when she was just seventeen. The plot parallels the progress towards acceptance of the lover, Dramaan, with the opposite trajectory of the villagers, who immediately buy luxuries on credit and whose greed becomes insatiable. The film ends, inevitably, with Dramaan's death. The Africanisation of the fable works remarkably well, not just because Diop Mambety punctuates the story and comments on its action with animal images, but also because the subject matter – love, betrayal, greed – is universal. The story gives the director plenty of scope for striking symbolic imagery: Lingère Ramatou's golden hand and foot (replacing limbs burned off in a plane crash), her visually striking entourage (including a Japanese chauffeur played by Diop's sister-in-law), the bright new imported yellow shoes everyone is suddenly wearing, the cloak that is all that remains of Dramaan at the end. There are also seemingly unrelated scenes cut into the narrative (a mosque that appears from nowhere, a funfair and firework display suddenly coming into view), perhaps, as Anny Wynchank argues, to broaden the film's meaning to take in the whole continent of Africa.[16] The drama is watched over by Diop Mambety himself as Gana, the judge who expelled Lingère Ramatou from the village (on the basis of false testimony produced by Dramaan) and who is now the wealthy woman's valet. While there are as many truths about Africa as there are ambiguities woven into the plot, *Hyenas* is indeed 'a parable that is radically different from the unobtrusive realism favoured by many African directors'.[17]

In the Maghreb too there is work of real insight and imagination, in the form of a handful of outstanding 1970s first features in **Morocco**. Most of these were independently produced and made by filmmakers who had studied filmmaking at IDHEC in Paris during the 1960s: Hamid Benani's *Wechma/Traces* (1970), Moumen Smihi's *El Chergui/El Chergui ou le silence violent* (1975) and Ahmed Bouanani's *Mirage* (1979). To these may be added the debut film of the Polish-trained director Mustafa Derkaoui, *About Some Meaningless Events/De quelques événements sans signification* (1974), which seems not to have been released. *Wechma* is the bleak tale of a boy who is adopted by a man to whom he cannot relate and who drifts into petty crime, only to die meaninglessly in a motorbike accident. *El Chergui* traces the equally unhappy fate of a woman who dies trying to prevent her husband from taking a second wife. Both films castigate the rigidities and superstitions of traditional patriarchal society, mixing realistic study of contemporary society with symbolic images and often disjointed and enigmatic narratives. *Mirage*, by contrast, adopts the motif of the journey from countryside to town, tracing the passage of a peasant who has found a sackful of money. But the town is a nightmarish, labyrinthine world, full of strange encounters and constant off-screen hints of violence, and the narrative, which is shot through with cinematic references (Chaplin, Fellini, and others), constantly shifts registers.

These lively and inventive 1970s films were largely without immediate sequels. Bouanani returned to film editing and, later, worked as scriptwriter with the young Daoud Aoulad Syad. Benani had to wait twenty-five years before completing his second feature, *A Prayer for the Absent/La Prière de l'absent* (1995), which did not find a distributor in Morocco.[18] Smihi moved towards mainstream filmmaking, but Derkaoui kept the experimental approach alive with a series of highly complex self-reflective films during the 1980s and 1990s, beginning with *The Beautiful Days of Sheherazade/Les Beaux jours de Chahrazade* (1982). In doing so, he became, as Ahmed Ferhat notes, 'the most prolific Moroccan filmmaker and paradoxically the one least seen by the public',[19] with three successive films in the 1990s getting no Moroccan public screening at all. However, he achieved one of the major commercial successes of the new century with his eighth film (and first comedy), *The Loves of Hadj Mokhtar Soldi/Les Amours de Hadj Mokhtar Soldi* (2001).

Very different is the work in **Tunisia** of the theatrically trained collaborators from the independently run Nouveau Théâtre de Tunis: Fadhel Jaïbi (born 1945), Fadhel Jaziri (born 1948) and their colleagues, Mohamed Driss, Jalila Baccar and Habib Masrouki: These developed a quite distinctive style, much influenced by twentieth-century European drama, in their two complex theatrical adaptations, *The Wedding/La Noce* (1978) and *Arab/'Arab* (1988). *The Wedding*, which was collectively signed, owed much to the insight and technical skill of Habib Masrouki who had studied filmmaking in Paris (he died, aged just thirty-three, two years later). The group's explicit aim was to renew a Tunisian cinema they described as hovering between a 'Zorro' level and a 'zero'

level, and 'to narrate through fables the relations between people, class relations, sexual relations'.[20] The film proved a critical success abroad but flopped
in Tunisia where, as they wryly confessed, they had thought 'that they were
going to beat imperialist productions on their own battle field'.[21] *The Wedding*
owed much, it seems, to Bertolt Brecht's work (it opens with the Kurt Weill song
Mack the Knife sung in German) and the filmmaking style (here and in *Arab*)
was consciously influenced by German expressionism.[22] Shot in 16mm and in
black and white, but with a very elaborate soundtrack, the film makes few concessions to the audience. It was shot in a single location (an old and crumbling
flat) and concentrates claustrophobically on a couple alone for the first time on
their wedding night. The camera focuses implacably on their words and smallest gestures, as they spend the night discussing sexuality and jealousy, potency
and failure, life and fantasy – more like an old married couple than newly-weds.
It is a film unlike any other in Tunisian cinema, except, that is, *Arab* which followed ten years later.

Jaïbi and Jaziri, credited as co-directors of *Arab*, here have access to 35mm,
colour, a fully professional production team and international co-production
finance, but the film has the same claustrophobic atmosphere, being largely shot
in a deconsecrated basilica on a hill at Carthage just outside Tunis. Jalila Baccar
again plays the lead, this time opposite an actor with no Nouveau Théâtre con-
nections: Lamine Nahdi. The film begins with the arrival in Tunis of an air
hostess Houria seeking news of her lover, who has disappeared, from Khélil,
a photographer wounded in the war in the Lebanon. The film is not a realistic
account of current political events, but a fable in which Houria is transported
back into the Arab past, a time of chivalry but also of fatal rivalries, abduc-
tions, jealousies and honour killings. In the course of a very complicated action
all the characters kill each other, except Houria who returns to the Lebanon
pregnant with Khélil's child. Despite the many deaths, the directors claim that
Arab is 'none the less a film of hope. You have to have reached the extreme of
tragedy and violence for change to be possible'.[23] As its title indicates, *Arab* sets
out to question Arab identity, not to show the fate of individuals but to point
to a collective failure of Arab culture, as expressed both in its historical past
and in its present wars and conflicts.

In **Algeria** the bulk of the state-controlled production followed a pattern of
conventional Western-style narrative, giving little scope for innovation. But a
handful of films did, to some extent, challenge the dominant orthodoxy. The
most commercially successful of these is the first film of Merzak Allouache
(born 1944), which brought a fresh look at young people in Algerian society
and an interesting stylistic approach. *Omar Gatlato* (1976) is basically a study
of male inhibition. The hero, Omar, likes to think of himself as a macho male,
but falls in love with a girl whose voice he has heard but whom he has never
seen. Faced with meeting the real flesh-and-blood woman who embodies his

dreams, he flees in terror. Allouache treats this light comic theme ingeniously through a play with the soundtrack, using three forms of verbal narration (direct address to camera, voice-over and inner monologue). Initially Omar has all the authority of a film narrator, presenting himself directly to the camera, describing details of his life in Algiers. He has a weakness for romantic music (Algerian *chaabi* and the soundtracks of Hindi movies) and when he loses his proudest possession, his tape recorder, his life is plunged into crisis. The replacement recorder comes with a tape bearing an unknown woman's inner thoughts, and this unexpected intimacy with a woman in Algeria's totally seg-regated society overwhelms him. His loss of inner certainty is revealed through shifts in the structure of the soundtrack, as his confident assertions to camera and authoritative voice-over predictions about events become querulous doubts voiced through a troubled inner monologue.[24] Allouache adopted a sim-ilarly experimental approach in his second feature, *The Adventures of a Hero/Les Aventures d'un héros* (1978), which traced a mythical hero's trajec-tory through time and space, but his subsequent work is in a more conventional realistic style and has been discussed in Chapter 6.

More controversial, and markedly less successful commercially, are the four features directed by the self-taught director Mohamed Bouamari (born 1941). The best known of these is *The Charcoal Burner/Le Charbonnier* (1972) which was widely shown (including at Cannes) as a pioneer example of the shift in direction in the Algerian state's priorities from depictions of the liberation strug-gle to advocacy of the so-called Agrarian Revolution. At the time it was seen as a film in the documentary-realist tradition – Jean-Louis Bory compared it to Robert Flaherty's *Man of Aran*,[25] while Ali Mocki (from a Marxist perspective) asserted that 'the director's ideological limitations prevent him from defining the class struggle in Algeria in a correct (materialist) way'.[26] Certainly Bouamari's statements of the time favoured such an approach: 'The camera must be focused on the people of the countryside, showing their difficulties, troubles and hopes. We must prepare the objective conditions for a radical transformation of their mentality'.[27] But re-viewed thirty years later, Bouamari's film seems very different. *The Charcoal Burner* has numerous early sequences of observational filming of the repetitive nature of the protagonist's work, but these are interspersed with silent comedy sequences and an inventive, non-nat-uralistic use of sound effects (simple phrases of music, natural sound and the repeated noise of forest frogs). In terms of the overall structure, some seemingly key scenes are missing or shot mute, and the transformation brought by the coming of the new ways is depicted not as a material event, but as the protag-onist's dream (even nightmare). Quite how the transition to the gleaming factory with its white-clad workers shown at the end is achieved remains a mystery. Though the film is, on the surface, a hymn to progress, the gaps in the narrative and frequent lack of synchronisation of image and sound undercut this message. As Sabry Hafez notes, the result is a profoundly ambiguous image of the Agrarian Revolution: 'The linear narrative of the story of the disintegration of the old world of Belkacem, the charcoal maker, under the onslaught of 'progress' clashes with the ostensible linearity and undermines its logic.'[28]

Bouamari had achieved a high reputation for his early short films and he continued to innovate throughout his career. But while his later features are characterised by an ability to create striking, even startling, scenes, he shows far less skill in sustaining a ninety-minute narrative. *The Inheritance/L'Héritage* (1974) deals with the reconstruction of a village destroyed by the war and is clearly intended to symbolise the creation of a new independent Algeria, but the actual story – interspersed with caricatured scenes of colonial life and oddly placed moments of comedy – seems to take place in a social void. *First Step/Premier pas* (1979), which ostensibly treats the new freedoms for women in Algeria, spends its first quarter of an hour introducing us to the director and cast, before the action they have assembled to enact begins. The narrative comprises a set of variations rather than a logically developing plot and the tone veers wildly between conventional fictional filming , straight-to-camera improvisation and self-consciously theatrical performance. *The Refusal/Le Refus* (1982) shifts its focus to immigrant life in France, with the dialogue largely in French, though the film was apparently shot in Oran (which would account for a number of inconsistencies). The film seeks to relate the nationalisation of the Algeria's oil-fields to a worsening of life for Algerian immigrants, but the storyline jumps disconcertingly between time levels, and the jumbled sequence of events never creates a plot in the accepted meaning of the term.

Aside from Allouache's debut film and the work of Bouamari, there are two other films – both the sole features in their directors' output – that stand aside from the mainstream of Algerian 1970s production (neither was produced by the state organisation ONCIC). A quite unique view of post-war Algiers was provided by Mohamed Zinet (born 1932), dramatist and theatrical director as well as actor in a number of Algerian and French films, who had fought and been wounded with the ANL during the liberation struggle. *Tahia ya didou* (1971) is a film produced on the margins, by the city authority, in which the action is punctuated by songs by the Algiers poet Momo (Himoud Brahimi) and accompanied by a vivid and original use of sound. The film uses the tourist activities of a couple returning to Algiers where the husband had served in the French army as the pretext for a vivid portrait of the diversity of the city and its people, shot in observational documentary style (it was originally planned as a short documentary). Initially the tone is light-hearted, with plenty of humour, comic chases and some good jokes ('What's capitalism?' 'The exploitation of man by man'. 'Then what's socialism?' 'The opposite'). The dramatic mood deepens, however, when it emerges that the man was previously involved in the torture of Algerian patriots, and it comes to a climax in a restaurant where he has to flee from the seemingly relentless gaze of a man he once tortured. But the victim (played by Zinet) is in fact blind because of his mistreatment in prison.

Farouk Beloufa (born 1947) succeeded in making only one feature, *Nahla* (1947), produced by Algerian television but shot in 35mm for cinema release. Beloufa's independence of spirit is shown by the fact that his earlier feature-length documentary, *Insurrectionnelle*, was censored and collectively re-edited to emerge as *Guerre de Libération* (1978). In *Nahla* he is one of the few Maghrebian directors to look at events abroad in the Arab world, in this case the situation in Lebanon in 1975, shot on location at a time when violence was again beginning to erupt. An Algerian journalist, Larbi, arrives in Beirut on the eve of the civil war and tries to get to grips with the situation there, through his contacts with three very diverse women – the tormented singer Nahla, the angry and aggressive journalist Mahda and the ever smiling Palestinian activist, Hind – together with the men (business men, politicians, journalists and guerrilla fighters) circling around them. The film is, in essence, a beautifully composed and fluently shot conversation piece, with Nahla's songs and contemporary newsreel material well integrated into the flow of the narrative (the film was co-scripted by Beloufa and the novelist Rachid Boudjedra). Beloufa also handles excellently the chaotic action scenes when the civil war suddenly erupts in street battles, in one of which Larbi is wounded. Though, at 140 minutes, the film is perhaps too long, it is excellently edited (by Moufida Tlatli) and sound is used imaginatively (as in the scene where the newly arrived Larbi wanders for the first time through the streets of Beirut). The film as a whole is a kind of collage of everyday events and conversations, coloured by fears, anticipations and echoes of the past. Inevitably, Larbi does not solve the puzzle of Lebanese politics and power struggles, and the film ends inconclusively with a ceasefire which is as unexpected as the initial flare-up of violence. Merzak Allouache, Beloufa's contemporary who followed the same training route, from INA in Algiers to IDHEC in Paris, paid a fine tribute to the film in *Les Deux Ecrans*:

> My pride in seeing this film, sequence after sequence, was to perceive the author's signature and that of the director of photography. A work based on an aesthetic, for me that's something capital, because slowly, and despite all the problems which our cinema is encountering, we are entering a period where we are going to have to debate, perhaps subjectively, cinema as cinema, film as film.[29]

The only other major experimental film of the 1970s north or south of the Sahara is the first Algerian feature-length work to be completed by a woman filmmaker: *La Nouba/La Nouba des femmes du mont Chenoa* (1978), directed by the French-language novelist Assia Djebar (born 1936). At one level this is the simple story of a woman returning home to meditate on the failure of her marriage. But on another the film is a deeply autobiographical work in which Djebar explores her own past in Cherchell, where she was born, and the surrounding mountains from which her family came. The 'nouba' of the title is a traditional dance form in which the musicians take turns in coming to the forefront, and the film has a very musical structure, reminiscent of the lyrical form of Djebar's novels. It mixes a variety of styles (drama and documentary, historical re-enactments and formal interviews, music and meditation) and time levels (that of the enacted tale of personal exploration, the recounted stories of the immediate past, the more distant history evoked by the grandmother and the filmmaker's own reflections recorded after the shooting). Djebar occupies the paradoxical position of an Algerian novelist whose first language is French and her voice-over commentary here is in the French language. But the film, rather than being simply an evocation of a place and its past from the outside, is more aptly seen as an exploration of Arab women's experiences from within, through their voices as they evoke their own lives. Far removed from the male-dominated realistic conformities of much state-sponsored Algerian mainstream cinema, *La Nouba* is concerned to retell the stories of the women of Djebar's native region, ending with a celebration of their (often hidden) strengths, typified by the legendary heroine, Zoulikha. On a personal level too, *La Nouba* was a truly creative experience, for it enabled Djebar to resume her novel writing after a ten-year blockage. The series of novels that follow in the 1980s and 1990s are full of references to the making of the film and to the characters it evokes, and in 2002 Zoulikha became the protagonist of a full-length novel, *La Femme sans sépulture*.

NOTES

1. Stuart Hall, 'Cultural Identity and Cinematic Representations', *Framework* 36, London, 1989, p. 72.
2. Nwachukwu Frank Ukadike, *Questioning African Cinema: Conversations with Filmmakers*, (Minneapolis: University of Minnesota Press, 2002), p. xviii.
3. Réda Bensmaïa, *Experimental Nations or The Invention of the Maghreb* (Princeton: Princeton University Press, 2003), p. 8.
4. Ibid.
5. Fadika Kramo-Lancine, cited in Olivier Barlet, *African Cinemas: Decolonizing the Gaze*, (London: Zed Books, 2000), p. 132.
6. Keven Dwyer, 'Un pays, une décennie, deux comédies', in Michel Serceau (ed.), *Cinémas du Maghreb* (Paris: Corlet/Télérama/CinémAction 111, 2004), p. 91. This is virtually the only sustained analysis of African film comedy apart from the chapter 'Black Humours' in Barlet, *African Cinemas*, pp. 129–42.
7. Barlet, *African Cinemas*, p. 141.
8. Hall, 'Cultural Identity', p. 7.
9. Moumen Smihi, 'Moroccan Society as Mythology', in John D. H. Downing (ed.), *Film and Politics in the Third World* (New York: Praeger, 1987), p. 82.

10. Olivier Barlet, 'Les Nouvelles stratégies des cinéastes africains', *Africultures* 41, Paris, 2001, p. 71.
11. Dominique Mondolini (ed.), *Cinémas d'Afrique* (ADPF/*Notre Libraire*: 149, Paris, 2002), p. 143.
12. Nar Sene, *Djibril Diop Mambety: La caméra au bout ... du nez* (Paris: L'Harmattan, 2001), p. 33.
13. Sada Niang, *Djibril Diop Mambety: Un Cinéaste à Contre-Courant* (Paris: L'Harmattan, 2002), p. 117.
14. Anny Wynchank, *Djibril Diop Mambety, ou Le Voyage du Voyant* (Ivry-Sur Seine: Editions A3, 2003), p. 67.
15. See, for example, Wynchank, *Djibril Diop Mambety*, pp. 55–6.
16. Ibid., p. 83.
17. Richard Porton, 'Mambety's *Hyenas*: Between Anti-Colonialism and the Critique of Modernity', *Iris* 18, Paris and Iowa, 1995, p. 97.
18. Ahmed Ferhat, 'Le Cinéma marocain aujourd'hui: Les atouts et constraintes d'une émergence annoncée', in Michel Serceau (ed.), *Les Cinémas du Maghreb* (Paris: Corlet/Télérama/*CinémAction* 111, 2004), p. 59.
19. Ibid., p. 57.
20. Mouny Berrah, Victor Bachy, Mohand Ben Salama and Ferid Boughedir (eds), *Cinémas du Maghreb* (Paris: *CinémAction* 14, 1981), p. 188.
21. Ibid., p. 190.
22. Fadhel Jaïbi, in Hédi Khelil, *Le Parcours et la Trace: Témoignages et documents sur le cinéma tunisien*, (Salammbô: MediaCon, 2002), pp. 84–5.
23. Fadhel Jaîbi and Fadhel Jaziri, in Touti Moumen, *Films tunisiens: Longs métrages 1967–98* (Tunis: Touti Moumen, 1998), p. 127.
24. For a full analysis of *Omar Gatlato*, see Roy Armes, *Omar Gatlato* (Trowbridge: Flicks Books, 1998).
25. Jean-Louis Bory, cited in Claude-Michel Cluny, *Dictionnaire des nouveaux cinémas arabes* (Paris: Sindbad, 1978), p. 156.
26. Ali Mocki, 'Reflections on the Algerian Revolution', in Hala Salmane, Simon Hartog and David Wilson (eds), *Algerian Cinema* (London: British Film Institute, 1976), p. 45.
27. Mohamed Bouamari, cited in Cluny, *Dictionnaire*, p. 156.
28. Sabry Hafez, 'Shifting Identities in Maghribi Cinema: The Algerian Paradigm', in Ferial J. Ghazoul, *Arab Cinematics: Towards the New and the Alternative* (Cairo: *Alif* 15, 1995), p. 70.
29. Merzak Allouache, 'Salut l'Artiste', *Les Deux Ecrans* 15–16, Algiers, 1979, p. 64.

8. EXEMPLARY TALES

It's the time when African filmmakers give up systematically being a mirror for their space and their people, a condition which had long been necessary for a reappropriation and decolonisation of thought. It was no longer time just to denounce the mimicry and corruption of the elites. If the established order is to be changed, there is a need for solid values: they explore their culture and, to illustrate the need for social change, they plunge into pure fiction.

Olivier Barlet[1]

INTRODUCTION

African filmmakers' quest for autonomy in the 1980s is matched, notes Nwachukwu Frank Ukadike, by 'compelling experimentation', which 'enables us to appreciate African cinema as innovative and diverse'. Instead of directly denouncing the Westernisation and corruption of postcolonial African elites in realistically depicted stories of contemporary life, they choose instead to re-examine the roots of African culture and to draw inspiration from African oral story telling. Manthia Diawara has argued that there are three reasons for the this shift to a precolonial past: to avoid censorship, to search for precolonial African traditions that can contribute to the solution of contemporary problems, and to develop a new film language.[2] In following this path, the new filmmakers also, and no doubt unexpectedly, created images of Africa that found instant success in the West, where their films won prizes at European festivals and received (comparatively) wide recognition and distribution.

These 1980s and 1990s films offered new ways of accessing an African cultural identity and hence constituted a source of opposition to the alien forces that have done so much to shape and distort Africa since independence. Such films are – potentially at least – the 'hidden texts' of which Stuart Hall speaks, which 'restore an imaginary fullness or plenitude'. They are 'resources of resistance and identity, with which to confront the fragmented and pathological ways in which that experience has been re-constructed within the dominant regimes of cinematic and visual representation of the West'.[3] With the so-called 'village' films of Gaston Kabore and the early Idrissa Ouedraogo films, or the trio of allegories made by Mohamed Chouikh and the studies of the Andalusian heritage by Nacer Khemir, we also find for the first time a series of works in which the same non-realistic styles can be explored and developed over a period of time, rather than the isolated experimental works of the 1970s. The fact that this cinema is novel in form and questions simple notions of cultural identity and social realism does not mean that it is any less concerned with the realities and contradictions of postcolonial Africa. Indeed, as Richard Porton has noted, 'since allegory depicts, and indeed revels in, the "brokenness" of the world, it is a genre that is well suited to the requirements of contemporary African directors'.[4] As we shall see in Chapter 9, this trend continues in the work of many of the younger filmmakers of the 2000s.

THE 1980s

The new pattern was set by Gaston Kabore (born 1951), who, in addition to being head of the film organisation in **Burkina Faso** (1977–88) and secretary general of the filmmakers' association, FEPACI (1985–97), has made a dozen or more documentaries in addition to his feature films. *Wend Kuuni* (1982), the first of his four features, is set at the height of the Mossi empire which could, according to its director, be 1420 or, equally, 1850.[5] The film tells the story of a boy found in the bush and adopted by a family in a nearby village. His experiences have rendered him mute, but his adoptive parents give him a supportive environment and name him Wend Kuuni (Gift of God). Much of the film's focus is on the everyday events of village life – weaving, preparing food, fetching water, herding goats – creating a largely idyllic vision of the African past set in an empty landscape. Then the peace of the village is destroyed when a young bride noisily rejects her aged husband because he is impotent. He commits suicide and the subsequent discovery of his body triggers Wend Kuuni's return to speech. At last he can tell his personal story and that of his dead mother, driven out of her own village when she refused to remarry after her husband had failed to return from hunting. Visually, the narrative has an almost documentary simplicity, but the audience's response is enriched and shaped by both a voice-over narration and René Guirma's musical score. *Wend Kuuni* brought a fresh sense of storytelling to African cinema, drawing on oral traditions to capture beautifully the slow, calm rhythm of life where man and nature are in harmony.

Kabore's second film, *Zan Boko* (1988), begins with the tranquil ordered life in a Mossi village where the inhabitants' lifestyle, gestures and words of greeting have not changed for centuries. Life quietly follows the rhythm of the seasons. In the evenings the men gather to drink beer and listen to traditional music, and the women sit together to talk of family matters, food and markets. Everything has its true place. But then abruptly surveyors appear, measuring the land and numbering all the traditional round huts, their intrusion underlined by a switch to jazzy modern music. The protagonist Tinga argues that if they stick together, the villagers will manage to keep their lifestyle, but this is not to be. Soon the French-speaking developers and politicians have succeeded, and a huge new villa, inhabited by a French-speaking bourgeois family, towers over Tinga's farmyard. Inevitably Tinga and his family are ejected, to make way for a swimming pool, and even the intervention of a sympathetic journalist cannot save them. The live television programme raising their plight is cut off on the orders of the state president and the journalist censured. Kabore tells his story simply but effectively, without recourse to suspense or dramatic confrontations (we do not see the actual expulsion of Tinga's family, for example). The basic contrasts are those found in twenty years of African filmmaking: tradition versus modernity, More speakers versus French speakers, powerlessness versus economic weight. What is new is the political edge – characteristic of the 1980s – that Kabore has added to his film: Burkina Faso is explicitly a corrupt society where wealth buys influence and laws are designed to benefit the urban rich.

Kabore's third feature, *Rabi* (1992), is his shortest and slightest, totally lacking the political dimension of *Zan Boko*. Apart from the odd touches of modern life, such as a bicycle and a radio, this could be set at any time in the last 100 years. The film is the timeless tale of a boy growing up within a close family and village environment, learning from everything around him: the old man Pusga he helps look after, the work of his mother (a potter) and his father (a blacksmith), his sister's growth to womanhood and the games of the other children. The particular story of Rabi revolves around the tortoise he loves but eventually returns to the wild. As in his previous films, Kabore shows immense respect for the rhythms of rural life and the sensibilities of children. The grey-bearded Pusga is the source of wisdom in the film and, as Hédi Khelil has pointed out, Kabore's style of direction can best be captured through one of Pusga's sayings: 'You must never limit yourself to what is visible. You have to spy out the vibrations of nature'.[6]

Kabore's fourth and finest film, *Buud Yam* (1996), which won the top prize, the Étalon de Yennenga, at FESPACO in 1997, is a further investigation of some of Kabore's favourite themes: memory, identity, the need to be true to oneself. Though village life is depicted as before, with its slow rhythms and parochial concerns, there is a new dynamism, as the protagonist does not just remain to suffer or face defeat. Here he has a mission which involves him in constant restless movement, and this, in turn, gives the film its lively pace, beginning with the opening pre-credit sequence of the hero riding furiously through the bush. Set at the end of the nineteenth century at a bend in the River Niger, the film updates the story of Wend Kuuni and Pughneere from Kabore's first feature (Wend Kuuni is played by the same actor, now fourteen years older). When Wend Kuuni remembers the past, it is clips from the earlier film that we see. At the beginning of the film, Wend Kuuni is full of anger at his fate and at his lost father (the title means 'spirit of the ancestors'). He is also at odds with the other young men who see him – the outsider – as responsible for all the troubles the village has suffered since his arrival. Still, the surface of life is fairly untroubled until his sister Pughneere falls ill with some inexplicable sickness. It is Wend Kuuni who must set out to find a legendary healer who alone can cure her. After multiple adventures, including meeting the very man who found him unconscious in the forest over ten years earlier (as shown in *Wend Kuuni*) and being lured by water genies (from which the voice of Pughneere saves him), he finds the healer, only to slip and injure himself. But he and the healer do finally reach Pughneere in time and she is cured. The film has all the simplicity and universality of a folk tale and it derives its pace and drive from the constant intercutting between Wend Kuuni's adventures and Pughneere's suffering. If Pughneere is the obvious beneficiary of his journey, Wend Kuuni recognises, in the last of his voice-over comments which have recurred throughout his travels, that he himself has learned most. Hailed as a hero and reconciled with his accusers, Wend Kuuni determines, in classic folktale style, to set out on a new quest, this time to find his father. As Olivier Barlet observes, 'The choice of a narrative structure not far removed from folk tale represents not so much a pursuit of timelessness as a desire for universality'.[7] Certainly the film has been consciously shaped by Kabore to form one of those works constituting 'resources of resistance and identity' of which Stuart Hall speaks.[8]

Following Kabore, his compatriot Idrissa Ouedraogo (born 1954) burst onto the international scene in the late 1980s with a loose trilogy of 'village' films – *Yam daabo* (1987), *Yaaba* (1989), *Tilaï* (1989) – all of which were premiered at Cannes. *Yam daabo* (the title means 'the choice') is set in contemporary Burkina Faso and reflects the director's earlier work making socially committed documentaries. It is a simple film, shot in a pared-down 16mm style and using little music or dialogue. It opens with crowds waiting in the empty drought-plagued landscape of Gourga in the north for handouts of international aid. But one peasant, Salam, opts to take his family in search of a new life. The focus is on everyday gestures and tasks, initially hunting for food and water in a desert landscape and later farming and preparing food in a simple village setting. One child is lost, but the family finds a river and fertile land where they can resettle. Life goes on – meeting old acquaintances, surviving predictable family tensions between the young men, enjoying the birth of a new child. Meanwhile, those who have stayed in Gourga still queue for aid handouts. Though his later work is more complex, *Yam daabo* remains one of Ouedraogo's own favourites, 'a film from the heart' made out of the director's direct knowledge of his country and its problems.[9]

In *Yam daabo* only the Ouagadougou scenes depict a world of modernity: elsewhere activities such as cooking and farming use totally traditional methods and utensils. In *Yaaba* (which means 'grandmother') this process is taken a stage further and we enter the same totally timeless world, untouched by colonialism, as that of *Wend Kuuni*. The film is set in a village where life goes on in the traditional way, with drinking and infidelity, quarrels and reconciliations, all of which are treated with sympathy: everyone has their reasons. The adult characters include stereotypical figures such as the wise drunkard and fake beggars and healers, but the children give the film a great freshness and spontaneity. Much of the film's focus is on the games, affections and rivalries of the two children, Bila and Nopoko, and their affection for Sana, an old woman excluded from the village as a witch. When Nopoko falls ill, it is Sana who fetches from the healer, Taryam, the herbs needed to cure the little girl. Back home Sana dies in her burnt-out hut and Bila fulfils his earlier promise to build her a new home by arranging her burial. Stylistically, the long-held landscape shots and sparse dialogue of the film closely echo *Yam daabo*. So does its tone of optimism, its acceptance of the movement from one generation to the next and its confidence in the young.

In *Tilaï* (which means the 'law') the style is even more abstract, with the setting comprising an Africa lacking any geographical or regional specificity and the action rooted in no particular African cultural tradition (though the language, as in the previous two films, is More). Most critics, both African and Western, have experienced it as a tragedy in the Greek sense, dealing with universal human values and laws. Certainly the law is absolute here and the tale has strong Oedipal overtones. Stylistically it can be seen as a development of the audio-visual procedures of the previous two works, but above all it reveals a heightened mastery of filmic structure and dramatic expression. Though music (by Abdullah Ibrahim) is used extensively, especially to accompany solitary figures in a desert landscape, the warm humanity of the earlier works is totally absent. The image is pared down, reducing to a minimum traditional greetings and forms of address and excluding any of the modern 'clutter' (gerry cans, plastic bowls, and so on) of a real African village. Nothing is allowed to take away from the terrible action that unfolds when Saga returns to his village after an absence of two years to find that his father has married his bride-to-be, Nogma, who still loves him. In the eyes of all, as his father's second wife,

Nogma is now his mother, so when they make love they are committing incest. When they are discovered, it is Kougri, Saga's brother, who is chosen by lot to kill him. Instead he helps Saga escape with a promise never to return. But when he learns that his mother is ill, Saga returns. Kougri, now himself banished from the village for disobedience, kills him. No-one emerges unscathed from the the the application of a rigid law to the lives of fallible human beings.

Though Ouedraogo continued to be a prolific filmmaker throughout the 1990s, with works adopting a variety of more realistic styles (which have already been discussed in Chapter 6), *Tilaï*, which won the top prize at FESPACO in 1989, marks the climax of his career in terms of critical acclaim. His one return to the pre-colonial past, *The Anger of the Gods/La Colère des dieux* (2003), was originally planned as a massive epic, but was eventually realised with very limited resources and was markedly less successful.

In **Mali**, Souleymane Cisse's *Yeelen* (1987) (the title meaning 'brightness') marks a clear break with the realist style of the director's earlier films (discussed in Chapter 6). The project, which illustrates perfectly the new ambitions of African filmmakers, was much interrupted by financial difficulties and the death of the initial lead actor, Ismail Sarr (which led to the doubling of the hostile patriarchal figure into Bafing and his brother Soma). It is in essence a simple timeless narrative, reconstituting/reinterpreting pagan Bambara tradition (though Cisse himself is a Muslim). It traces the journeys of the young Nianankoro, first with his mother and then alone, through sin (the seduction of a young Peul woman which leads to the birth of his son) to a ritual purification by his true mentor, his blind uncle, Soma's identical twin. The film's climax comes with the final confrontation between Nianankoro's newly acquired powers and the misused Komo magic of his father. Both die in the battle, but Nianankoro's son clearly represents the future hope of the community. The film ends, as it had begun, with images of childhood. In contrast to *Tilaï*, *Yeelen* is deeply rooted in specific African traditions, and for Cisse, the rediscovery of Bambara tradition was 'an extraordinary lesson': 'It was the discovery of a new thing that I knew existed but which I had not experienced in real life. And discovering the ritual scenes was like taking part in the activities; it was like an initiation for me.'[10] This sense of discovery is very apparent in the film, which is full of dazzling imagery in its scenes of ritual and magic. Yet to see the film simply as an exotic fairytale is to misread it. As Suzanne H. MacRae notes in her informative analysis of the film, 'African audiences recognise serious contemporary issues in the narrative and perceive the direct relationship of the film to their own social and political problems'.[11] This view is backed up by Manthia Diawara, who argues that such a return to the African past 'does not therefore mean a subordination to tradition for the director who uses oral literature. It is a questioning of tradition, a creative process which enables him to make contemporary choices while resting on the shoulders of tradition'.[12] With its multilayered narrative texture, *Yeelen* is the perfect filmic recreation of the riches of African oral tradition and proved enormously successful with both African and international audiences.

In **Tunisia** two films of the early 1980s about emigration show – though in very different ways – a similar shift away from everyday reality and towards a sort of formal abstraction. The most sophisticated and universally relevant parable about emigration, exile, borders, rules and bureaucracy is *Crossing Over/Traversées* (1982) by Mahmoud Ben Mahmoud (born 1947), where two passengers are trapped on a cross-channel ferry. The film begins on 31 December 1980 and plots the parallel fates of two refugees, a working-class Polish dissident and an Arab middle-class intellectual, both trapped on the same ferry. Because they both lack the necessary passport documents – a new year begins at midnight – neither the British nor the Belgian authorities will allow them ashore. Separated by language, class and culture, they are unable to take a common stand, and each goes a separate way, the Pole towards the suicidal killing of a policeman, the Arab towards an inner world, strengthened by a casual sexual encounter. A settled life in Western Europe is never a possibility in this Kafkaesque tale, which moves with total narrative logic from an almost documentary style of realism (with details of precise time and place noted on screen) to a world of myth and imagination. Ben Mahmoud went on to make two further features but much of his later output has taken the form of video documentaries, many of them striking pieces of historical research.

Taïeb Louhichi (born 1948) made *The Shadow of the Earth/L'Ombre de la terre* (1982), another exemplary tale. It tells of an isolated rural family community – patriarchal father with his sons and nephews and their families – whose life is slowly torn apart by natural forces and the impact of the modern world. As natural disasters increase pressure on the group, the young men leave for exile or are conscripted. The film is an elegy for the passing of a traditional way of life, but the emigration of the young is seen to offer no solution and the film ends with the frozen image of the coffin in which the body of young man who has chosen emigration is returned to his family. Despite the realism of the detail, the setting is abstract: the location is never made explicit, the 'border' leads to an unnamed country, the port at the end could be anywhere in the Maghreb. *The Shadow of the Earth* is a fable with universal application.

Even more distinctive are the worlds conjured up by the multi-talented Nacer Khemir (born 1948), who is sculptor, designer, actor, performing storyteller and author of a dozen children's books, as well as video and filmmaker. Both his features explore the lost domain of a legendary Andalusia, the Arab empire that stretched from Damascus to Grenada. *The Drifters/Les Baliseurs du désert* (1984) begins with a young teacher arriving in the remote, ancient village to which he has been sent. All the young men of the village are cursed to drift endlessly, 'marking out' the desert, just as an old man digs endlessly for buried treasure. This is a world of strange children's games (they are making a mirror garden), enigmatic old people, a mysterious fifteen-year-old girl. When the villages set out on a three-day pilgrimage, the young teacher is entrusted with handing over to the drifters a book whose secrets will free them from the curse. Instead he is led off into the desert by the woman whose image appears in the ancient volume. The focus now shifts to a second storyline, that of a white-uniformed police officer who arrives to investigate the teacher's disappearance and to discover the truth about a mysterious boat, supposedly belonging to Sindbad, found outside the village. When the policeman disappears, walking back to civilisation in the dark, the film turns to the young boy who organised the children's games and who now decides to travel to Cordova. As a new story is about to begin, the 'markers of the desert' are heard passing on their endless march and the credits roll. In *The Drifters*, loosely linked stories succeed each other before being erased rather than resolved.

Khemir's second film, *The Dove's Lost Necklace/Le Collier perdu de la colombe* (1990), is a homage to the golden age of Andalusian culture. Again there are two stories, but this time they run alongside each other, sometimes interweaving, sometimes going in their own directions. Hassan, the trainee calligrapher, is seeking the meaning of love by collecting as many of the sixty Arab terms for love as he can. His dream, triggered by a book illustration, is of the Princess of Samarkand. Zine, still just a boy, serves as messenger and go-between for young lovers. His longing is for the return of his father (though his mother asserts he was a djinn who claimed her when she was sleeping on the roof terrace). The opening sequences depict an idyllic tranquillity, an ordered world of learning and calligraphy, where everyone is safe. It is filled with the elements of fairy tales and dreams: a monkey said to be a prince who has been bewitched, a poet driven mad by love, an old man who sets out on a pilgrimage to Mecca, a vision of the mosque at Cordova, a prince who dies when the last letter is stitched onto his shroud. Hassan meets a mysterious horseman, Aziz, who is, it seems, the Princess disguised as a man, and Zine meets his father (or perhaps this is a dream). As Hassan sets out on his quest, the ordered world collapses, as the beggars invade and burn the city. Hassan is reunited with Aziz and they get a precious copy of the book, *The Dove's Necklace*, but the threatened violence of the beggars leads them to jump off a cliff. Aziz vanishes, the book is lost and Hassan returns alone to the devastated city.

Khemir's vision is unique in African cinema. His imagined world has a total coherence, with certain constantly recurring themes and characters – a mixture of dream and reality, a beautiful and mysterious virgin, small boys, the lost grandeur of Andalusia, tales of journeys, treasure, magic and, always, the mysterious power of books and the written word. This world is created through precise camerawork, sumptuous colour imagery, a multitude of expressive faces and exquisite costumes. Khemir's narratives too are unique. Just as the desert shifts in the wind, constantly uncovering and obliterating, so Khemir's stories start up but peter out. His characters hold stage for a while and then vanish in some unexplained way from the narrative.

One of the few filmmakers to develop a truly distinctive style under the state system in **Algeria** (and to continue to work in Algeria after its collapse) is the former actor, Mohamed Chouikh (born 1943). In a remarkable trio of films – *The Citadel/La Citadelle* (1988), *Youssef – The Legend of the Seventh Sleeper/Youcef, la légende du Septième Dormant* (1993) and *The Desert Ark/L'Arche du désert* (1997) – Chouikh turns his back on realism to explore the possibilities of parable and allegory. In this way, as Denise Brahimi notes, 'he constructs revealing situations and invents images with a strong symbolic charge'.[13] In *The Citadel*, which was released at the height of the disorders in Algeria, the autocratic power of the old men of the village is depicted as akin to the stultifying impact of thirty years of FLN rule.[14] Significantly, the film – like the contemporary 1980s Tunisian films noted above – is not precisely located in time and space: this is a fable about Algeria, not a social study. The action takes place in a stultifying village somewhere in the mountains. Poverty and superstition are everywhere, but this is a divided society: the self-indulgent world of the village elders contrasting with the sufferings of the women held in polygamous marriages. Kaddour, an isolated figure and a dreamer, is obsessed with the shoemaker's flirtatious wife and is cruelly punished for causing what his father sees as trouble. Though most of the film is shaped as a farce, complete with comic beggars and scenes of women outwitting their husbands, the ending is riveting. Kaddour is told he is to be married, but when the 'bride' is unveiled, she is a tailor's dummy. Jeered at and humiliated, Kaddour has no option but to throw himself to his death from a cliff top. The film ends with the frozen image of a little girl crying 'Let me free!'.

The full title of *Youssef* refers to the Arab legend of seven warriors who slept for three centuries and woke to find themselves in a very different world. The notion is used ironically here in the film, as Youssef, an amnesiac who has spent thirty years in hospital after being wounded in the war of liberation, escapes to find a country he assumes is still colonised. Confronted with the truth, he cannot accept that the oppression, suffering, poverty, injustice and humiliation he has found everywhere are the characteristics of the independent Algeria he and his comrades fought for. As is so often the case with parables, in *Youssef* the madness lies in the society, not in the apparent madman. *The Desert Ark* is a further parable, this time about the meaninglessness of violence between two communities, triggered, as in *Romeo and Juliet*, by the innocent love of two young people. The film is set not in contemporary Algeria but in a timeless Saharan village,where a boat is mysteriously stranded in the dunes. Here the observer (and judge) is not a holy fool but a small boy who sets off, at the end, to find a land where children are not slaughtered senselessly. Chouikh's work, with its mixture of tenderness and grotesquery, tragedy and farce, is a power-ful answer to mainstream Algerian cinema's crippling lack of originality of form and conformity of message.

THE 1990S AND 2000S

The new decade saw a continued increase in film production both north and south of the Sahara. In the Maghreb comparatively few of the new filmmakers followed the trends towards abstraction which we have identified in the 1980s work of Ben Mahmoud and Chouikh. But there are a number of examples in Tunisian cinema of films – whether depicting urban or rural subjects – that are not precisely located in time or place, but instead allude to an ill-defined epoch viewed or remembered with nostalgia. The prime example of this approach in **Tunisia** is Ferid Boughedir's *Halfaouine/Halfaouine, l'enfant des terrasses* (1990). Boughedir (born 1944) is the complete *cinéaste*: feature filmmaker, documentarist, academic, film historian and critic. His first solo feature follows Nouri Bouzid's initiative of introducing an autobiographical tone into Tunisian cinema, but Boughedir lacks Bouzid's concern to create a 'new realism'. Here there is neither precise historical reconstruction nor the depiction of contempor-ary issues. Rather the film's aim is to create a timeless, dreamlike world of child-hood and the subsequent acquisition of the experience that allows it to be left behind for ever. The hero Noura is depicted at just that point where his small stature allows his unsuspecting mother to continue to take him to the women's baths (or *hammam*), while he is in fact – like his contemporaries – developing a growing obsession with women's bodies. Expelled from the hammam, Noura recreates it at home with a servant girl little older than himself. The result is her ejection from the household and his freedom to roam the rooftops of the medina. The whole world of adolescence – another world *par excellence* – is sen-sitively captured in perfect detail and with immense humour and *joie de vivre*. The film proved to be Tunisian cinema's biggest box-office hit at home and its most successful export to the overseas market. Boughedir's only other feature, *One Summer at La Goulette/Un été à La Goulette* (1995), is a study of three families – one Muslim, one Catholic and one Jewish – living in harmony in a suburb of Tunis before the Six Day War. Though less successful with audiences, it was a deeply felt plea for tolerance which contains the warmth, humanity and humour so characteristic of all Boughedir's work.

Another strikingly original film set in the timeless world of the Tunis medina is *The Sultan of the Medina/Soltane el Medina!* (1992), directed by Moncef Dhouib (born 1952), who had worked in street theatre and as a theatre direc-tor, and was already known for his innovative short films.[15] Nothing could be further from Boughedir than the dark claustrophobic world conjured up by Dhouib's fable. The central characters are a young virgin Ramla, locked up by her future in-laws, and her only friend, Fraj, a holy fool who can move freely in the medina – even entering the women's quarters – but only naked like a child, to be used by women seeking cures and spells. The couple's innocence is set against the cruel world around them, which is characterised by lust, cruelty, male rivalries and violence. Ramla dreams of escape, but when she succeeds with the help of Fraj, she finds an even more violent world outside, where her future husband abandons her to be raped and destroyed by his men. Dhouib's bleak world, static and cut off from modernity, is full of mysteries and enigmas and constitutes a unique vision of Tunis and its past.

Another filmmaker who plays with time to get at an essential truth about Maghrebian life – in this case in **Morocco** – is Mohamed Abderrahman Tazi, whose early realist films of the 1980s have been discussed in Chapter 6. *Looking for My Wife's Husband/A la recherche du mari de ma femme* (1993) is in many ways a fresh departure, being a hilarious comedy which became the biggest box-office success in Moroccan film history. The film's plot concerns the misfortunes of a polygamous middle-aged husband, Haj Ben Moussa, who repudiates his young third wife for the third time and then discovers, when he wants reconciliation, that Islamic law demands that she should have had a (consummated) marriage to someone else in the meantime. The husband's attempts to resolve this dilemma create much of the comedy, which ends in disaster, when the new husband disappears back to Belgium before his planned divorce can be arranged. The narrative is perfectly linear and the gags beautifully timed, but the handling of time and space is totally unconventional. The film is set in a single city, Fez, but the time-scale is double: the scenes in the Haj's house and the old city (the medina) are situated in the 1970s, while the exteriors depict the contemporary Fez of the early 1990s when the film was shot.[16] This use of what Tazi calls 'atemporality' captures perfectly an aspect of any major Moroccan city obvious to every tourist: the contrast between the medina, with its total lack of modern features (cars, street furniture, department stores), and the bustling newly-built streets that surround it. The stylistic device allows Tazi to move away from the social realism of his earlier films and yet still to offer a historically based critique of contemporary society which underlines the co-existence of tradition and modernity in African culture.

Earlier, in 1991, there had been an attempt to revive the Moroccan experimental impulse of the 1970s with two 16mm films: *The Waiting Room/La Salle d'attente* – 'a patient relives in disorder the key moments of his life' – by Noureddine Gounajjar (born 1946), and *Ymer or the Flowering Thistles/Ymer ou les chardons florifères* – 'a series of situations where it is difficult to know what people do or say' – by Tijani Chrigui (born 1949). However, neither film seems to have had much, if any, impact, and neither director made a second feature.[17]

By contrast, the end of the decade saw the debut of Daoud Aoulad Syad (born 1953), who has a wide range of interests and accomplishments, being an academic (with a doctorate in physics and a professorship at the University of Rabat), a still photographer (with three books of photographs published), a graduate of FEMIS in Paris, an occasional actor and an award-winning documentary filmmaker). His film work has been made in collaboration with the veteran filmmaker and professional film editor Ahmed Bouanani (author of *Mirage* in 1979), who edited his three shorts and scripted both his features. Aoulad Syad is one of the few Maghrebian filmmakers not to claim a screenwriting credit, but *Bye Bye Souirty/Adieu forain* (1998) and *The Wind Horse/Le Cheval de vent* (2001) reveal a unified vision. The first tells the story of a travelling showman whose show includes a young transvestite dancer and who is accompanied by his estranged son; the second traces the chance encounter of two men – one old, one young – who go in search of their past (the grave of his second wife in one case, the mother he had never known in the other). Both films are muted road movies that go nowhere, dealing with characters who never quite come together and full of encounters that lead to nothing. The past – from which the characters are mostly fleeing – weighs down on them and there is no sense of a future opening up. Both films are slow paced, even and meditative. Everything is underplayed, since Aoulad Syad never pushes his material to make big dramatic scenes or confrontations. The films are full of silences, and words are seldom tools of communication. For Mohamed Bakrim, the parallel is Samuel Beckett: 'As in Beckett's theatre, talking signifies being outside of one's self: he who possesses nothing, who is hidden from himself, has to speak'.[18] With inevitably inconclusive endings, both films reveal a longing for a lost past, show wasted lives, misfortunes which are undeserved. The coherence of this hermetic, nostalgic world and the sense of an authorial presence controlling it recalls – in the sureness of touch, though not at all in the tone – the Tunisian medina films of the early 1990s.

South of the Sahara too we find a profusion of exemplary tales in the 1990s. In **Mali** Cheickh Oumar Sissoko turned away from the basically realistic approach of his first two features (discussed in Chapter 6) with *Guimba The Tyrant/Guimba, un tyran, une époque* (1995). Already, in *Finzan*, Sissoko had drawn on the popular Malian koteba theatrical tradition in the portrayal of Bala, the village idiot. Now in *Guimba* he moved further in the use of African oral traditions to shape the whole film – creating a narrative full of abrupt shifts in time and place and unexpected digressions – the shift in style typified by the appearance of a *griot* at the beginning and end of the film, introducing the tale and commenting on its aftermath. The inset story, which focuses squarely on tyranny and the need to oppose it, has obvious contemporary relevance, as many commentators have noticed, to the overthrow of the Malian dictator Moussa Touré in 1991. But the film is shaped as a fable mixing elements of farce and the supernatural and with constant shifts in mood and direction. It chronicles the rule of Guimba and his dwarf son Jangine, putting emphasis on their brutality, on the constant praise-singing of their eloquent but two-faced personal griot, and also on their ludicrous sexual desires: Jangine rejects the beautiful Kani, to whom he was betrothed as a child, in favour of her more than amply proportioned mother, Meya. The exile of Meya's upright husband by Guimba, who coverts Kani for himself, triggers the ruler's eventual downfall, chronicled in an often confusing sequence of confrontations played out in splendidly evocative costumes within the visually impressive setting of Djenné, one of Mali's ancient Saharan trading centres. As Sissoko has rightly said, *Guimba* 'opens the door to audiences for understanding our history through our cinema. Obviously, some aspects will seem odd or not readily comprehensible, but the door to dreaming and discovery is open to those who wish to enter it'.[19]

In *Genesis/La Genèse* (1999) Sissoko applied the same African oral narrative procedures to a story of universal dimensions: the fratricidal relations between Jacob, Esau and Hamor as related in chapters 23 to 37 of *Genesis*. Though the film was scripted by a Frenchman, Jean-Louis Sagot Duvauroux, the focus is very much on aspects of the story relative to ethnic strife in contemporary Africa. Approaches to the rival use of limited land resources are incorporated in the three lead figures, all played by key star African performers: the singer Salif Keïta (as Esau, the leader of the hunters) and the actors Sotigui Kouyaté (as Jacob, the head of the nomadic pastoralists) and Balla Moussa Keïta (as Hamor, whose people live a settled agricultural life). The film's narrative itself constantly digresses into other related stories (such as the circumstances of the father Isaac's marriage and the son Judah's seduction by Tamar) as the biblical story is reshaped and its elements are rearranged, But as brother turns against brother and cousin against cousin, the key theme that emerges is the need for reconciliation, here enacted between Jabob and Harmor in the totally African context of a tribal discussion (in the impressive Dogon structure of a 'toguna' or meeting place), enlivened by vigorous re-enactments of key contradictory elements of the biblical story. While the film as a whole benefits enormously from the complex visualisation incorporating both the striking setting of Mount Hombori Tondo and Kandioura Coulibaly's costume designs,[20] it also has a complex verbal pattern in Bambara (to which the subtitles cannot, it seems, do full justice), reflecting Sissoko's concern with the African oral traditions which have inspired him. As Olivier Barlet notes, the film's message is 'rich and complex, in political, human and spiritual terms'.[21]

Sissoko, who followed these two striking oral narratives with *Battù* (2000), starring the American actor Dany Glover, has always been politically active, and with the change of government in Mali in 2002, he became Minister of Culture. His film work throughout his career, despite its stylistic diversity, is consistently committed to addressing social and political issues concerning the current state and future progress of Mali, and indeed of Africa as a whole.

Also in 1990s Mali, Adama Drabo (born 1948) made his debut with *Fire!/Ta dona* (1991), the tale of a young idealist, Sidy, who is both a modernist, attempting to explain the reasons for the new ban on traditional bush-burning to villagers, and a traditionalist searching for fundamental elements of Bambara culture. The overall narrative has the same expansiveness as Sissoko's work, embracing inventive and engaging children, elements of magic and very contemporary glimpses of overwhelming corruption. Drabo's approach has aptly been characterised by Jonathan Haynes as 'myriad-mindedness': 'There is a staggering breadth of material in this movie, as if Drabo were trying to define the parameters of the Malian imagination, getting everything into one film'.[22]

At the beginning of Drabo's second film, *Skirt Power/Taafe fanga* (1997), a griot turns off the television images of a Hollywood musical and, provoked by a woman's aggressive entry into the gathering, begins a story about women in a Dogon village, who reverse the power relations with their menfolk after one of their number has seized the traditional mask of power. Like Drabo's first film, it uses the patterns of oral narrative, shifting constantly between its various individual stories, mixing legend and immediacy and, of course, drawing huge amounts of humour (particularly for an African audience) from the depiction of men reduced to wearing skirts and coping ineptly with basic women's tasks, while women sit smoking and drinking in the shade of the men's palaver tree. At the end of the film, men are restored to their customary position of power, but not before Drabo has praised the role, wisdom and importance of women, though he has not, as Valérie Thiers-Thiam has noted, given them the role of narrator, who remains, as usual, a male griot.[23] Drabo has said that he is not interested in making films just for aesthetic effect. Given the good fortune of being allowed to make a film, he has to 'encourage people to think, to encourage people to ask themselves questions, to surpass themselves, and thus participate in the effort to reconstruct our countries'.[24]

In **Senegal** three newcomers, all born in the 1950s and trained in Paris, made their mark with their first features. Mansour Sora Wade (born 1952) made *The Price of Forgiveness/Ndeysaan* (2001), after completing ten very varied short films, both documentary and fiction, over a period of twenty years. The film is a complex narrative, related by a griot and using oral storytelling techniques, but it is also one of the rare African films (apart from those of Ousmane Sembene) to be based on a French-language novel (in this case by Mbissane Ngom). On one level the film is the story of a poor fishing village's struggle for survival, but it also draws on the supernatural, concern for the ancestors' continued presence, animal symbolism, folk ritual and, at one moment, simple animation. It is also a study of generational change, showing the young rebelling against – but still being in many ways dominated by – inherited ancestral roles: hunter, fisherman or griot. *The Price of Forgiveness*'s visual style, backed up by a complex musical score, is highly composed, sometimes in static long-shot, sometimes in big facial close-up. But the visual impact is also shaped by the fact that much of it is shot in mist or half-darkness, with very toned down colours and clothing. The film's ambiguity is enhanced by the fact that there is no forgiveness: the protagonist cannot live with his own weakness, which has driven him to murder, and the sea is pitiless.

Joseph Gaye Ramaka (born 1952) made a number of shorts and even a feature-length documentary *Nitt . . . Ndoxx!* (1988), as well as working extensively in production and distribution, before directing his sole feature, *Karmen Geï* (2001), based loosely on the Prosper Mérimé story that inspired Bizet. The film, with its nude lesbian love scene, is deliberately provocative and inevitably provoked a censorship debate in Senegal. Its settings – the Gorée island slave prison in which it opens, the lighthouse which forms the smugglers' base and the ever-present sea – are key elements in its visual style. But Gaye Ramaka's desire to universalise the story is typified by the musical accompaniment he has chosen – a modern jazz score by David Murray, interspersed with vigorous performances by noted Senegalese singers, drummers and dancers – and a script that mixes passages of conventional French dialogue with lively Wolof chants and debates spiced with traditional maxims. This Carmen is bisexual, and the opening dance, in which she seduces the prison warden Angélique, is a *tour de force* of energy and provocation, followed almost immediately by an equally stunning performance in which she breaks up Corporal Lamine's wedding and then seduces him. She drives Angélique to suicide, by rejecting her love as too sad, and Angélique's requiem mass, celebrated by hundreds, is the film's turning point, the first moment at which Karmen is silent and isolated. Thereafter Karmen moves from man to man, but the sense of joy and provocation is lost, as she becomes increasingly aware of her own impending death. When Lamine kills her, her ending could not be farther from that of Angélique, as she is carried to her grave, alone and wrapped anonymously in a carpet, by her sole true friend. While maintaining this single trajectory from lust to lonely death, Gaye Ramaka indulges in constant shifts of mood, time and place, creating an exemplary tale of passion, desire and death.

Moussa Sene Absa (born 1958) is a man of many talents: painter, writer and musician, as well as filmmaker. In the years following his debut in 1988, he produced a startling array of films: fictions varying from twenty minutes to full feature length – in 16mm and 35mm format as well as video – and documentaries on subjects ranging from bus drivers and farmers to Islamic sects and the singer Aminata Fall. His first 16mm fictional feature, *Ken Bugul* (1991), seems to have attracted little attention, perhaps because it was made at a time when French funding schemes were making possible the switch throughout Sub-Saharan Africa to 35mm filming. Sene Absa was a pioneer of the video feature film with *Twist Again/Ça twiste à Poponguine* (1993), a lively if nostalgic look back at the lure of foreign music (French pop and American rhythm and blues) and at adolescent rivalries in a 1960s Senegalese fishing village. Equally impressive is his one-hour video *And So Angels Die/Ainsi meurent les anges* (2001), a highly personal film which tells with great fluidity the familiar tale of an uprooted intellectual, here the poet Mory (played by Sene Absa himself), who is unable to find roots or success in either Europe or Africa. The angels of the title are the hopes and dreams of love and innocence which all of us carry within us, to which Sene Absa's poetic voice-over constantly returns. The film mixes black-and-white images of childhood and adolescence with colour sequences of the present in Paris and Senegal. The logic of the moves between past and present is less one of narrative necessity than of a response to the inner turmoil of Mory's life, and the film illustrates perfectly Sene Absa's contention that there is no linearity in African narrative: 'Everything is in concentric circles, it's always a spiral, a story is a spiral. Not something that has a beginning and an end, because the beginning is the end and the end is at the beginning.'[25]

The same structural principles apply in the film on which Sene Absa's international reputation largely rests, his first 35mm feature, *Tableau Ferraille* (1996) – the title is the name of the district of Dakar where Sene Absa was born and has connotations of a 'scrap heap'. Early scenes in the film show Daam and his first wife Gagnesiri making a forlorn exit from Dakar and pausing at the cemetery. We constantly return to this scene throughout the film, while in between the life of the couple is shown in fragmented and often disjointed flashbacks. Daam's success as a politician grows, and since Gagnesiri is sterile, he takes a second wife, the Western-educated Kiné. But as his domestic life falls apart, his rise to Minister is followed by an abrupt and total fall. Daam's transparent honesty and dogged commitment contrasts sharply with the approach of his friend and eventual rival, the businessman Président, whose rise parallels his fall and whose speed of manoeuvre is symbolised by his ever-changing headgear: French beret, baseball cap, cowboy's stetson and, finally, traditional African headdress. In the film's final return to the cemetery, while Daam is alone, asleep on a bench, Gagnesiri leaves him and sails off into the unknown from the beach where the film began. All the figures can be seen as in some way symbolic of the fate of Senegal after thirty-five years of independence: the (sterile) traditional and the (treacherous) modern wives, the clash of honesty and corruption, the impotence of labour in the face of African capitalism. Sene Absa has an overt political message: 'Africa wake up! They're asking you to go too quickly . . . Africa has got onto a train without knowing where it's going. I'd rather we waited for another train, where we could find our place knowing where the train is going'.[26] But the real attraction of the film lies in the fluency of Sene Absa's camerawork – especially in the exteriors – and the brilliant use of colour and costume. Key too is the use of music, especially the songs of the blue-clad band of fishermen-singers, the *faye ball* (led by the director himself), which warn Tableau Ferraille of the dangers throughout the film.

Sene Absa's second feature, again with largely French dialogue, is *Madame Brouette* (2002) which adapts the first film's structural pattern to what is basically a whodunit. The film opens with a striking sequence showing a man in drag with white make-up and a red dress (Naago) shot dead when he returns home (it turns out to be the day of a cross-dressing carnival). The rest of the film is a more or less chronological, but certainly non-linear, account of events leading up to the killing, beginning with his meeting with the woman accused of his murder. This is the plucky market seller Mati who calls herself Madame Brouette (meaning 'pushcart woman'). The account of her stormy relationship with the corrupt policeman Naago is paralleled by the innocent love between her own little daughter and the boy next door, and both narrative threads are constantly interrupted by returns to the police investigation. There is also a powerful musical score which, together with the songs of a group of griots continually intervening to comment on the action, make the film almost a musical. At the film's ending, the truth about the shooting is genuinely unexpected. The versatile career of Moussa Sene Absa, who was born just two years before independence, provides the perfect introduction to the range of approaches which become so striking among the generation born after the end of colonial rule.

NOTES

1. Olivier Barlet, 'Cinémas d'Afrique noire: Le Nouveau malentendu', Paris: *Cinémathèque* 14, 1998, p. 107.
2. Manthia Diawara, *African Cinema: Politics and Culture* (Bloomington: Indiana University Press, 1992), p. 160.
3. Stuart Hall, 'Cultural Identity and Cinematic Representations', *Framework* 36, 1989, p. 70.
4. Richard Porton, 'Mambety's *Hyenas*: Between Anti-Colonialism and the Critique of Modernity', in *Iris* 18, University of Iowa, 1995, p. 97.
5. Gaston Kabore, cited in Françoise Pfaff, *25 Black African filmmakers* (New York: Greenwood Press, 1988), p. 177.
6. Hédi Khelil, *Résistances et utopies: Essais sur le cinéma arabe et africain* (Tunis: Édition Sahar, 1994), p. 91.
7. Olivier Barlet, *African Cinemas: Decolonizing the Gaze* (London and New York: Zed Books, 2000), p. 66.
8. Hall, 'Cultural Identity', p. 70.
9. Idrissa Ouedraogo, interview in Amna Guellali (ed.), *Idrissa Ouedraogo* (Tunis: ATPCC/*Cinécrits* 15, 1998), p. 49.
10. Souleyman Cisse, in Nwachukwu Frank Ukadike, *Questioning African Cinema: Conversations with Filmmakers* (Minneapolis: University of Minnesota Press, 2002), p. 22.
11. Suzanne H. MacRae, '*Yeelen*: A Political Fable of the *Komo* Blacksmiths/Sorcerers', in Kenneth W Harrow (ed.), *African Cinema: Postcolonial and Feminist Readings* (Trenton, NJ and Asmara, Eritrea: Africa World Press, 1999), p. 127.
12. Diawara, *African Cinema*, p. 39.
13. Denise Brahimi, 'Images, symbols et paraboles dans le cinéma de Mohamed Choikh', in Michel Serceau (ed.), *Cinémas du Maghreb* (Paris: Corlet/Télérama/ *CinémAction* 111, 2004), p. 154.

14. Michel Chouikh, in CamilleTaboulay, *Le Cinéma métaphorique de Mohamed Chouikh* (Paris: K Films Editions, 1997), p. 42.
15. See Andrea Flores Khalil, 'Images that Come Out at Night: A Film Trilogy by Moncef Dhouib', in Ida Kummer (ed.), *Cinéma Maghrébin*, special issue of *Celaan* 1: 1–2, 2002, pp. 71–80.
16. Mohamed Abderrahman Tazi, in Kevin Dwyer, *Beyond Casablanca: M. A. Tazi and the Adventure of Moroccan Cinema* (Bloomington: Indiana University Press, 2004), p. 32.
17. Quotations from the films' publicity material cited in *Les Cinémas d'Afrique: Dictionnaire* (Paris: ATM/Karthala, 2000).
18. Mohamed Bakrim, '*Adieu forain* de Daouad Aoulad Syad, un film beckettien', in Michel Serceau (ed.), *Cinémas du Maghreb* (Paris: Corlet/Télérama/CinemAction 111, 2004), p. 185.
19. Cheikh Oumar Sissoko, interview, in Ukadike, *Questioning African Cinema*, p. 194.
20. See Debra Boyd-Buggs, 'Les Costumes de Kandioura Coulibaly pour *La Genèse*', in Samuel Lelièvre (ed.), *Cinémas africains, une oasis dans le désert?* (Paris: Corlet/Télérama/CinémAction 106, 2003).
21. Olivier Barlet, '*La Genèse*', *Africultures* 18 (Paris: L'Harmattan, 1999), p. 69.
22. Jonathan Haynes, 'Returning to the African Village', *Jump Cut* 40, Berkeley, 1996, p. 65.
23. Valérie Thiers-Thiam, *À chacun son griot* (Paris: L'Harmattan, 2004), p. 137.
24. Adama Drabo, interview in Melissa Thackway, *Africa Shoots Back: Alternative Perspectives in Sub-Saharan Francophone African Film* (London: James Currey, 2003), p. 184.
25. Moussa Sene Absa, interview in P. -G. Despierre (ed.), *Le Griot, le psychanalyste et le cinéma africain* (Paris: Grappaf/L'Harmattan, 2004), p. 130.
26. Moussa Sene Absa, interview in *www.africultures*, 3 September 2002.

PART IV

THE NEW MILLENNIUM

If it's important to know where we come from, it's even more important to know where we are, that is to define our place as African filmmakers in the world. This positioning, which is in fact a taking stock, will help us clarify our gaze at Africa . . . Taking stock of our place in the world does not mean distancing ourselves from it. We are for the most part filmmakers on the move, in contact with other people. We are the filmmakers of wandering, of nomadism. Like every good nomad, we need to have a good mount in order to move forward, and our mount is the cinema.

Guilde Africaine des Réalisateurs et Producteurs[1]

9. THE POST-INDEPENDENCE GENERATION

African intellectuals live a duality which they suppress most of the time. However, they speak French among themselves, they eat in French at the table at home, and often, they live in France; but when they shoot a film, they shoot it in their own language!

Moussa Sene Absa[2]

A New Generation

In one of his last articles on African cinema, written in 2000, Pierre Haffner posited the existence of three waves of African filmmaking (the 1960s, the 1970s and the 1980s–1990s).[3] This present chapter argues that it is now possible to see the outlines of a new wave or generation, the first to be comprised entirely of film-makers who, because of their date of birth, never experienced life under colonial rule. Filmmakers born since independence now make up about 15 per cent of the total number of francophone African filmmakers – and a far greater proportion of those currently active (they are responsible for almost a third of all features made in the five years since the beginning of 2000). They have also begun to dominate African film festivals, with Ayouch and Sissako winning at FESPACO in 2001 and 2003 respectively, and Asli at the JCC in 2004. Forty filmmakers – five of them women – have given us over fifty feature films in the years since the late 1990s. About two-thirds of these new filmmakers come from the Maghreb: one from Algeria, thirteen from Morocco and ten from Tunisia. The rest come from nine of the independent states south of the Sahara.

Though there is considerable continuity with the work of the slightly older filmmakers, such as Abdoulaye Ascofaré, Daoud Aoulad Syad and Moussa Sene Absa, who preceded them in the 1990s, the new younger filmmakers do have enough specifically in common to constitute a distinctive group, with largely shared backgrounds and particular modes of approach to filmmaking. The characteristic profile for the group is, firstly, birth in Africa, though Nadia El Fani (born 1960), Gahité Fofana (born 1965), Nabil Ayouch (born 1969) and Alain Gomis (born 1972) were born in Paris, of partial Tunisian, Guinean, Moroccan and Senegalese descent respectively. Their dates of birth are mostly in the 1960s, though some, such as Gomis and the Maghrebian directors Raja Amari, Narjiss Nejjar and Elyes Baccar (all born in 1971), are a little younger. Most of the group lived in France for a number of years while studying, and some have settled there permanently. Most of them – from the oldest of the Tunisians, Mohamed Zran (born 1959), whose first feature, *Essaïda*, appeared in 1996, to the youngest arrival, Mohamed Ladjimi (born 1975), who showed his first feature, *Summer Wedding/Noce d'été*, at the JCC in 2004 – made their feature film debuts in their twenties or thirties. But a few have established their careers elsewhere: Hakim Belabbes (born 1961) at Columbia University in Chicago, Nawfel Saheb-Ettaba (born 1959) in Quebec, Nidhal Chatta (born 1959) in England, and Mohamed Asli (born 1957) in Italy, for example. These 'outsiders' tend to be the oldest of the group at the time of their first feature – in their forties.

Virtually all are film-school trained, with no less than twenty-three of them having studied in Paris, though again there is a group from the Belgian film school INSAS – Jamal Belmejdoub (born 1956), Hassan Legzouli (born 1963), François Woukoache (born 1966) and Yasmine Kassari (born 1968) – and a few 'outsiders': Abderrahmane Sissako (born 1961) studied in Moscow, Idrissou Mora Kpaï (born 1967) in Munich, Asli and Ahmed Boulane (born 1956) in Italy, and Imane Mesbahi (born 1964) at the Cairo Cinema Institute. The filmmakers as a whole comprise one of the most highly educated of such groups in the world. Dani Kouyaté (born 1961), who followed his DEA in film at the University of Paris VIII with further studies at the Sorbonne, set a pattern followed by most of these filmmakers. Many have additional academic qualifications acquired in Paris in subjects other than film. Ayouch also studied drama, Gahité Fofana literature, Camille Mouyeke (born 1962) art, Omar Chraïbi (born 1961) photography, Issa Serge Coelo (born 1967) history, Mahamet Saleh Haroun (born 1963) journalism, and François Woukoache (born 1966) mathematics and physics. Only three filmmakers – El Fani (who worked as assistant and production manager), Jean Odoutan (born 1965) and Mohamed Camara (born 1959) (both actors) – seem to have learned their filmmaking by working from the start, without formal training, within some area of the film or television industries. Having completed their film training, most of the others made fictional or documentary short films which were shown at foreign festivals, and a few – most notably Faouzi Bensaïdi (born 1967) and Régina Fanta Nacro (born 1962) – achieved an international reputation with their short films.

QUESTIONS OF NATIONALITY

French dominance and the paucity of African film finance and production infra-structures have important influences on how we must regard the work of these 'new millennium' African directors. The first issue is that of nationality. Though, for convenience, films are referred to here as Cameroonian or Congolese, in fact, the 'nationality' of a contemporary African film often reflects little more than its director's place of birth. Certainly it does not necessarily reflect his or her place of residence, particularly as, until recently, the possession of a production base in France has been a considerable asset when applying for funding. Eight of the group (Coelo, El Fani, Gomis, Haroun, Mora Kpaï, Mouyeke, Nacro and Odoutan) belong to the Paris-based Guilde Africaine des Réalisateurs et Producteurs, which exists specifically to promote the work of French-based African-born filmmakers. Several older filmmakers – Mama Keita (Guinea), Taïeb Louhichi (Tunisia), Raymond Rajaounarivelo (Madagascar), Jean-Marie Teno (Cameroon) and the Swiss-based Mohamed Soudani (Algeria) – are also members, as are directors from outside the francophone area, such as Zeka Laplaine and Mweze Ngangura from the Democratic Republic of Congo. A number of other members of the 'millennium' group, such as Ayouch, Sissako, Ladjimi and Amari, also reside in France. The sense of unity among the group is strong. For example, Haroun had three fellow directors, Laplaine, Coelo and Nacro, to assist him in various ways on his first two features.

The shaping influence of France is clear from the credits of all their films, such as Haroun's *Abouna* which shows the range of funding available to these Paris-based filmmakers. The film was co-produced by Cinénomad (Paris) and Goï Goï Productions (Chad), with the participation of Fonds Sud Cinéma, the ADC-Sud, the Fonds Européen de Développement, the Agence Intergouvernementale de la Francophonie and Arte France Cinéma, as well as the Chadian Ministry of Promotion and Development and Télé-Tchad, the Hubert Bals Foundation and Cinemart-IFF in the Netherlands. The situation of living in France also makes a significant input into the subject matter of their work. Gomis's *L'Afrance* (2001), for example, is based directly on his own immediate experiences of growing up within the Parisian migrant community. Fofana, after a number of document-aries, played the lead in his own *Immatriculation temporaire* (2000), a fiction-alised account of a possible return to Guinea in search of an unknown father, which leads to disappointment and plunges the protagonist into a life of crime. Two 'road movies' of 2004, made as their feature debuts by Paris-based Moroccans, also offer young men's reflections on growing up in France and discovering only later the values of their fathers. In Hassan Legzouli's *Tenja* the son has to drive his father's body for burial in a Morocco he scarcely knows, while in *The Long Journey/Le Grand voyage* by Ismaïl Ferroukhi (born 1962) a non-religious Europeanised young man drives his devout, Arab-speaking father overland to Mecca. Similarly, after shooting his first film in his native Benin (*Barbeque Pejo*, 1999), Jean Odoutan has made three studies of the African community in France, where he lives, though all were given French government funding as 'Benin' films.

At first sight these filmmakers seem to constitute a typical exile group of the kind so ably chronicled by Hamid Naficy.[4] Certainly, as we shall see, many of their films carry the marks of exile and diaspora and chronicle a return to the filmmaker's origins. Perhaps the most remarkable work in this respect is Idrissou Mora Kpaï's sixty-three-minute documentary *The Queen Mother/Si-Gueriki* (2003), which marked the filmmaker's first return home, after ten years of living in Germany, to the Borgu region of Northern Benin where he was born. He had originally intended the film as a homage to his father, a local 'wasangari' or nobleman. But his father died before the film could be made, and instead Mora Kpaï discovered the hitherto unknown female half of his family: his mother, stepmother and sister. In traditional Borgu society boys were brought up in an exclusively male environment from the age of five, and the girls were sent away to live (often as virtual servants) with aunts or cousins. For Mora Kpaï the film was a double discovery. Firstly, there was meeting and talking with a mother he had never known in childhood, a woman living modestly and seemingly concerned only with traditional domestic tasks. Then there was the surreal discovery that, as a direct descendent of the 'wasangari' king, she was 'si-gueriki', the ceremonial head presiding over the annual 'gaani' festival reuniting the whole clan, before whom all – men and women alike – had to prostrate themselves.

But these Paris-based African filmmakers have an advantage not shared by other exiles, in that their decision to reflect cinematically on life in the countries where they were born has intermeshed precisely with the French government's desire to maintain its cultural links with all its former African colonies. Their problem is less exile than potential integration and loss of African identity. This is what has happened to a group from which they can now hardly be distinguished, namely the dozen or so of their contemporaries who are second-generation immigrants, mostly of Algerian origin, resident in France. Back in the 1980s the first immigrant filmmakers, such Mehdi Charef, Abdelkrim Bahloul and Rachid Bouchareb, commonly known as *beurs* (the term is derived from a slang inversion of the letters 'r' and 'b' of the word 'arabe'), constituted a clearly defined group. But twenty years later they could no longer be considered as constituting an entity apart from the rest of French cinema.[5] Indeed, in 2005 one of their number, Abdellatif Kechiche (born 1960 in Tunis), won no less than four

'Césars' (the French film industry's own Oscars) – for best film, best director, best script and most promising female newcomer – with *The Scam/L'Esquive*.

In the case of the Maghrebians, it is really only their funding sources that set the two groups apart and even then the results can be contradictory and confusing, as a comparison between Nabyl Ayouch and Nadir Moknèche shows. Moknèche was born in Paris in 1965, but he returned to Algiers at the age of one month and was brought up there. He was, in his own words, a product of independent Algeria, of the Algeria of Boumediene and Chadli, of Arabisation (he learned French only at the age of nine) and of Islamisation.[6] Yet he is generally considered a *beur*, simply because his films are funded through the normal mechanisms of low-budget French national production and he uses the French language, even when filming, as in *Viva Laldjérie* (2004), in Algiers. On the other hand, Nabil Ayouch, born of mixed (French and Moroccan) parentage in Paris, where he grew up and has his current production base, is usually defined as a 'Moroccan' filmmaker, simply because all his features have received government funding through the aid scheme administered by the CCM in Rabat.[7]

Another striking example of confusions about nationality concerns the *beur* filmmaker Fatima Jebli Ouazzani, whose Dutch-produced *In My Father's House/In het Huis van mijn Vader* (1997) won the top prize in 1998 at the Fifth Moroccan National Film Festival. The director was, it is true, born in Meknès in 1959, but she has lived in the Netherlands since the age of eleven and has had no contact with any Moroccan film production structures. What makes her award even more remarkable is that the film's subject matter (female sexuality) precludes it from ever getting a commercial release in Morocco, though it does, however, now appear in the official listings of Moroccan films produced annually by the CCM. The film's formal pattern of weaving together autobiography, fiction and documentary does, however, anticipate many aspects of the work (to be discussed in coming chapters) of Haroun and Sissako. The result, in the case of *In My Father's House*, is a complex exploration of questions of virginity, sexuality and marriage, which is fascinating but has no real connection with how cinema has developed in Morocco.

Perhaps the most startling confusion over national identity concerns the 1998 award of the top prize (the Tanit d'or) at the JCC in Tunis to an allegedly 'Algerian' film, *Living in Paradise/Vivre au paradis*. The parents of the director, Bourlem Guerdjou (born 1965), are, it is true, of Algerian origin. But Guerdjou himself was born in France, has French nationality and works as a writer-director in French television. His film, a French-Belgian-Norwegian co-production, is the adaptation of a French-language novel, co-scripted with two French writers, and has Europeans in all the key production roles. Though shot in Tunisia, it is set in France, in the slums of Nanterre during the early 1960s and uses largely French dialogue. Set against a background of real historical events, it tells of a migrant worker, Mokhtar, who dreams of a better life and summons his family from Algeria. But things do not develop as he hopes. Though his wife finds a new identity with other immigrant women and in the liberation cause, he fails miserably to do so. This is a bleak story handled with care and skill, convincingly recreating the period setting and tracing the characters' progress with a clear-eyed, documentary-style attention to detail, but it is hardly an Algerian film.

One common factor uniting virtually all filmmaking – within the *beur* community in France, in francophone West Africa, in contemporary Algeria, and to an increasing extent in Tunisia – is its reliance on French government initiatives. The French government's current concern seems to be to sponsor 'prestige' African productions which can get European festival screenings, ideally at Cannes, and a successful release in one or more Parisian art cinemas. There is also a very conscious effort to make French film aid all-embracing. It is hardly by chance that during the four-year existence of the funding body ADCSud (2000–3), aid was given filmmakers in over sixty countries in Asia, Africa and Latin America. In terms of Africa, assistance was given to at least one filmmaker from eleven of the independent states created by the break-up of the former giant French colonies of French West Africa and French Equatorial Africa, as well as to Algerian, Moroccan and Tunisian filmmakers. In addition, funding was given to filmmakers from the former Portuguese colonies of Angola, Cape Verde, Mozambique and Guinea-Bissau; Egypt, Ethiopia, Burundi, the Democratic Republic of Congo (ex-Zaire) and Madagascar; South Africa, Namibia and Zimbabwe. No doubt the new French funding body, the Fonds Images Afrique, set up on 1 January 2004, will adopt a similar policy.

The Films

The paradoxical notion that the filmmaking of the first African generation born after independence would be essentially a cinema in exile was not apparent in the early 1990s when the first members of the age-group made their appearance. The first to achieve a breakthrough – Malek Lakhdar Hamina (born 1962) in Algeria and Imane Mesbahi in Morocco – were both in privileged situations in that their fathers were well established filmmakers in their own right. Lakhdar Hamina's *Autumn – October in Algiers/Automne – octobre à Alger* (1992), in which the director played the lead after his return from film study in the USA, brought together a team of very experienced Algerian technical collaborators, many of whom had worked with his father. The film offers a powerfully dramatic look at the experience of a family caught up in the riots and demonstrations of 5 October 1988. At the age of thirty, Lakhdar Hamina was by far the youngest director then active in the Maghreb, but though the film was well received, he has not made a second in the fifteen or so years since its release. Imane Mesbahi, who like Lakhdar Hamina had appeared as a child actor in some of her father's early films, was markedly less successful with her debut film, made after the completion of her film studies in Cairo and the making of a couple of short documentaries. *An Immigrant's Song/Le Chant d'un immigré* was based on a script by her father and shooting began in 1994. But Mesbahi abandoned the project for five years, while she worked directing téléfilms for Moroccan television. In 1999 she began shooting new sequences and re-edited the project, but even then it was not until 2002 that the film was eventually released in Morocco, under a new title, *The Paradise of the Poor/Paradis des pauvres*.

In general, the films of the millennium generation follow, with some significant variations, one or other of the dominant tendencies outlined in the four previous chapters. On the one hand, there has been a continuation of the kind of realist filmmaking chronicling the problems of post-independence societies which has been characteristic of African filmmaking since its origins and which has been discussed in Chapters 5 and 6. Among key figures renewing the realist impulse are filmmakers from two Sub-Saharan African countries lacking a strong filmmaking tradition – Ivanga Imunga (born 1967) from Gabon, and Issa Serge Coelo from Chad – together with Régina Fanta Nacro from Burkina Faso, the Tunisian Nawfel Saheb-Ettaba and the Moroccans Nabil Ayouch, Mohamed Asli and Yasmine Kassari.

Ivanga Imunga made his feature debut – after half-a-dozen shorts – with *Money/Dôlè* (2000), the winner of the top prize (the Tanit d'or) at the JCC in 2000. Though this was the first Gabonese film for twenty-two years, there are links with the veterans of the 1970s, in that it was co-scripted by Philippe Mory and co-produced by Charles Mensah. As was always the case in the 1970s, the film's dialogue is in French. *Dôlè* is an engaging study which offers a vivid picture of a group of children living largely on the streets of Libreville, the country's capital. Though they indulge in petty crime – stealing radio equipment, car tyres or batteries – they all have their private dreams, even performing a pagan ritual to ensure success. There is a real sense of the young actors living out their own lives, and their street encounters have a totally convincing immediacy (such as their meeting with a slightly crazed preacher of doom). The gang leader Baby Lee wants to become a rap star (and his singing leads us into and out of the film), Akson has real ambitions of succeeding as a boxer, while Joker dreams of becoming a sea captain. The central figure, Mougler, has deeper problems. His mother, who has been abandoned by his father, is sick and in need of expensive medication. So Mougler conceives of a daring plan to attack and rob the latest craze in Libreville, the new scratch-card game, Dôlè, which promises 1 million CFA francs to its winners. Inevitably the raid goes wrong, Baby Lee is killed and, in any case, Mougler's mother is already dead. But in the final scenes the film switches gears. The kiosk raid goes unpunished by the authorities and Baby Lee turns out not to be dead after all, able to lead them in a final rap number which continues over the credits, as they set out for a sea trip with their friend, 'Uncle' Charlie.

Issa Serge Coelo's *Daresalam* (2000) is one of the very few recent African films to confront the wars that have wracked the continent since independence. Coelo had worked as a documentary cameraman in French television and made several short films before beginning his first feature, set in an imaginary African country. *Daresalam* begins by showing the impact of heavy-handed treatment by government troops imposing the collection of taxes and the 'national loan' on impoverished villagers. Forced from their homes and fleeing through a landscape of rape, torture and violence, two friends, Djimi and Koni, end up in a training camp run by the FRAP rebels. After just two days of training, they are in action, but soon a heavy defeat splits the FRAP ranks and separates the two friends. A final confrontation between the two of them makes clear the divisive contradictions of a civil war, tearing even close friends apart. The film ends with the wounded Djimi meeting spectral figures from the past, as he hobbles through his old village. There are no false heroics in the film and Coelo makes very clear the ideological and resource limitations of the rebels, as well as the confusions of the actual fighting. But his observational style, perhaps rooted in his early work in documentary, keeps us at a distance from his characters. In addition, Coelo is convinced that 'cinema should ask questions rather than give answers',[8] so his work lacks the passion which Med Hondo brought to his 1970s studies of the Polisario rebels. But *Daresalam* remains a sincere and serious study of a key aspect of contemporary Africa.

Also set in a fictional African country but again confronting the tragedy of civil war caused by atrocious ethnic rivalry is Régina Fanta Nacro's much praised *The Night of Truth/La Nuit de la vérité* (2004). In the short films which earned her an international reputation, Nacro deftly treated serious issues with humour and a lightness of touch, but here in her first feature the tone is unrelentingly bleak, leading to a climax of almost unwatchable horror. The director, who co-scripted the film with Marc Gautron, has said she wanted to create a 'Shakespearian' drama,[9] and the main focus is on two families, President Miossoune and his wife Edna and the charismatic rebel leader Colonel and his wife Soumari. There are even a kind of 'court jester' – in the form of the ex-soldier Tomoto (an awkward figure, since he is not the familiar wise fool, but an active embodiment of racial hatred) – and a Cassandra-like figure, Fatou, who foresees the outcome and carries the film's final meaning of reconciliation.

The action is compressed into a few hours as the two rival groups, summoned by the Colonel, come together to try to create peace after ten years of civil war. The immediate awkwardnesses of this attempt at peace-making are well captured, as each couple has to eat the other's gastronomic speciality (caterpillars and snakes respectively). The real underlying tensions between the two groups of soldiers, haunted by the memory of their own dead, are also well conveyed and, above all, the scenes featuring children injured in the war making up little stories about their horrific mutilations are stunning. Less convincing are the two lead characters, the Colonel and the President's wife Edna, who are both depicted as deeply flawed tragic individuals. From the years of war, the Colonel is haunted by one single incident of a massacre in which he personally killed and mutilated a child, and Edna, whose son that child was, is driven only by thoughts of bloody revenge. While the Colonel seeks forgiveness for his crime, Edna offers only vengeance, persuading her husband's troops to capture him and then slowly spit-roast him over an open fire (a fate which, the director tells us, also befell her own uncle). *The Night of Truth* is a passionately sincere film, but it is perhaps over-ambitious. The writing and directing both have an over-explicit theatricality, and the acting cannot quite reach the intensity needed to capture these extraordinary personal stories, in which the whole horror of ethnic hatred is intended to be encapsulated. But though in some ways a flawed work, *The Night of Truth* is immensely apposite and courageous, and a reminder that the new generation of African women directors have real ambition and are no long willing simply to chronicle women's domestic oppression.

Nabil Ayouch's three films to date are very varied. The first and third are thrillers based on Hollywood models (the latter with very explicit, Western-style sex scenes which caused censorship problems in Morocco). But his second film, *Ali Zaoua* (1999), is very different: a much darker study of three Casablancan street children that recalls both Italian neorealism and the Luis Buñuel of *Los Olvidados*. Based on lengthy research, the film has a carefully devised dramatic structure built around the efforts of the three kids to devise a worthy funeral for the leader of their little band (the Ali Zaoua of the title). The same care has been expended on the performances as on the structure, with the naturalness of the orphans who play the central roles counterbalanced by the experienced actors playing the adult roles. The whole was co-scripted with a French screenwriter, Nathalie Saugeon, with the Arab adaptation and dialogue by the dramatist Youssef Fadel. While showing the plight and helplessness of the children (their sheer inability not to steal or sniff glue, for instance) and the lack of hope their lives offer, Ayouch's view incorporates their hopes and dreams as well as the bleakness of their immediate surroundings, ending, like *Dôlè*, with a boat trip into a hopefully better future. While in no way romanticising their plight, Ayouch has constructed a moving dramatic tale that became the second most popular Moroccan film ever at the box office and won the top prize (the Étalon de Yennenga) at FESPACO in 2001.[10]

Another film with echoes of neorealism is Mohamed Asli's debut feature, *In Casablanca Angels Don't Fly/A Casablanca les anges ne volent pas* (2004). This is not surprising since the director trained (and subsequently worked) in Italy and many of his crew are Italians. The film traces another aspect of poverty in Casablanca: a trio of Berber waiters who are exploited and live in poverty at the mercy of the restaurant owner. The core of the film is the tragic story of Said, who is unable to be with his wife for the birth of their second child, but has to watch her die on the way to hospital. Said's story is paralleled by the comic tale of his colleague Ismail's obsession with a pair of shoes that cost a month or more's wages (there is a marvellous scene – an almost religious ritual – as he puts them on for the first time). The third, less developed, story is that of Ottman, a Berber horseman who rides his horse into Casablanca, only to have it throw him and bolt (one of the film's most spectacular scenes). All three stories end in defeat, but Asli shows great sympathy for his protagonists' lives and he dreams and weaves their tales beautifully together by means of a sensitive handling of the soundtrack. The film won the top prize (the Tanit d'or) at the JCC in 2004.

After a well received documentary about Moroccan workers in Europe, *When Men Weep/Quand les hommes pleurent* (1999), Yasmine Kassari turned her attention to the women left behind in rural Morocco in her first fictional feature, *The Sleeping Child/L'Enfant endormi* (2004) (the title refers to the folk belief that an unborn child can be 'put to sleep', that is, put on hold until the husband's return). This is a reticent film, depicting two illiterate, unassertive women who largely submit to the situation to which they are reduced by their husbands' absence. Halima abandons her children and returns to her parents after being wrongly suspected of a liaison with another man and beaten by her in-laws. Zeinab persists, but eventually loses hope and throws away the spell which she thinks will allow her to reawaken the child conceived on her wedding night. Another understated study of difficult personal relations, this time in a very confined urban space, is the Tunisian Nawfel Saheb-Ettaba's debut feature, *The Bookstore/El kotbia* (2002). This chonicles the marital difficulties of a repressed bookseller, Tarek, and his more forceful wife, Leïla, who has ambitions as a singer. The couple are eventually reunited, but though Tarek's widowed mother and his much younger assistant, Jamil, are drawn to each other, social pressures keep them apart. This is a discreetly told story of real commitments but largely repressed emotions.

The alternative African approach, whose history has been chronicled in Chapters 7 and 8, has found an even stronger echo among the post-millennium filmmakers. One filmmaker who tried to open up new subject matter for African cinema and also explore new ways of shaping a film stylistically is Mohamed Camara who, like other filmmakers from Guinea, uses French dialogue in his films. After two shorts exploring very controversial subject matter – mother-son incest in *Denko* (1992) and child suicide in *Minka* (1994) – Camara confronted homosexuality head-on in the feature-length *Dakan* (1997). This film begins with a deliberately provocative scene of two young men kissing passionately in a car, and it follows the lives of the two protagonists as they try, under parental pressure, to change their lives. Manga (a role initially conceived by Camara for himself) submits to a traditional healer (who fails to 'cure' him) and begins an affair with a white girl. His friend Sory quarrels with his over-bearing father (played by Camara), gets married and has a son. But the end of the film sees the pair of them driving off together towards a very uncertain future. Camara treats his subject in a deliberately formalised manner, using explicitly worked-out, patterned dialogue, deliberate paralleling of scenes and incidents, and some very carefully composed visual images. There is no space here for instinctual response, and this stylistic choice prevents real audience involvement in the unfolding of the characters' lives, seen as their destiny (the literal meaning of the title).

The filmmaker who really set the pattern for the most experimental work of the new generation – and who has vanished from view of late – is the Cameroonian Jean-Pierre Bekolo (born 1966), who studied as a television pro-ducer and editor at INA and was based in Paris for many years. Bekolo is the author of two unclassifiable features – *Quartier Mozart*, made in 1992 when he was just twenty-six, and *Aristotle's Plot/Le Complot d'Aristote* (1996), together with *Grandmother's Grammar/La Grammaire de grand-mère* (also 1966), a short documentary about the African filmmaker he most admires, Djibril Diop Mambety. The pattern is set from the very opening of *Quartier Mozart* when the characters introduce themselves, with their nicknames, direct to camera and Bekolo's voice-over commentary introduces the key element of magic: the trans-formation by the local witch of the schoolgirl who calls herself Neighbourhood Chief into a man, MyGuy, so that she can enjoy the 'best of all lives', that of a woman in a man's body. The film continues in similar vein with the witch's adventures as a man, Panka, who can make a man's penis disappear simply by shaking hands with him (except, that is, for the police chief, Mad Dog, who hires 'him' as a watchman). The film develops as an often hilarious study of urban life in Yaoundé, focusing particularly on its sexual problems, such as the police chief's difficulties with his two wives, the predicament of the shopkeeper Good-as-Dead (who has shaken hands with the witch), and the growing passion of the police chief's liberated daughter, Saturday, for the outsider MyGuy. There is, it seems, a good deal of autobiography in the film (Bekolo was born in Yaoundé and his father was a polygamous police chief).[11] The whole film is shot in a dis-jointed style that recalls Bekolo's earlier experience of making pop videos and the influence of Spike Lee (particularly the handling of dialogue) and Jean-Luc Godard (using stills and handwritten messages, a blank screen sequence and direct-to-camera dialogue). The whole is accompanied by lots of contemporary references (to Michael Jackson and Denzil Washington, 'Lady Di' and Princess Caroline, for example) and a very lively pop music soundtrack. But the ending is disappointingly conventional, with Neighbourhood Chief, restored to her schoolgirl identity, concluding, after her adventures, that before she goes out with a boy, he will have to prove he loves her and that it is the real thing.

Bekolo's second film, *Aristotle's Plot*, has the same pattern of a continual voice-over by the director (this time in English) and a fragmented, sometimes incoherent, storyline. This mixes talk (with plenty of swearing) with action and parody (especially of gangster films and westerns), apparently improvised scenes and a style full of jump cuts and unexpected transitions. Again, as in *Quartier Mozart*, one of the central characters is a large policeman whose actions and words are laughable (he is given the task of finding out how it is that people who die in one film can be seen alive and well in the next). The subject matter this time is cinema itself, and the film begins with two opposed characters chained to the policeman: the Filmmaker, variously referred to as Cinéaste (and hence 'silly ass'), Essoumba Tourneur or ET, and the gangster who calls himself Cinema, because he has seen 10,000 films, few of them African because 'African films are shit'. Cinema's range of fake identity cards bear the names of well-known African filmmakers – Diop Mambety, Kabore, Lionel Ngakane, Sembene, Hondo, Cisse, Haile Gerima and Kwah Ansah – but his own taste is for violent American movies, and the members of his gang have all taken on the names of their heroes: Van Damme, Schwarzenegger, Bruce Lee, Nikita and so. On the soundtrack, Bekolo speculates on why he has been chosen by the British Film Institute to direct a film for their series celebrating 100 years of cinema (along with Scorsese, Godard and Bertolucci), meditates on Aritotle's *Poetics*, quotes his grandfather ('a filmmaker is an outlaw who doesn't have enough personality to be a gangster'), and asks questions of all kinds. The action, such as it is, involves ET having Cinema's gang evicted from the Cinema Africa which forms their headquarters and which he renames Heritage Cinema. In response, the gang members steal the projector and the stock of films and improvise a cinema, the New Africa, only to find the films they have are African ones, which they mock but find oddly fascinating. There is a parody shoot-out in which ET is killed and then brought back to life by the director, and a return to the film's opening scene. *Aristotle's Plot* ends enigmatically with a series of disjointed scenes concerning death and resurrection, and the end titles unroll to the sound of a song telling us to remember that a movie is a movie.

Bekolo has said of his approach that 'each film should give a definition of film. Otherwise I do not learn anything and I do not feel interested. It is like an adventure and my definition of film is changing'.[12] It is a great loss to African filmmaking that having made two films quite unlike any others in the continent's filmmaking history, Bekolo was not able to continue his exploration of the medium. Jonathan Haynes aptly describes Bekolo as 'a cagey and attitudinous guerrilla roaming the post-modern globalised mediascape',[13] and certainly his work opened the way for the successful and award-winning films of Haroun, Sissako and Kouyaté, which are discussed in subsequent chapters.

There is plenty of craziness in Bekolo's work which carries real conviction. But the actual depiction of madness in Maghrebian cinema has been much less successful. The Tunisian Jilani Saadi's *Khorma* (2002), for example, is an uneven study of a village idiot. At first we are amused by Khorma's antics, then we come to laugh at the discomforture of those whom he confronts when he has a little power. But his transition into a tortured Christ-like figure in the hands of the villagers at the end strikes a discordant note. Another film of considerable ambition is the Moroccan Narjiss Nejjar's *Cry No More/Les Yeux secs* (2003), which began, she tells us, as an idea for a documentary on rural prostitution. But there is little evidence of this in the actual film, a grindingly slow, sumptuously shot, two-hour symbolic melodrama. *Cry No More* begins with the return to her native village of Mina, a woman who has spent over twenty-five years in prison. Only women now live in the village, supporting themselves and their aged mothers higher up the mountains by prostitution, systematically killing all their children at birth and adding a new red flag to a nearby 'cemetery of virginities' as any new girl reaches puberty and takes up the village trade. The initial confrontations between Mina and Hala, the forceful daughter who does not recognise her, and between Hala and Fahd, the prison-warder turned bus-driver who drove Mina home, are promising. But the film begins to lose its direction when Fahd puts on a Charlie Chaplin costume to entertain the women. Then, having done nothing to prevent the child Zinda being prostituted, a weeping Fahd dresses in drag (complete with eye make-up and badly applied lipstick) in some kind of symbolic taking-on of the prostitutes' pain, which also involves him dancing and screaming naked on a snowy mountain top. After this burst of ill-inspired grandiloquence, the film returns to a banal semblance of reality with Mina staying on to teach the village girls weaving and Fahd driving off into the unknown with Hala and Zinda.

CONCLUSION

As can be seen from the above – and as will become apparent in subsequent chapters on specific filmmakers – the new generation of francophone African filmmakers has kept largely to the paths opened up by their elders, even though African societies have seen huge transformations in the course of the past forty years. In many ways this is admirable, since, as Milan Kundera argues in a discussion devoted largely to music and the novel,

> Great works of art can only be born within the history of their art and as *participants* in that history. It is only inside history that we can see what is new and what is repetitive, what is discovery and what is imitation; in other words, only inside history can a work exist as a *value* capable of being discerned and judged.[14]

The films of the younger generation are increasingly autobiographical, exploring the immediate issues of exile and identity and making innovative advances in story structure, and, in the process, creating, as Elisabeth Lequeret notes, 'an art of the unsaid, of the ellipse, a dislocation of classical narrative'.[15] Partly as a result of their freedom from many of the social and political concerns which were so vital to their elders (one thinks of the contrast between the two Mauritanians, Med Hondo and Abderrahmane Sissako), the newcomers have shown, in Tahar Chikhaoui's words, 'more confidence in the camera and in reality, from which stems the place accorded to the suggestive force of the image, liberated from the process of narration, and the growing interest in the documentary'.[16] They have also shown real willingness to explore many of the new potentialities offered by video technology. But these advances have largely been limited to a stylistic level, as a comparison with Nigeria shows.

When Françoise Balogun wrote her survey of Nigerian cinema in 1984, she surveyed a scene not that different from the situation in neighbouring francophone countries: thirty-six fictional features, over half of them shot in 16mm, produced in fifteen years. Looking at film production structures, she noted that the state sector 'is characterised by bureaucratic inertia and bad organisation which paralyse the production of films', while the private sector 'is shackled by the lack of financial means'.[17] The leading filmmaker, Ola Balogun, author of eight of these films, was even a characteristically francophone intellectual, educated at the University of Caen, trained at IDHEC and author of two French-language plays before he turned to filmmaking.[18] But she did note perceptively that film production was far from satisfying popular demand, and by 1997 Jonathan Haynes had a quite different focus: 'Nigerian video films – dramatic features shot on video and marketed on cassettes, and sometimes also exhibited publicly with video projectors or television monitors – are being produced at a rate of nearly one a day.'[19] By 2005, Pierre Barrot could look back at a body of some 7,000 Nigerian video films produced since 1992 and see a current output of around 1,200 such videos a year, though he noted that the 59 million euro budget of France's most expensive film of 2004 – Jean-Jacques Arnaud's *Deux Frères* – would have funded 3,500 Nigerian video films.[20] Film finance is always an opaque matter, and it can be argued that very few European films cover their costs at the local box office (making a profit depends on television and video rights and overseas sales). But the form of filmmaking we find in francophone Africa is an extreme example of this economic fact. The lack of box-office success of African films in African cinemas (for whatever reason) has virtually no effect on whether or not the films are made, since the funding continues to come from France. By contrast, Nigerian video production is totally commercial, with films shot in days and needing to recover their costs in months. Most Nigerian video films have little artistic worth, but the occasional exception has emerged. Tunde Kelani, a fifty-seven-year-old Nigerian London

Film School graduate, has, as Barrot notes, 'developed a mode of production adapted to Nigerian economic conditions, directed at a popular audience and local video market', and merited a retrospective at the New York African Film Festival in 2004.[21] Nothing this revolutionary has occurred in francophone Africa – the mode of production as well as the established traditions of style and subject matter continue largely unchanged.[22]

NOTES

1. www.bulletin de la guilde africaine des réalisateurs et producteurs 3 – internet publication (March 2001).
2. Moussa Sene Absa, interview in the pressbook of his *Madame Brouette* (needless to say, a French-language film), p. 6.
3. Pierre Haffner, 'D'une fleur double et de quatre mille autres: Sur le développement du cinéma africain' (Paris: La Documentation Française), 2000, pp. 27–35.
4. Hamid Naficy, *An Accented Cinema: Exilic and Diasporic Filmmaking* (Princeton: Princeton University Press), 2001.
5. René Prédal, *Le Jeune cinéma français* (Paris: Nathan, 2002), p. 136.
6. Nadir Moknèche, pressbook for *Viva Laldgérie*.
7. See Roy Armes, *Postcolonial Images: Studies in North African Film* (Bloomington: Indiana University Press, 2005).
8. Issa Serge Coelo, www.africultures – internet publication (30 August 2002).
9. Régina Fanta Nacro, www.africultures – internet publicaion (29 May 2005).
10. For a full analysis of the film, see Armes, *Postcolonial Images*, pp. 169–77.
11. Jonathan Haynes, 'African Filmmaking and the Postcolonial Predicament: *Quartier Mozart* and *Aristotle's Plot*', in Kenneth W. Harrow (ed.), *African Cinema: Postcolonial and Feminist Readings* (Trenton, NJ and Asmara, Eritrea: Africa World Press, 1999), p. 31.
12. Jean-Pierre Bekolo, interview, in Nwachukwu Frank Ukadike, *Black African Cinema* (Berkeley: California University Press, 1994), p. 233.
13. Haynes, 'African Filmmaking', p. 27.
14. Milan Kundera, *Testaments Betrayed* (London: Faber & Faber, 1995), pp. 17–18.
15. Elisabeth Lequeret, 'Afrique noire: Des lumières dans le désert', in Jean Michel Frodon (ed.), *Au Sud du Cinéma* (Paris: Cahiers du Cinéma/Arte Editions, 2004), p. 50.
16. Tahar Chikhaoui, in Frodon (ed.), *Au Sud du Cinéma*, p. 36.
17. Françoise Balogun, *Le Cinéma au Nigéria* (Paris: OCIC, 1984), p. 13.
18. Ola Balogun, *Shango, suivi de Le Roi-Éléphant* (Honfleur: Pierre Jean Oswald, 1968).
19. Jonathan Haynes, Nigerian Video Films (Jos: Nigerian Film Corporation, 1997), p. 9.
20. Pierre Barrot (ed.), *Nollywood: Le Phénomène vidéo au Nigeria* (Paris: L'Harmattan, 2005), p. 5.
21. Barrot, *Nollywood*, p. 14.
22. Olivier Barlet notes a new trend for low-budget filmmaking in Burkino Faso in the work of Boubakar Diallo and Boubacar Zida (known as Sidnaaba): feature-length films made for about €30.000 each and able to recover their costs locally in a couple of months. In two years (2004–5), Zida has made and shown two features (*Ouaga Zoodo* and *Wiibdo*) and Diallo four (*Traque à Ouaga, Sofia, Dossier brûlant* and *Code Phénix*). See Olivier Barlet, 'Les Nouveaux paradoxes des cinémas d'Afrique noire', Paris: *Africultures* 65 (October–December 2005), pp. 39–40.

10. MAHAMAT SALEH HAROUN (CHAD)

Because cinema, more than any other art, is above all national, a film-maker is often the mouth-piece of his community. Even if I have chosen to live in France, I cannot forget that part of me which is over there, those founding roots, that lively memory, in spite of exile. Consequently I shall fight for the visibility of my people.

Mahamat Saleh Haroun[1]

INTRODUCTION

Mahamat Saleh Haroun was born in Chad in 1963. He moved to France and studied first filmmaking at the CLCF in Paris and then journalism at the IUT in Bordeaux. He worked for five years in print journalism and radio before returning to filmmaking, working from a base in Paris (through his company, Les Productions de la Lanterne) and becoming a key figure in the Guilde africaine des réalisateurs et producteurs. In the Guild's first bulletin he defined his (and their) ambitions:

Because a certain spirit of resistance animates us at the heart of the Guild, because we are conscious of belonging to the same community destined to meet the same problems, our group is aware of a responsibility which should guide us towards the light, around these two words: freedom and independence.[2]

From the first Haroun has been a prolific and eclectic filmmaker. His early shorter films alternate between documentary and fiction and are in a number of media: 16mm film – *Maral Tanie/La Deuxième épouse* (1994, fiction); Beta SP video – *Bord'Africa* (1995, documentary), *Sotigui Kouyaté, un griot moderne* (1996, documentary), *Un thé au Sahel* (1998, fiction); 35mm film – *Goï Goï le nain* (1995, fiction), *B 400* (1997, fiction). His first feature, *Bye Bye Africa* (1999), similarly mixes fiction and documentary, black-and-white and colour sequences. It was shot on Beta SP and transferred to 35mm film for its release, and features the director himself as its protagonist. By contrast, Haroun's second feature, *Abouna* (2002), is a more distanced, unambiguously fictional feature, beautifully composed and shot in 35mm colour. Since making his feature debut, Haroun has completed two further video documentaries: *Letter from New York* (2002) and *The Essential/L'Essentiel* (2003), a short dealing with the problem of AIDS, made for the Global Dialogue Trust.

The most substantial of Haroun's early works is his study of Sotigui Kouyaté, the celebrated *griot* and actor, who is the father of Dani Kouyaté (see Chapter 11). The film gives a fascinating picture of a man who thrives by living across cultures, with a family in Burkina Faso and a French wife and children in Paris. Largely through interviews backed up by film clips, Haroun focuses on his work in Paris on *La Mahabharath*, produced by Peter Brooks, for whom Sotigui is the perfect instinctual actor. We also hear of his contributions to African theatre and film, see him with his childhood friends in Ouagadougou, and witness him in his role as a *griot* versed in African traditions of storytelling and healing. A key sequence in the middle of the film is his return to Mali, where he was born, to meet his extended family there for the first time in thirty years. Despite the complexities of Sotigui's character, his message is simple. For a *griot*, all violence and hatred comes from ignorance and a lack of understanding of others. The film ends with an exchange of songs between Sotigui and the Malian singer Fanfani Touré.

BYE BYE AFRICA

Despite its title, *Bye Bye Africa*, Haroun's first feature, is the story of a homecoming, the filmmaker's return to Chad after ten years of exile. But unlike the simple emotionality of Sotigui Kouyaté's return to Mali, *Bye Bye Africa*'s mixture of observation and enactment is so complex that it is difficult to know whether to call it a documentary fiction or a fictional documentary. Particularly complex is Haroun's own status not only as director and scriptwriter, but also as both authenticating voice-over narrator, Haroun, and lead actor, a seemingly fictional version of himself, referred to here as 'Haroun'. The film's opening sets the pattern. It begins as an enactment, with Haroun, in bed with his French wife, being woken in the middle of the night to be told his mother has died.

Almost immediately we hear Haroun, in voice-over, commenting on the mother's death, treating it, documentary style, as a real event in his life. When 'Haroun' arrives in Chad, the film's visual aspect is similarly doubled, as the colour images of the main narrative are intercut with the first of the black-and-white images (taken by the video camera which 'Haroun' carries with him at all times) which will recur throughout the film.

As a result, when we move on to Haroun's meeting with his bereaved father, we have no way of knowing whether this is what really happened as the two came face-to-face (as when Sotigui Kouyaté visited Mali) or whether the scene was scripted by Haroun. The second scene between the two clarifies matters since it is clearly scripted, referring to a film about Freud which does not appear in any Haroun filmography and underlining the two key themes of the film. Here the father questions what is the use of cinema and, in particular, rejects the approach of 'Haroun': 'Your films are not made for us. They are for the whites'. He also warns about exile: 'The white people's land is nice, but it's not yours and never will be. The day you think you belong there, you'll lose your soul'. In response 'Haroun' screens film footage of his mother, shot at his sister's wedding by his friend Garba, and explains that he makes films for the sake of memory, quoting Jean-Luc Godard's adage that 'cinema creates memories'.

In the following colour sequence, this questioning of cinema is taken further as Haroun, in voice-over, laments not having been there for his mother's funeral and talks about his need to find refuge by making a film about her. This leads directly to an enacted scene in which 'Haroun', riding pillion on Garba's scooter, talks about the film he is going to make in a year's time, which is, of course, to be called *Bye Bye Africa*. Asked what it is about, Haroun compares it to a set of Russian dolls, dealing with 'cinema, exile, family, love, about life in short'. There are two questions confronting him: 'how do you film life?' and 'what is the point of making films which no-one in Chad will see?'. These questions are probed further in a series of seemingly authentic black-and-white interviews with various people once involved with cinema in Chad, who are asked about their view of the future of cinema there. The interviewees include Garba who, it turns out, was once projectionist at Le Normandie and inspired 'Haroun' to become a filmmaker, and the daughter of the founder of the Étoile, who still dreams of renovating it. Haroun's doubts remain: how to believe in cinema in a country where war has become a culture?

After this seeming documentary sequence, the film plunges back into fiction with 'Haroun' beaten up in the street by a man who accuses him of stealing his image. The scenes of 'Haroun's face being treated by Garba are intercut with shots of 'Haroun's nephew and a friend playing with a toy camera made out of recycled cans. Garba explains the attacker's motives. In Chad, people distrust the camera and have a great problem with images. They cannot separate fiction and reality (a knowing comment perhaps on audiences of the real *Bye Bye Africa*?). This problem of the inability to separate fiction from reality is illustrated by what is the weakest section of the film, the story of the actress Isabelle who appeared in a film about AIDS made by the character 'Haroun' (a film which the real Haroun had not yet made). Her life has been ruined because everyone thinks she must be HIV positive, since, as she tells him, 'Cinema is stronger than reality'. Though 'Haroun' wants sex with her, he brutally refuses any commitment or responsibility.

'Haroun' next meets a Chadian film producer who likes the script of the fictional *Bye Bye Africa*, but finds it too expensive to produce. When he suggests using video, Haroun protests that he wants to make *real* cinema – again ironic, since the real *Bye Bye Africa* was in fact shot on video. 'Haroun' next meets his friend Issa Serge Coelo (the real-life director of *Daresalam*) and persuades him to allow his film-mad nephew Ali to stay and watch the day's filming. Ali had earlier tried to steal 'Haroun's video camera and then offered to exchange his toy camera for it. Despite the lack of the producer's backing, 'Haroun' goes ahead with his auditions, filming the actor's responses with his video camera. Again, the black-and-white images we see could show real actors hoping for a film role or be improvised scenes directed by Haroun. A letter from the (real) Congolese director Jean-Pierre Fila is then read out in voice-over, confirming that the situation in Congo is the same as that in Chad. This series of scenes concerning cinema concludes with another black-and-white interview, this time with the owner of one of the video rooms which have replaced cinemas.

We then return to the fictional story with Garba winning the lottery which will allow him to achieve his ambition of emigrating to the United States. At the celebratory party in a nightclub a spectral Isabelle accuses 'Haroun': 'Reality scares you, so you cower behind your stupid dramas. I'm not a fictional character, I'm real'. After a visit to his grandmother, 'Haroun' hears the voice of his father, urging him to take responsibility. He then sets out to locate Isabelle, only to find her dead body. A video she has left behind explains why she has killed herself. 'Haroun' is left in tears, protesting it was just a casual affair. Our first real sight of the grandmother, a distant figure hobbling across a courtyard, is accompanied by Haroun's voice-over talking tenderly of her and explaining that she brought him up. Then it is time for farewells. 'Haroun' gives his camera to his nephew who films his departure while the voice-over ends the story. As the final credits unroll, we learn that all the scenes, even the meeting with the father and the black-and-white interviews and auditions, were played by actors.

Bye Bye Africa is a good example of the kind of stylistic innovation we can increasingly expect from the millennium generation, as they are faced with limited budgets but all the new potential of video technology. The narrative

Figure 10.1   Mahamat Saleh Haroun: *Bye Bye Africa*

pattern, whereby we see the film we are actually watching ostensibly being made, may not be new, but the way in which the on-screen action is reinforced by the authoritative, documentary-style voice-over creates some interesting tensions, and the handling of the black-and-white material and its insertion into the narrative is excellent. The film deals with the uncertain relationship between cinema and reality and creates a real ambivalence in audience response. Of Haroun's stated list of themes – his set of Russian dolls – only cinema gets any real exploration; exile and family are underplayed and 'love', if that is what it can be called, is both unconvincing and totally lacking in any moral perspective.

ABOUNA

Nothing could be further from *Bye Bye Africa* than Haroun's second feature, *Our Father/Abouna*, with its 35mm format, its beautiful and composed style, and its intensely moral tone. Haroun claims that he choose the subject for its relevance to contemporary Chad where, it seems, 'there are daily messages on the national radio from women seeking their husbands who have gone off without saying a word'. Instead of the usual focus on the man who emigrates, Haroun chose to focus on the suffering of the women and children who are left

Figure 10.2   Mahamat Saleh Haroun: *Abouna (Our Father)*

behind. His three other key points of reference are indicated by the posters outside the cinema: Charlie Chaplin's *The Kid* (Chaplin is Haroun's 'first reference'), Idrissa Ouedraogo, who, in *Yaaba*, 'achieves something truly magical', and Jim Jarmusch, whose cinema, exemplified by *Stranger Than Paradise*, is 'nomadic, searching, setting a possible dream under way, profoundly anchored in life'.[3] Haroun worked closely with his designer, Laurent Cavero, and director of photography, Abraham Haïlé Biru, to ensure that 'everything in the frame was significant, so as to attain a dimension that was essentially sacred'. In addition, he worked with his friend, the Chadian painter and calligrapher Kader Badawi, to ensure 'the harmony of the colours so that the film would flow like a river, strong in tonality and harmony'.[4]

The tone of *Abouna* is set in the credit sequence, which comprises just two very formally composed shots. In the first shot a man is seen in long-shot walking with a suitcase in an empty, hilly landscape. In shot two, which is closer, the man turns and looks directly at the camera, then turns away, moves off and vanishes beneath the brow of the hill. The credits unroll over this long-held shot. Then, as the final credit (the director's name) vanishes, the man reappears in extreme long-shot, beginning to climb the next hill. We later discover that we are witnessing a tragic moment in the man's life – he is abandoning his family and going into exile – but emotion is held back and nothing is allowed to disturb our feelings directly.

The same mood of tranquillity holds during the opening scenes of the narrative. It is only when their father fails to turn up to referee a children's football game that the two brothers, fifteen-year-old Tahir and eight-year-old Amine, begin to wonder where he is. When their mother arrives home, she tells them that their father has been irresponsible and has gone. Touchingly, Amine gets out the dictionary to look up the word, concluding that 'irresponsible' means his father was not responsible for going away. It is typical of Haroun's elliptical style that we never learn precisely what made the father leave or what his relationship with the mother was. The narrative, which is pared down from the beginning, becomes more and more sparse as the film continues. Next day the two boys go to the Chad-Cameroon border to see if their father is there, but find nothing. A pair of beautifully contrived panning shots captures their situation perfectly. The long-shot of their journey out emphasises their fragility amid the squalor of N'Djaména, while the answering shot of their return brings out the fraternal closeness which is their strength. On their return we see the sorrow etched into their mother's face.

Some sort of normality returns. Tahir fulfils his father's role in reading to Amine from the copy of Saint-Exupéry's *Le Petit Prince* which he carried with him at all times. Amine has an asthma attack from which he soon recovers. The pair continue their search for their father only to discover that he was dismissed from his job over two years ago. Again, there are gaps in the narrative. We never learn why he was fired or what he did in the two years of unemployment, when he left 'for work' every morning. Everything is told at the level of the children's experience. Then comes a magical moment. While they are watching a film, they see an actor who looks just like their father from the back and who turns round to say 'Hello, children'. The resemblance is so striking that Amine even talks back to the figure on the screen. Next morning, at Amine's suggestion, they skip school and go instead to the cinema where they saw the film. This, incidentally, is the kind of modern cinema with plush blue seats that 'Haroun' in *Bye Bye Africa* argued no longer exists in N'Djaména (marking yet another point of difference between the two films). The pair steal the film reel, roll it home like a hoop and take it apart looking for the image of their father. They are surprised by their mother, to whom Tahir lies, but the cinema owner and the police are already there. They are taken to the police station and only escape a beating through their mother's intervention. On the way home the mother laments: 'Shame on me. A husband who leaves. Children who steal'.

Next day, in another unexplained twist in the narrative, the mother drives with them to a koranic school, a much harsher environment, where the master assures her that he will make good people of them. For a time they seem to settle in. Amine is spoilt by the master's wife, because he looks like her drowned son Moussa, and Tahir meets a beautiful girl who is, it transpires, mute. But soon trouble occurs and both are beaten, with Tahir, who is unrepentant, even tied to a post. Then they receive news that their father is in Tangiers and has sent them a present, a picture of the beach and the sea. Their joy is short-lived, as Amine falls ill and his medicine is missing. The treatment of his death shows Haroun's stylistic approach to perfection. We see Amine smiling in close-up as *Le Petit Prince* is read to him, then we cut to a beautifully composed shot of the window from the outside and, as the camera pulls back, the reading turns into a lament. Tahir, left alone with just the dream image of Amine and himself playing on the beach in Tangiers, makes his second escape attempt. This time it is successful and he is joined by the mute girl in her customary gold dress.

Up to this point the narrative has flowed continuously, though with many of the key moments concealed from us: the boys' capture when they first try to escape, Tahir swearing on the Koran that he will not try to escape again, Amine's death. After Tahir arrives back at N'Djaména with the girl and they cut their wrists and mix blood to symbolise their union, the film becomes a succession of very loosely linked tableaux, each ending with a cut or fade to black and each marking a stage in Tahir's progression from a child to a fifteen-year-old with adult responsibilities. We see the couple in a dream image smiling and waving from a scooter, then, without narrative transition, we see Tahir learning that his mother is in a psychiatric hospital and going with the girl to 'free' her. In the final scene, all the elements are brought together: the mother in a seemingly unconscious state, the couple very much in love, Tahir with his father's map. As he begins to sing, the mother joins in and the film cuts to a long-shot of the trio and then fades to black.

Inevitably, there can be no resolution to this story and it is hard to imagine what will happen next. At least until the final series of tableaux, the pace is steady and deliberate, indeed so reverential that one hardly dares to laugh at what are clearly comic incidents, such as Tahir discovering the girl is twenty ('You're old!') or the girl creeping up behind the hospital attendant and hitting him over the head with a pan. This Chaplinesque mixture of humour and pathos is rare in African cinema. Visually, the film is sumptuous, with a succession of perfectly framed images, though at times the use of complementary colours (orange for Amine, blue for Tahir, gold for the girl) seems overcontrived in its overt colour-coding. As with Mansour Sora Wade's *The Price of Forgiveness*, the care given to formal composition is almost oppressive. Haroun's strength lies in his ability to depict so precisely the unspoken ties that bind people and their inner strengths – the links that unite Tahir first with his brother Amine and then with the mute girl who becomes, as it were, his 'blood-sister', when they mingle their blood to give witness to their unity.

NOTES

1. Mahamat Saleh Haroun, 'Un certain esprit de résistance', www.bulletin de la guilde africaine des réalisateurs et producteurs – internet publication (March 2000).
2. Ibid.
3. Mahamat Saleh Haroun, interview, *Africultures* 54, Paris, 2003, p. 166.
4. Ibid., p. 167.

11. DANI KOUYATÉ (BURKINA FASO)

Why am I so interested in oral dramaturgy? In my view, if Africa is to bring its dance contribution to the universal rondo, where each civilisation brings its own dance, then the technical and dramatic richness of oral dramaturgy can help us.

Dani Kouyaté[1]

INTRODUCTION

Dani Kouyaté (the name is sometimes spelt as Dany) was born in Bobodioulasso, in Burkina Faso, in 1961. Descended from one of the most celebrated families of griots, his father was the celebrated griot and actor Sotigui Kouyaté, who plays the leading role in Dani's first feature. Within traditional Mande society, with its three-caste structure of nobles, artisans and slaves, griots were ranked in the middle category, alongside blacksmiths and leather-workers, as men of the word. In a society without writing, their role was the preservation of memory and mediation between people and power. Given their control of verbal expression, as both historians and genealogists for their peoples, griots had considerable power and authority. Valérie Thiers-Thiam notes that, 'The griot enjoys a great freedom of speech, he uses flattery and well as mockery; no-one, not even senior dignitaries, escapes the risk of hearing home truths and seeing himself ridiculed by a griot.'[2]

Though Dani Kouyaté himself was never initiated as a young man (as his father had been), he believes that 'cinema can be an extraordinary means of allowing the griot to survive'.[3] It was only later in life, paradoxically, that he learned about traditional culture, from books, and he admits that in terms of his education, he has 'benefited more from Cartesian culture than traditional culture'.[4] But, in interviews, he slips easily into the suggestion that he is indeed a griot in the traditional sense: 'my function as a griot is to transmit, communicate, defend, and for that you have to use all the means which are available today'.[5] And again, 'I think that cinema can be an extraordinary means of allowing the griot to survive'.[6] Whereas his father is a natural, untrained actor, Dani Kouyaté studied anthropology and filmmaking in Paris (the latter at both the Université de Paris III and the Sorbonne). While living in Paris, where he is still mostly based, he also founded a theatre company, 'The Griot's Voice' / 'La Voix du griot', which did several tours in Europe. In addition, before embarking on his first feature, he directed or co-directed several shorts: *Bilakoro* (1989), *Tobbere Kosam/Poussière de lait* (1990) and *The Crocodile's Sacred Tears/Les Larmes sacrées du crocodile* (1992). He has also set up his own production company, Sahélis Productions, in Burkina Faso and participated in the production of the twelve episode téléfilm series, *Life is Ours/À nous la vie* (1998) for Burkinabè television (TNB).

KEÏTA! L'HÉRITAGE DU GRIOT

In his first feature, *Keita! The Heritage of the Griot/Keïta! L'Héritage du griot* (1994), Kouyaté deals with the epic of Sundjata, which constitutes 'the founding myth of Manding culture: it recounts the history of the foundation of the Mande empire by Sundjata Keïta, a great thirteenth-century warrior'.[7] Mande is the area around the upper reaches of the river Niger, roughly comprising what is now Mali and Guinea and the nearby coastal states, and the epic of Sundjata is a tale that can be told only by a griot and thereby 'gives the griot his place in Manding society and ideology'.[8] The Kouyaté family, from whom Dani is descended, were by tradition the griots of the ruling Keïta family. In passing, it is interesting to note, as Valérie Thiers-Thiam points out, that a filmmaker descended from a family of griots should base his film account on the version written by a historian, Djibril Tamsir Niane.[9]

The film begins with the griot, played by Sotigui Kouyaté and referred to in the film by the Mande term Djeliba, asleep in his hammock. We see his dream or vision of the origins of the world, narrated by Sotigui himself:

> The world was born out of chaos. The shadows and darkness of pre-life had just been dissipated. Wagadu was the theatre for the first meeting of all the creatures of the universe. At that time no-one commanded men and then one man, Maghan Kan Fatta got up and spoke to all the others: The world shouldn't be like this, without a leader. I want to be your king.

Figure 11.1   Dani Kouyaté: *Keïta! l'Héritage du griot* (*Keita! The Heritage of the Griot*)

Are you agreed?' They all replied together, 'Konate' ('no-one hates you') and immediately Maghan Kan Fatta took the name Konate and proclaimed himself king of the Mande.

Djeliba is roused from his sleep by the mythical figure of the hunter and sets out for the town, with just his stick, his water pouch and his hammock. The subsequent narrative is based not just on the juxtaposition of myth and reality, Djeliba's story and everyday life, but also on the contrast of two contemporary worlds. The first is that of the griot, who is immersed in Mande tradition, lives a simple rural life, sleeps outdoors and hates the town. The other is the very different life of the schoolboy Mabo Keïta, who is growing up in a French-speaking household in town and being given a very Westernised education. When Mabo returns from school and asks about his ancestors and why he is called Keïta, Djeliba reveals that his mission is to answer these questions, though this will take not a day or even a year, but a whole lifetime.

Djeliba begins his story, 'It all began with a poor antelope, at a time of drought. A hunter was passing . . .', and we see a simple reconstruction of Maghan Kan Fatta's court. Here there is nothing spectacular of the kind found in Sissoko's *Guimba* or *La Genèse*, just a stress on the ordinary and everyday. The mythical figure of the hunter, whom we have already seen rousing Djeliba, reads his cowrie shells and tells the king that he must marry a very ugly girl who will come his way, because their son will become heir to the Mande empire. When the huge and ugly Buffalo Woman of Do (daughter of a buffalo which terrorised the country and killed ten hunters) is brought to his court, the king has to follow the cowries' prophesy. The child Mabo, who is totally caught up in this tale of a mythical past which involves his ancestors, begins to skip school to hear more of the story. There is a a great ceremony, but the king needs seven months to conquer his wife's resistance. The pregnancy lasts eighteen months and the boy, Sundjata, to whom she gives birth is a cripple, unable to stand and scorned as a worm by the villagers.

Mabo's neglect of his studies prompts his teacher, Fofana, to visit his parents to warn them what is happening. The result is a memorable confrontation with Djeliba, who argues that if he does not know the meaning and origin of his own name, he is unfit to teach. On learning that Fofana does not set the pattern of the school year, but that this is done by a government minister, Djeliba reveals his own unconscious arrogance in his reply: 'Send for him then, I'll wait here'. But the question of what is appropriate knowledge is forcefully put. In his claim that griots work for everyone and for nothing, Djeliba sets up the familiar dichotomy between 'real' griots (like himself) and 'false' ones (like the griotte who sings praise songs to Mabo's father for money at a party). This is a contrast that runs through African cinema from Ousmane Sembene's pioneering short *Borom Sarret* in 1963 onwards, and, as Valérie Thiers-Thiam ruefully notes, with the sole exception of Ababacar Samb-Makharam's *Jom*, griottes (female griots) are always depicted as 'false and avaricious'.[10]

Djeliba continues his story. When the king dies, he names Sundjata as his heir and appoints Balla Fassehe as his griot, but his first wife seizes the throne for her own son. By now Mabo is not only missing school, but also getting two of his friends involved by retelling the story to them daily, while all three are perched in the baobab tree. Within the story, years pass. When the queen insults his mother, the now fully grown Sandjata is faced with a crisis, but this too has been foreseen. The old blacksmith made him an iron bar with which to struggle to his feet. This first attempt fails, but a second try, aided this time by a branch brought by his mother, is successful. Now he can walk and show his strength by tearing up a baobab tree single-handed.

But at this point, Mabo's storytelling days are at an end, as he is expelled from school and his two friends are punished by their teacher. But Djeliba can tell one last episode – Sundjata's confrontation with his half-brother which results in him being sent into exile – before his storytelling has to cease, long before the origins of the Keïta name have been reached. When the two other parents confront Mabo's father angrily, Djeliba realises it is time to go, telling Mabo that this is only the beginning and that the story, like the wind, is unstoppable. Abandoned, Mabo has for company the bird which Djeliba has said will watch over him, and he is consoled by the hunter, who now appears to him: 'The world is old and the future grows out of the past – and there will be other griots'.

Keïta! L'Héritage du griot is a film that recaptures the verve, humour and apparently artless simplicity of the late 1960s and early 1970s work of the Niger directors Oumarou Ganda and Mustapha Alassane. Like them, Kouyaté is working with a limited budget (though in 35mm) but is still able to apply a light touch to Africa's past and adopt a nicely tuned approach to the present. The film is, in fact, carefully structured, with tellingly placed appearances by the legendary hunter (as much at home in the twentieth century as in the thirteenth) and an excellent narrative progression, whereby the storytelling by Djeliba is taken over midway through the film by Mabo himself. Kouyaté draws humour as well as strangeness from the legend and one can understand how captivating it becomes for Mabo. At the end, one wants a sequel, for surely there are many other tests and trials for Sundjata (descended on his father's side from the prophet Mohamed and on his mother's from the Buffalo Woman of Do) before he comes into his inheritance. Sotigui Kouyaté is never less than riveting as the griot, giving huge vitality to a character who, in the script, was a dying old man,[11] but one can see that the griot's time has passed for ever. At the same time there is a real sadness about this new generation of children growing up with a knowledge of Europe, but none of their own African past. Olivier Barlet summed up the film precisely when he wrote that *Keïta!* is 'attractive, profound, sensitive and above all successful'.[12]

SIA, LE RÊVE DU PYTHON

Sia, The Dream of the Python/Sia, le rêve du python (2000), 'freely inspired' by the Mauritanian Moussa Diagana's play, *La Légende du Wagadu vue par Sia Yatabéré*, goes back even further into the past to examine one of the founding myths of West Africa itself. *Sia*, which opens with a dark mysterious ritual, is an altogether more sombre film, full of madness, intrigue and death. A title introduces the plot: 'The legend tells us that at one time, the empire offered its most beautiful girls to the Python-God in return for prosperity'. It answers the question, 'Where does this story unfold today? In which epoch?', with a quote from Jean Cocteau: 'Legends have the privilege of being ageless', and allows us to decide for ourselves. The first character to introduce himself is a madman, Kerfa, who scornfully salutes the suffering and poverty of the people of Koumbi and denounces the king, Kaya Maghan. At court, the priests come to demand the sacrifice of Sia Yatabéré, the virgin named by the oracles. The king agrees, though the head of his armies, Wakhane (Sotigui Kouyaté as convincing as an evil schemer as he was as an innocent griot), disagrees, since she is engaged to his nephew Mamadi. When Sia flees, the king's first response is to have Wakhane arrest and brutalise all who knew her. But Wakhane is more subtle. He refuses to punish Kerfa, who continually sings his favourite refrain, 'He who sows misery, reaps only penury', on the grounds that he will be more trouble dead (as a martyr) than alive (as a madman). Stung by the vehement protests of Sia's friend Penda, who offers herself for sacrifice in her place, Wakhane releases everyone who has been arrested, much to the queen's anger.

But Wakhane has his own agenda, and keeps the whereabouts of Sia secret until his nephew has been able to say his farewells. Kerfa meanwhile thoroughly enjoys his role as Sia's saviour, giving her both warnings and enigmatic hints of survival: 'You'll know when the story has run its course – if you're alive of course'. He enjoys even more a confrontation with Kaya Maghan whom he openly insults and who reveals himself more in need of Kerfa than Kerfa is of him. Later, Kerfa complains to Sia that the king had wanted his dreams, his madness and indicates her personal powerlessness: 'Whatever you do, the story will take its course'. When Mamadi arrives, he shows himself determined to kill the Python-God, in whom his uncle still believes, and free Sia. But when he and his men enter the Python's lair, they learn that there is indeed no python, just the priests who rape and murder their annual victims. They save Sia's life, but only after she has been raped and left wanting to die. Here Wakhane shows his true ruthlessness, killing all who know the truth, including Mamadi's faithful soldiers, so that Mamadi can become the new Kaya Maghan, the heroic slayer of the Python-God. Though he saves Sia from his uncle's ruthlessness, she refuses to marry him because his new kingdom is built on the same falsehood and violence as the old one. Kerfa had once told her that not everyone could become mad, madness had to be earned. Sia has earned her madness and now has the true insight once possessed by Kerfa: 'The new king is dead, dead in the well of falsehood'. She strides, bare-breasted, out of the palace and, in one of African cinema's most startling transitions, the film's last shot shows her in modern-day Koumbi, calling on the people to rise up and chanting Kerfa's song, 'He who sows misery, reaps only penury'.

Kouyaté's stated aim in *Sia* was to tell a universal story, not to recreate faithfully the African past (the costumes in the film, for example, were designed by a Swiss woman, Judith Hentz, who had never even been to Africa), and he was delighted when audiences in Burkina Faso saw immediate political relevance in the film.[13] Kouyaté is always keen to remind his audience that what they are watching is a story, with the particular viewpoints and conventions of fiction. In *Keïta*, the hunter explains to Mabo that the hunters always win in stories because they are the ones who tell them: 'If the lion told them, he'd win sometimes'. Here Kerfa muses to Sia, when he is hiding her, that, 'Stories always have madmen, but madmen never have stories'. The dialogue too is full of (perhaps invented?) African sayings, such as the king's 'The corpse doesn't play hide-and-seek with

Figure 11.2   Dani Kouyaté: *Sia, le rêve du python* (*Sia, The Dream of the Python*)

the undertaker', or Kerfa's 'A father and a mother are but a mere trifle – a simple meeting'. Kouyaté's stories may be simple fables, but they are told with elegance, an extreme lightness of touch and a clear sense of narrative structure. Perhaps the major reason why they are so captivating is that his characters refuse to bow down to some preordained fate. Surely at the end of *Keïta*, Mabo will pursue the story of his ancestors, and even if he completes his school studies, he will not become the unquestioning francophone his parents intended. Here in *Sia*, Mamadi, though he finally succumbs to his uncle's web of deception, has earlier taken a clear personal stand in refusing a tradition that requires human sacrifice, going far beyond anything his uncle can imagine.

OUAGA SAGA

Kouyaté's third film, *Ouaga Saga* (2004), was a fresh departure for Kouyaté in almost every way, since he was here shooting on high definition video (which allowed the inclusion of a generous sprinkling of special effects), and working not from his own script but from one written by two Frenchman as a kind of homage to the city of Ouagadougou which they know and love. This is a totally optimistic vision of Africa today, enthusiastically acted by its team of young performers and full of little gags and lightly handled touches of magic (including a fetisher who summons up fake visions of horse racing results, and even a

Figure 11.3   Dani Kouyaté: *Ouaga Saga*

talking donkey). The focus is on a band of adolescents who live largely as a community on the streets, while each possesses a private dream (often reflected in a nickname): Moussa, eager to have his own garage; Bouremah and his brother Bouba who want to run a dance band; Bouftout who longs for a restaurant; Pele who is a budding football star; and Sherif who dreams of cinema. Sherif's passion for westerns imbues the whole film, which begins with clips from *Rio Bravo* and adds typical music from the film when a group of angry mothers march on the police station to demand the release of their sons. The boys are clearly delinquents (they steal and dismantle a motor scooter early in the film), but they retain their good humour at all times, buoyed up by the film's constant bursts of music and dance. The gang's exploits are never censured, and the film allows them a lottery win which enables them all to realise their dreams. In particular, Sherif is able to transform the Ouagacinema of the opening into his own personal Ouagamultiplex in a final magical transformation. The film is well matched to its intended poplar film and television audience and shows yet again the versatility of the new millennium generation. In an African cinema dominated by realism and serious intentions, Kouyaté's lighter mixture of everyday life, humour and magic offers an equally valid insight into the continent's contradictions.

NOTES

1. Dani Kouyaté, '*Sia, le rêve du python*', www.bulletin de la guilde africaine des réalisateurs et producteurs 4 – internet publication (May 2001).
2. Valérie Thiers-Thiam, *À chacun son griot* (Paris: L'Harmattan, 2004), pp. 15–16.
3. P. G. Despierre (ed.), *Le Griot, le psychanalyste et le cinéma africain* (Paris: Grappaf/L'Harmattan, 2004), p. 138.
4. Ibid., p. 141.
5. Dani Kouyaté, interview in Despierre, *Le Griot*, p. 136.
6. Ibid., p. 138.
7. Thiers-Thiam, *A chacun son griot*, p. 23.
8. Ibid.
9. Ibid., p. 138.
10. Ibid., pp. 137–8.
11. Dani Kouyaté, interview, *Africultures* 49 (Paris, 2002), p. 91.
12. Olivier Barlet, '*Keïta! L'Héritage du griot*', *Africultures* 2 (Paris, 1997), p. 51.
13. Dani Kouyaté, interview, www.africultures – internet publication (February 2002).

12. RAJA AMARI (TUNISIA)

The only problem with being a woman filmmaker and having a woman as the film's subject is that the woman is often seen as the victim and is soft-spoken . . . I really want to break out, to go beyond that and tackle really difficult subjects and not be so sweet and soft-spoken about it. I think that's the tendency for women filmmakers making films about women.

Raja Amari[1]

INTRODUCTION

Raja Amari was born into a middle-class family in Tunis (her father was a civil servant and her mother designed children's clothes) in 1971. She studied French literature and civilisation at the University of Tunis I, before going on to study film at FEMIS in Paris, from which she graduated in 1998. She currently divides her time between Paris and Tunis. Before making her first feature, she worked as a film critic for various Tunisian film reviews, contributing, for example, articles to the early issues of *Cinécrits* on filmmakers as diverse as Mahmoud Ben Mahmoud, Pier Paolo Pasolini, Raymond Depardon and Michel Khleifi, and on subjects ranging from the depiction of space in Tunisian films to the amateur film movement. Her stated preference (when asked in 2004) was for Italian and French filmmakers, Pier Paolo Pasolini having been an early influence. She added that she felt very close to the new French cinema, to young French filmmakers like François Ozon and Arnaud Despleschin: 'It's not that they come out of the same school as me, FEMIS, it's more that I like the way they deal with their characters.[2] Though she has a particular fondness for the actresses, such as Samia Gamal, who appeared in the classic Egyptian musicals of the 1940s and 1950s, which she first saw with her mother as a child, it is certainly difficult to see antecedents for her first feature in any area of Arab or African cinema.

Before making her first feature, *Satin rouge* (2002), Amari also made three short films, beginning with *The Bouquet/Le Bouquet* (1995). Her best known short is *April/Avril* (1998), an atmospheric thirty-minute piece shot in 35mm and dealing with a ten-year-old girl, Amina, who comes to Tunis to work as a maid to two lonely sisters. Gradually Amina is drawn into the games of sickness and suffering that the sisters play out daily, becoming a sort of doll to be cosseted and cared for. Amari followed this with a further twenty-seven-minute short, *One Evening in July/Un soir de juillet* (2001), a gain in 35mm, which deals with the close relationship that grows between Miriam, a young woman hesitating on the brink of marriage, and Saida, an old woman whose role is to help brides on their wedding day, with henna, make-up and massage. In 2004 Amari completed her first video documentary, *Tracking Oblivion/Sur les traces de l'oubli* (2004), which deals with an emblematic figure in North African feminism, the nineteenth-century European explorer Isabelle Eberhardt, who lived with all the freedom of a man and had a particular regard for the spartan life of the Bedouin tribes.

SATIN ROUGE

If, as Tahar Chikhaoui has observed, *Satin Rouge* (2002) is 'undoubtedly the most remarkable Tunisian film of recent years',[3] this is more because of the way the subject matter is handled than because of any particular stylistic innovation. The subject has a filmic origin in Amari's love of Egyptian 1940s and 1950s musicals rather than in personal experience. She had never set foot in a cabaret before she started seeking locations for the film, though she had grown up living almost next door to one (that used in the film) and, like the daughter in the film, had taken bellydancing lessons. The film was not intended as a general study of women's role in Tunisian society, but as the investigation of a particular woman, Lilia: 'I just started out with that specific character. I wanted to study her evolution and how she's going to journey through the film. I didn't want to set the character against society'.[4] By choosing a foreigner, Hiam Abbass, a Palestinian who lives in Paris, to embody her image of Tunisian womanhood, Amari was following a well established tradition in Tunisian filmmaking. After using the French actress, Juliette Berto, for the lead in his first feature, Abdellatif Ben Ammar chose an Algerian actress (Dalida Ramès) and a Lebanese actress (Yasmine Khlat) for the key roles in his masterpiece, *Aziza*. Similarly, Taïeb Louhichi, after choosing an Italian, Despina Tomazini, to play the Bedouin matriarch in *Shadow of the Earth*, cast a Roumanian actress, Anka Nicolaï, as

Figure 12.1   Raja Amari: *Satin Rouge* (*Red Satin*)

the dream embodiment of Arab beauty in his adaptation of the classic tale of Leila and Majnun, *Leila My Reason*.[5] In personal terms, *Satin Rouge* changed Amari's relationship with her parents, 'For the first time I was able to talk with them about subjects like sexuality . . . I had grown up'.[6]

The essential aspects of the situation of the protagonist, Lilia, are beautifully captured in the complex three-minute panning and tracking shot which precedes the main film title. Lilia is first seen cleaning windows and, as she continues around the room, dusting and tidying, the camera initially precedes her to some key object in her life (two photographs of her husband, her simple toilet accessories and a photograph of her daughter as a baby) each time she moves into shot. Pausing before the mirror, she seems to hear for the first time the rhythm of the popular Egyptian music which has been playing on the radio since the beginning, catches the rhythm and begins to sway to and fro. She lets down her hair and begins to dance demurely but sensuously round the room. But when she comes back to the mirror, she frowns, pulls back her hair and resumes her dusting.

The film proper begins with a series of little scenes, divided by fades to black which sum up Lilia's life as the dutiful mother. First we see her sewing and watching an Egyptian melodrama on television, waiting for her daughter who is late. The film's dialogue has relevance to the way the plot will unfold, though at the moment it looks like a glimpse into a totally alien fictional world: 'If

Figure 12.2   Raja Amari: *Satin Rouge (Red Satin)*

I were really a liberated woman, would that upset you?' 'It all depends'. 'Then I'm yours'. Next Lilia is shown eating and watching television alone, then fetching her daughter, from her dancing class, where she notices Salma's closeness to the drummer playing for the class. When she sees him again on the street, she follows him to the cabaret where he works, glancing in timidly, as she had at Salma's dancing class.

One reason why *Satin Rouge* has such an impact is that these opening scenes, showing Lilia as a widow, concerned with domestic issues and worried about her daughter's welfare, echo the stereotypical role of a woman in Tunisian cinema and indeed in Arab cinema in general. Ferid Boughedir has observed that the most striking difference between Tunisian cinema and all other Arab cinemas is the fact that 'families are almost always deprived of fathers and the woman has the predominant role. The fathers are either dead (sometimes they die at the very beginning of the film) or are defective, drunks, lacking a sense of responsibility. Always negative.'[7] But though predominant in the narrative, women do not dominate the action. The woman is 'either the victim of centuries of unjust traditions which have made her no more than a token of exchange and a slave who must be freed, or the mother who is the guardian of tradition and acts to protect it'.[8] In this first sequence, Lilia seems to fit this latter role exactly.

But when her daughter stays overnight at a party, Lilia is drawn out of the house after dark and goes to the cabaret, ostensibly in search of her daughter. Here she crosses a line since, as Amari explains, giving the reason why she herself had never been to a cabaret before making the film: 'In Tunisia, as in all Arab countries, it's a place with too bad a reputation for a respectable woman to go to'.[9] When Lilia first enters the world of the cabaret with its exclusively male audience, its colour, lights, dancing and music, the effect is too much for her and she faints. Here we see for the first time what will be the basic structure of the film, the meeting of two opposed worlds, 'the world of the day, strict, dominant and prudish, and the world of the night, relaxed, marginal, lascivious'.[10]

Back home next morning she quarrels with Salma and then makes up. When she goes shopping next day, she meets Folla, the dancer who helped her and whose dance she had watched admiringly, and we learn she is a dressmaker. Doing little jobs for Folla brings her back to the cabaret, and one evening she tries on one of the costumes and dances to herself in front of the mirror, then finds herself dragged out on stage as 'the surprise of the evening, the new star'. She appears in the line-up and gives a very spirited performance. The boss criticises her, however, for letting herself go too much and not being professional. He signs her on, but on condition that she takes lessons. The colourful, animated atmosphere among the girls, all laughing and helping each other, conveys a world that one can understand the lonely Lilia being drawn to, so the first stage of her double life begins. In conventional social terms, the cabaret dancers are dishonourable. As the ethnographer Karin van Nieuwkerk notes, 'Female performers are evaluated primarily as women and only secondarily as performers, and because they are women who exhibit their bodies, they are shameful'.[11] But none of this is apparent backstage among these basically happy, uninhibited and seemingly unexploited (if underpaid) women.

Lilia's double life gradually takes its toll on her life as a respectable widow and devoted mother. She fails to do Salma's mending and is out shopping for high-heeled shoes when her uncle turns up from the country to make his monthly visit. Eventually the two halves of her life clash when Folla turns up at her apartment and reveals the truth to Lilia's sanctimonious neighbour (who has come round to warn Lilia that she thinks Salma is smoking). Life is complicated too for Salma, who is having an affair with the drummer Chokri and – unaware of the change in Lilia's life – is scared of her respectable mother finding out. This central portion of the film intercuts between them, giving the film its rhythm and onward drive. Lilia's life gets even more complicated when Chokri declares his interest in her and saves her from the attentions of an importunate customer. Lilia's immediate response is to plunge back into housework, but back at the cabaret, she flirts outrageously with Chokri during her dance. They make love that night in the bed we had last seen occupied by her daughter and now it is Lilia who creeps home like a guilty adolescent. Woken by the phone, it is Salma to say she wants to introduce her to her boy friend, the drummer from the dancing class. At their next meeting Chokri, still unaware of Lilia's true identity, breaks it off with Lilia when he comes home to find her in his bed. The last two scenes show an almost regal Lilia greeting Salma and her future son-in-law Chokri, full of the confidence her secret life has given her, and then dancing, in red satin, at their wedding.

The narrative of *Satin Rouge* is beautifully shaped, moving easily between its two worlds and its two generations, and with the constant leitmotif of the dance in all its social forms – as private self-contemplation, adolescent amusement, cabaret turn and as a key to the celebration of marriage. The parallels, contrasts and dramatic ironies are well worked out, and the pace maintained through the intercutting of the various segments is admirable. The use of music by Nawfel El Manaa in the dance scenes is exhilarating, and elsewhere it is used quietly but to great effect. This is indeed a striking feature debut and one that goes outside the normal parameters of the Maghrebian film.

One important difference between Maghrebian filmmaking and cinema in the West is the development (or non-development) of the characters during the course of the narrative. In any cinema built on the Hollywood model, the notion of freewill is crucial, and the characters are constantly required to make choices and to act on them, whatever the risk. Hence Hollywood-style characters change and develop in the course of the narrative. When Kevin Dwyer, in his excellent series of interviews with Mohamed Abderrahman Tazi, explored why this never seems to happen in Maghrebian filmmaking, the Moroccan director's response was fascinating:

> Perhaps part of the explanation may have something to do with Islam, because we may be guided by a certain notion of the predetermined fate of the person, the idea that people have a destiny traced for them, that they aren't in control of their future but that this is controlled by the Creator.[12]

Whatever her religious beliefs, Amari has created in Lilia a character who functions on Western lines and therefore has room to develop, The difference between the housewifely Lilia at the film's opening and the splendidly self-assured Lilia at the end could not be more striking. In a sense she drifts into her dancing at the cabaret, but before she embarks on her affair with Chokri, there is the classic close-up of her face – the moment of decision. In true Western fashion, the end is one that she alone constructs. Having defied society, she now puts things back together, though from a very different standpoint from that which she occupied at the beginning. In a context where social realist filmmaking has been the dominant tradition for some fifty years, Amari's refusal to offer any sort of social analysis also makes her stand out from most Maghrebian cinema. Her explanation – 'I've minimised to the maximum the social setting in order to concentrate on the story of a character evolving in a modern-day and very real Tunisia, which there are stories can also have a universal dimension'[13] – is only partly satisfying. The empty night-time streets along which Lilia is able to pass without harassment do not ring wholly true, and the outside figures representing social pressures – the uncle and the censorious neighbour – lack their expected weight and authority.

Amari had doubts about how the (very European-style) love scenes would be received: 'In an Arab context, these scenes will probably shock certain people, because you don't show "those sorts of things" in such an explicit way in the cinema'. Certainly they are the kind of scenes that the young filmmakers living in France (such as the Moroccan Nabil Ayouch) are increasingly creating in their films and ones that, within the context of French filmmaking, are by no means remarkable or excessive. But what caused the real scandal surrounding the film is Lilia herself. She does not fit the social stereotypes of the older woman as victim or upholder of tradition. She is depicted as a widow with strong sexual feelings and desires for which she seeks a real outlet with a much younger man. Unlike the heroines of those Egyptian musicals of the 1940s and 1950s which Amari so admires, Lilia actually transgresses and instead of being punished, as women who act outside male guidance always are in Arab cinema, she is shown flaunting herself before her respectable wedding guests almost as brazenly as in the cabaret. Shocking indeed for the respectable middle-classes who make up the bulk of the audience for Tunisian cinema in Tunisia.

NOTES

1. Raja Amari, interview in www.indiewire – internet publication (2004).
2. Ibid.
3. Tahar Chikhaoui, 'Maghreb: De l'épopée au regard intime', in Jean-Michel Frodon (ed.), *Au Sud du Cinéma* (Paris: Cahiers du Cinéma/Arte Editions, 2004), pp. 35–6.
4. Raja Amari, indiewire interview.
5. See Abdelkrim Gabbous, *Silence, elles tournent!: Les femmes et le cinéma en Tunisie* (Tunis: Cérès Editions/CREDIF, 1998), pp. 43–61.
6. Raja Amari, cited in Nancy Ramsey, 'An Initiate in the Night Rhythms of Tunis', *The New York Times* (New York, 25 August 2002), 2, p. 2.
7. Ferid Boughedir, 'Le Cinéma tunisien avant *La Trace*: une thématique féministe', in Gabbous, *Silence*, pp. 174–5.
8. Ibid., p. 175.
9. Raja Amari, interview in the press book for *Satin Rouge*, n.p.
10. Ibid.
11. Karin van Nieuwkerk, *'A Trade Like Any Other': Female Singers and Dancers in Egypt* (Austin: University of Texas Press, 1995), p. 182.
12. Kevin Dwyer, *Beyond Casablanca: M. A. Tazi and the Adventure of Moroccan Cinema* (Bloomington: Indiana University Press, 2004), p. 181.
13. Raja Amari, press book interview, n.p.

13. FAOUZI BENSAIDI (MOROCCO)

I would like us to be considered as filmmakers who bring a certain gaze to bear upon the world . . . When you see the films of certain film-makers, you don't ask yourself questions about their nationality, you are experiencing the universality of cinema: I hope that our films can achieve that.

Faouzi Bensaidi[1]

INTRODUCTION

Faouzi Bensaidi was born in 1967 in Meknès and, after completing his diploma studies of acting at ISADAC in Rabat, he spent a further period of drama study in Paris from 1990 onwards, first at the Institut d'Etudes Théatrales at the University of Paris III and then at CNSAD. He also did courses in various aspects of filmmaking at FEMIS in 1995. His long academic training allows him to be unusually articulate about the choices he makes when filming and the nature of his own *mise-en-scène*. But he also has wide practical and professional experience, having worked extensively in theatre in Morocco as both actor and director. On screen, he has had important roles in Nabil Ayouch's *Mektoub* (1997), Jillali Ferhati's *Braids/Tresses* (1999) and Daoud Aoulad Syad's *The Wind Horse/Le Cheval de vent* (2001). In addition, he has worked as co-writer and actor on the French director André Téchiné's feature *Far Away/Loin* (2001), a story of drug trafficking which was shot in Morocco. Bensaidi is very much a product of the Moroccan government's project to support younger filmmakers.

He has received CCM support for all his personal projects, and he completed the stipulated three shorts before beginning his first feature. He began his film-making career in 1998 with an eighteen-minute fictional piece, *The Cliff/La Falaise*, which was followed by two further shorts, *Journeys/Trajets* (1999) and *The Wall/Le Mur* (2000). His first feature, *A Thousand Months/Mille mois*, was shown in the 'Un Certain Regard' section of the Cannes Film Festival in 2003, winning the award for most promising newcomer.

A key element of Bensaidi's style is his particular approach to the camera. He chooses 'lengthy fixed takes, long shots in which the distance from the subject is important, a sort of "powerless gaze" contemplating what happens to the characters'.[2] The rhythm is created by 'the movement of bodies in a limited space and a precise frame. The appearance, encounters and disappearance of figures in this space are as important as a musical note in a score'.[3] What does not appear on the screen is as important as what does and Bensaidi's films demand an active spectator whose 'intelligence and imagination are constantly addressed'.[4] All this is already apparent in *The Cliff*, a black-and-white fictional story, with no commentary and virtually no dialogue, which has won more international prizes than any other Moroccan film. The film chronicles a day in the life of two boys, Hakim and his younger brother Said, who scavenge for empty bottles on the beach and sell them to a blind alcohol vendor. When Hakim tries to cheat him, he is chased, caught and loses his meagre hoard of money. A group of drunken bikers spotted on the beach from a clifftop offers the prospect of good pickings and Hakim steals a sack in readiness. But the bikers use their empty bottles for target practice, smashing them with stones from the beach, and Hakim is left mortified.

Of particular interest here is the extreme use of depth and distance, with the camera regularly looking down on the action from a considerable height. Bensaidi likes 'working with the "off-screen": what happens not at the centre of the image but in the periphery, in the margins'.[5] Here the elements shown close-up in the foreground – a passing funeral, a gesticulating drunk, a moving lorry – are less important than the figures in the extreme background, the boys' powerlessness emphasised by their tiny image on the screen. Bensaidi also likes 'not following the character', but lets him 'leave and re-enter the frame'. In *The Cliff*, shots begin well before a character enters and are held long after characters have exited the frame. The slow pace of such scenes is offset by the precisely chosen camera angles and crisp cutting of the chase scenes, together with the occasional use of exaggerated close-up. In typical Bensaidi fashion, the film ends not with the boys' reunion after the difficult incidents of the day, but with the tiny figure of Said trudging presumably towards his desolate elder brother. Alternative ways of seeing are always of interest to Bensaidi, and here there is a long-held shot of distant waves distorted when seen though the bottom of a bottle Hakim has just found in the sea.

Asked about his multiple career on stage and screen, Bensaidi has spoken of his admiration for directors who 'direct, draw, produce opera . . . a multitude of activities' and he has mentioned Orson Welles and Francis Ford Coppola as among those who have influenced him.[6] Until *Mille mois* he had kept acting and directing separate in his theatre and film work. Though he was drawn to give himself roles to play on stage and parts in his own short films, he resisted the temptation. But in *Mille mois* he takes a small but important role, because he 'wanted to try an experiment', to see if he 'could be at ease, and if switching between being in front of and then behind the camera would harm the film'.[7] The decision was no doubt helped by the fact that his scenes were played opposite his wife of ten years standing, Nezha Rahil. He has always like to mix professional and non-professional actors in his films and, in *Mille mois*, he uses the inhabitants of the village where the film was shot, finding that this is both 'stimulating for everyone' and also lends 'a certain accuracy'.[8] But while he enjoys acting, 'the vital necessity of directing is the fact that it allows me to create worlds'.[9]

MILLE MOIS

The world of *Mille mois* is precisely set in time: in 1981 and at the start of the month of Ramadan, during which all Muslims are obliged to fast. Despite the precision of this choice of 1981, Bensaidi has no desire to confront history head-on: 'even if the period was one of great social confrontations, there are no demonstrations, strikes or riots in the film'.[10] Instead, Bensaidi is interested in an 'intimate' form of history, 'its traces and after-effects on the lives of people who do not see it occurring, because they are caught up in a present where no holds are barred in the fight to survive'.[11] Equally, though religion plays an important role in the film, Bensaidi is not concerned to express his own particular beliefs about Islam, but 'to grasp its place in the daily lives of the characters, the formation of their personality and their relationship with the world'.[12] He chose Ramadan as the film's setting because it allowed him 'to place the film in a time and place of social ritual which occurs in a natural way', allowing him 'to show how the protagonists live their relation with it'.[13] Within Ramadan, the Laylat al-Qadr (Night of Power), is of particular importance, being the very night on which the first revelations came to the Prophet.

Mille mois applies the approach explored in *The Cliff* to a two-hour narrative, and the result is a complex film which simultaneously excites and frustrates the spectator. There is a mass of fascinating individual detail and lots of tiny moments of comedy to draw in the spectator, though the overall narrative is bleak and unrelenting. But the choice of a strictly chronological unfolding of the plot and the wide spread of characters included means that the spectator has to hold a myriad of stories simultaneously in mind, constantly switching from one to another, with no clear indication of what is important and what is not. This is a deliberate strategy by Bensaidi who defines his stylistic approach as 'polyphonic'. From the start he attempts

> to lure the audience along a path that seems to be marked out and reassuring, only to make them lose it instantly. The centre keeps shifting and what seems to be the margin becomes the magnet that attracts all the rest to it, only to disappear, replaced by other peripheral elements. This disappearance of the centre allows us to approach each character and each sequence with the same intensity.[14]

As a result of this approach, key moments are underplayed, either because they are omitted from the on-screen narrative or because they are shot in such remote long-shot that their impact is diffused.

A further difficulty for the spectator is the fragmentary nature of the information we are given in any particular scene, which results in the spectator having to wait for considerable periods of time before getting the information needed to fill in the gaps and to understand fully how the scenes cohere and how precisely the plot is unfolding. Bensaidi has said that he likes a cinema on several levels, 'a film being something you can rediscover at a second viewing, with what you hadn't seen first time'.[15] Certainly this is true of *Mille mois*, and the film's opening sets the pattern for the unfolding two-hour narrative. It begins with a couple of little mysteries for the spectator. The first is why are all the villagers standing on the hillside watching the sky? This is swiftly resolved when a title tells us that this is Ramadan, the beginning of which is marked by the first sight of the waxing moon For an answer to the second question – why is seven-year-old Mehdi carrying a chair around all the time? – we have to wait about ten minutes, when we learn that it is Mehdi's honour and privilege to be in charge of his schoolteacher's chair.

Bensaidi has admitted to 'liking to play with the spectator at the level of form' and 'keeping the audience's participation in this way and not giving him everything on a plate from the start'.[16] But this is only the beginning of the problems which the film sets the spectator, since there is no way of knowing at this point of revelation, for example, the importance the chair is to play as a leitmotif running through the whole unfolding narrative. In fact, the film could easily have been entitled 'The Chair', on the lines of *The Cliff* and *The Wall*. The chair is the means by which his fellow pupils get their own back on Mehdi, by getting him blamed for negligence by distracting him and knocking a nail into it. But the chair's story does not end here. To buy new clothes for Mehdi to wear on Laylat al-Qadr, Mehdi's grandfather (who has already sold all his own furniture to make ends meet) steals the chair and sells it. As a result, the teacher refuses to teach, proclaiming that 'a teacher without a

Figure 13.1   Faouzi Bensaidi: *Mille Mois* (*A Thousand Months*)

chair is not a teacher' and forcing the community to buy him a replacement.
The chair turns up again among the hired furniture at the wedding of the local
caïd (or district administrator), is recognised by the teacher and almost leads
to the grandfather's exposure and punishment as a thief by a mob of villagers.
While the chair itself is part of the film's final conflagration, the discovery of
the theft drives the grandfather to leave his village with Amina (Mehdi's
mother) and Mehdi in the film's final shots. The differing roles played by the
chair as the story progresses are paralleled by the shifting perceptions we have

Figure 13.2   Faouzi Bensaidi: *Mille Mois* (*A Thousand Months*)

of the various characters as new layers of information about them are given to us.

Despite Bensaidi's claims of a 'polyphonic' narrative, the key to the understanding of the film is Mehdi. Though the story is not shown through Mehdi's eyes, it is his level of perception (or failure to perceive) which shapes the whole of *Mille mois*. Because of the temporal compression of the narrative into just a week or two, there is no space for Mehdi to develop: he is exactly the same seven-year-old at the end of the film as he was at the beginning. He does what little boys do: tells stories when he has lost his satchel, beats up a small boy who annoys him, wants to pee when out walking with his mother. As the teacher's pet he is given his 'first lesson in being a teacher' when he is made to cane other boys. The boys in the class beat him up in turn, though the effect of this is defused by being filmed in extreme long-shot. Key things happen in his immediate family circle (his friend Malika tells him the truth about his father's imprisonment before she dies, his grandfather becomes a thief, his mother is tempted by the thought of a new husband), but he can comprehend none of this and therefore it does not affect him. The film mirrors his level of perception, in that moments of real adult emotion and understanding are underplayed or elided altogether, and we are left with a flattened-out narrative, where carrying a chair and losing a friend, failing to make one's first fast and thinking you can see France in a sweet wrapper are events on the same level.

Amina, Mehdi's mother, has the typical Maghrebian role of female victim, with her husband in prison without trial for almost a year and little money to live on, despite working as a servant for the caïd. When she wants to go back to live with her mother in Casablanca, her father-in-law makes it clear she will not be able to take Mehdi with her. Refused permission to see her husband, she raises her voice in protest, only to be accused of insulting the state and beaten by the police. Bensaidi's handling of this incident is typical of how key actions occur off-screen in his films. We see only the grandfather on his knees begging for her to be spared as she is dragged off. Next a shot of the family travelling home in silence (shot from outside the taxi) and then the mother silent at home, bathing her wounds. No word is said about what has happened. Bensaidi relies on the gestures of the grandfather and the mother to tell all that needs to be said.

Later, raising money to live on by selling her wedding ring, Amina is promptly robbed of it all by rapacious beggars in a scene worthy of Buñuel at his best. The scenes between Amina and Samir (played by Bensaidi), in which the possibility of a new life seems to offer itself, are abortive, but beautifully played by the couple. The grandfather too is a victim, penniless after his land has been confiscated by the state, forced to sell his furniture and eventually to steal in order to survive. The domestic scenes between him and Amina, when each knows the other's deepest secret, are also sensitively handled.

We get only fragmentary pictures of the other characters. We are introduced to Mehdi's friend, Malika, the liberated student daughter of the caïd who is the only character to show any interest in politics and popular dissent and who dies (we eventually discover) in a car crash. The handling of this scene too shows the characteristic Bensaidi approach. When Amina arrives for work at the caïd's house, there is commotion – Malika has not returned home. As his mother works, Mehdi wanders through the empty house, going into Malika's room. There is a straight cut to Mehdi's mother hanging sheets over mirrors and pictures, and the house is now full of silent weeping women. Like Mehdi, we see from a distance Malika's body being prepared for washing, then a door is shut to block off our view as well as his. We see no more of the family, whose grief and mourning are never shown.

We only gradually piece together the story of Hocine, one of those marginal characters for whom Bensaidi has such affection. He is first seen in a Christ-like pose carrying water to his fields. It eventually transpires that he killed his wife on his return from the war, and is now building his own mosque as an act of atonement. When he commits suicide, it is implied (but not explicitly stated) that he is taking on himself the sins of the community. Compared to Hocine, the other characters are merely sketched in: Marzuk, the authoritarian school-teacher (and would-be poet) who is hopelessly in love with Mehdi's neighbour, Saadia; the beautiful seventeen-year-old Saadia herself, a 'good girl' despite her many suitors; the local electrician, Abdelhadi, also in love with Saadia, who amuses himself by regularly cutting the power to the village television and who triggers the final conflagration at the new caïd's wedding, and the new caïd, whose wedding; celebration brings out all the simmering tensions in the village and ends with him trying to shoot his own brother, while the wedding tent burns out of control.

Bensaidi's own comments on his approach help to clarify why this is a key film among the millennium generation's explorations of new narrative structures. He states that, 'it's a film about looking, about what you see and what you don't . . . The question is knowing what you allow people to see or not. I ask myself this question about cinema: what do I show?'[17] What he chooses to show are the details of life and behaviour, striking little incidents which are often comic moments in the overall bleak description of Morocco in 1981. He leaves to his audiences the task of fitting together the pieces of the mosaic, giving each piece its appropriate weight. *Mille mois* is a remarkable work, and, in considering Bensaidi's style, one can only echo Lindley Hanlon's verdict on Robert Bresson:

> His modernism can first and foremost be located in his severe reduction of narrative form in film . . . He has started from degree zero and reinvented a cinematic language with only those elements absolutely necessary for the movement of the narrative in his particular style.[18]

This is not in any way to imply either that Bensaidi's work is derivative or that he will eventually create a body of work to equal Bresson's. But it does point to a first feature that has an austerity and authority rare in modern filmmaking.

NOTES

1. Faouzi Bensaidi, interview in www.africultures – internet publication (May 2003).
2. Faouzi Bensaidi, unsourced interview cited in the National Film Theatre programme (London, July 2004).
3. Ibid.
4. Faouzi Bensaidi, africultures interview.
5. Ibid.
6. Ibid.
7. Faouzi Bensaidi, NFT interview.
8. Ibid.
9. Faouzi Bensaidi, africultures interview.
10. Ibid.
11. Faouzi Bensaidi, NFT interview.
12. Ibid.
13. Faouzi Bensaidi, africultures interview.
14. Faouzi Bensaidi, NFT interview.
15. Faouzi Bensaidi, africultures interview.
16. Ibid.
17. Ibid.
18. Lindley Hanlon, *Fragments: Bresson's Film Style* (Rutherford: Fairleigh Dickinson University Press, 1986), p. 20.

14. ABDERRAHMANE SISSAKO
(MAURITANIA)

The cinema is a gaze which has its source in the personality of each of us.
A personality forged by our lives, our education, our trajectory . . . I am
a filmmaker and I have never left my continent, because I carry it within me.

Abderrahmane Sissako[1]

INTRODUCTION

Born in Kiffa, Mauritania in 1961, brought up in Mali, trained at the VGIK film
school in Moscow thanks to a Soviet bursary, and resident in Paris since the early
1990s, Sissako is the archetypal filmmaker as exile. He is very much the product
of the European exile that foreign film school training entails. Though he tells
us he read the militant theorists Frantz Fanon and Aimé Césaire when he was
young (quoting the latter in the commentary of *Life on Earth/La Vie sur terre*),
his film tastes are very Westernised. Asked about the films that have influenced
him, he cites not his African forerunners, but Fellini's *La Strada*, Tarkovsky's
Ivan's Childhood and *Andrei Rublev*, Fassbinder's *Fear Eats the Soul* and
Antonioni's *The Passenger*.[2] Sissako's notion of African cinema also differs radically from that of the pioneers of the 1960s, for whom the notion of truly
African voices in cinema was so important. Talking to an interviewer in 1995,
Sissako said:

If there are a lot of African filmmakers, there will be a lot of African
images made by African filmmakers, but I don't think that that should be

a priority in itself. I believe that life, the image, the continent belongs to everyone . . . It is good that Africans make films here that they feel strongly about, that Europeans come here to make films that they feel strongly about too.[3]

The difference between Sissako's approach and that of the pioneers was very clear too when he admitted to an interviewer that what interests him in cinema is 'poetry, but not necessarily revolutionary poetry'.[4]

Sissako regards with equanimity his personal situation as a half-forced, half-voluntary exile and never dwells simply on the disadvantages. His attitude is more fundamentally ambiguous: 'I share this fate with many people who will always remain anonymous. I've lived in different continents and consider myself both rich and poor as a result'.[5] Sissako's *Life on Earth* begins with the questioning words of a letter to his father: 'Is what I am learning far from you worth what I am forgetting about us?' and, throughout his career, Sissako has been a filmmaker who uses his own situation and experience as the basis of his work, with each stage being 'a sort of autobiography': 'For me cinema is above all a search for yourself. It's through cinema that I attempt to construct myself, as others do through writing or painting or even making shoes.'[6] This use of his own experience is very conscious: 'Autobiography is a pretext which gives me considerable freedom'.[7]

His graduation film at the Moscow film school (VGIK) was *The Game* (1988), which intercuts the stories of a little boy Ahmed, who plays war games from which his mother can rescue him, and his father, a real-life soldier sent on a spying mission and summarily executed. The film ends with a quotation from Paul Valéry: 'War is a massacre by people who do not know each other, profiting people who do know each other but never massacre each other'. Sissako subsequently made a trio of very varied short films. *October* (1993), shot in Moscow, traced the separation of a pregnant Russian girl and her African lover, who is leaving Russia to return home. *The Camel and the Floating Sticks/Le Chameau et les bâtons flottants* (1995) was a six-minute adaptation of a La Fontaine fable made for a French television series. The twenty-six-minute *Sabriya* (1997), by contrast, was shot in Tunisia and forms part of the international television series 'Africa Dreaming'. A study of erotic obsession, it tells of the story of two young men, Saïd and Youssef, who are locked in a close physical and emotional friendship and spend their time endlessly playing chess in a café on an isolated beach. One day Youssef meets a mysterious Westernised woman, Sarah, on a train and neglects his friend to follow and spy on her as she poses seductively in a mini skirt, a swimsuit and a clinging wet dress. When the disgusted Saïd leaves, he too meets another mysterious woman, who strangely resembles the first, on the same train.

Sissako's later longer works show a development from personal document-ary to autobiographical fiction. The hour-long video *Rostov-Luanda* (1997), accompanied by a French-language commentary spoken by Sissako himself, traces his search in Angola for an old friend, Alfonso Baribanga, an ex-freedom fighter with whom he had studied Russian in Rostov. Armed only with a sev-enteen-year-old group portrait taken in Russia, Sissako explores Luanda and the surrounding towns and villages in search of his friend. He encounters a ruined, war-torn culture and meets a range of ordinary people with variously broken lives: drinkers and drivers, elderly married couples, musicians and orphans. The film remains on this level of individual encounter and there is no attempt to explain the historical situation or to offer a coherent picture of Angola's present-day politics or future prospects. As Sissako has said, 'What interests me in people is their present state, the moment when I'm face to face with someone'.[8] The picture that emerges from this series of sympathetic and often humorous interviews is one of hope and faith in the human spirit, together with nostalgia for a lost world of firm belief. Only on his very last day in Luanda does Sissako meet people who actually know Baribanga and can give him his current address, in Berlin. Talking about his first post-film-school film, Sissako has said, 'I like telling the story of everything which doesn't really happen: meetings which don't occur, as in *October*, impossible love, everything which is spoilt by a second's delay.'[9] This is borne out by *Rostov-Luanda*. When Sissako makes his final journey to Berlin and actually finds his friend, we do not see the meeting nor get a clear view of Baribanga himself. Instead, the film ends abruptly, with Baribanga just a voice-off answering the doorbell and a figure briefly glimpsed in long-shot at an upstairs window.

LA VIE SUR TERRE

The short sixty-minute feature that established Sissako as a leading figure in African cinema was made as part of a ten-episode international series aiming to show the impact of the new millennium on people throughout the world. But Sissako's film, set in the Malian village of Sokolo where his father was born, actually does nothing of the sort, since this is a world where time has no meaning. This is a paradoxical film, as remarkable for what it omits – inter-views, conversations, meals, domestic interior scenes, work and a clear sequence of passing days – as for what it contains. Hajer Bouden captures its place in Sissako's work and its particular tone very well, defining it as, 'a suc-cession of images, situations, phrases and sounds unfolding in his head, like a dream provoked by the desire to rediscover a place and developing at the whim of the feelings experienced'.[10] In place of a defined succession of the days making up the visit to Sokolo (four weeks of shooting in total), we have a pattern of extreme fragmentation, juxtaposition, repetition and symmetry.

The film's opening six shots – showing Sissako in a Paris store or at the airport buying, of all things, a cuddly white polar bear – are set against the sequences shot in Sokolo. The film proper begins with Sissako's letter to his father, announcing his impending visit and his wish to film there. It mentions an earlier communication sent via a friend returning to Sokolo. At the end of the film, Sissako himself will likewise carry to Paris a letter from a Sokolo inhabitant to his brother in exile. Though the ostensible reason for Sissako's visit is to meet his father again, the two are seen together in only three shots: two parallel panning shots (first from Sissako to his father, and then from his father to Sissako) placed near the beginning and the end of the film, and a long-held shot of them walking in long-shot through the fields. We hear none of the words they exchange; indeed, since Sissako never indulges in real conversation, the only verbal indications of Sissako's feelings are in his voice-over comments, many of which are quotations from Césaire's poems and political writings. The real richness of the soundtrack is the music: Salif Keïta's song 'Folon' (heard at his arrival and when he is with his father in the fields at the end) and a number of lyrical pieces by Anouar Braham. Significantly, the only indication of the coming of the millennium is the overheard sound of French radio programmes (including an interview with a correspondent in Japan).

We see a range of activities in Sokolo to which the film returns: broadcasting by the local radio station ('Radio Colon – La Voix du riz'), the local post office, where people – including Sissako himself – are continually attempting (with very little regular success) to make contact with outsiders, and the booth of the local photographer set up on the village square. A number of anonymous passers-by are also seen several times: a man on a motorbike, a lone boy kicking a football through the streets, customers for the village photographer. These repetitive actions and gestures give the film its sense of timelessness and, iron-ically, the only real progression of successive shots in the film depicts a group of the idle young men of the village who are seen initially sprawled out in the shade but who are subsequently constantly driven back towards the shelter of a wall. It is only when there is no longer any shade, even when they are stand-ing pressed against the wall, that they give up – to a brief flourish from a Schubert quintet (the only Western music in the film).

The only named character in the film, apart from Drahmane (Sissako himself), is a young girl, Nana, whom the filmmaker meets during the initial stage of his incessant cycling back and forth through the village (in traditional garb completed with a woven straw hat). She chats with him when they meet, indicating that she is from a neighbouring village, Kourouma, but subsequently, though they both continually cycle to and fro, they always just fail to meet. Nana meanwhile visits the village tailor, tries to make a phone call and has her photograph taken on the square. In this sense she is a potential source of nar-rative, but Sissako preferred her to keep her reticence, because he sensed that

Figure 14.1   Abderrahmane Sissako: *La Vie sur Terre* (*Life on Earth*)

she 'had something secret, that she was more than her very apparent beauty': 'I wanted to construct a whole mystery about her and make people understand that she shouldn't be seen as just a pretty hair-do and a beautiful smile'.[11] For this reason he did not invent a story for her, show her falling in love, or whatever: 'What is hidden in people, that's what is the most magnificent and strongest'.[12] *La Vie sur terre* bears this out.

HEREMAKONO

After *La Vie sur terre*, which was made in his father's village of Sokolo in Mali, Sissako felt the need to make a film about his relationship with his mother, to

Figure 14.2   Abderrahmane Sissako: *Heremakono* (*Waiting for Happiness*)

whom the new film is dedicated and who died on the last day of the film's shoot-ing. The film is also a return to Mauritania, emanating, he says, 'from an anxiety which I have always had about speaking about Mauritania, my country, which I have always missed. Going back there to make a film was an essential and necessary intimate act'.[13]

Sissako is not interested in pre-scripted filmmaking. He claims that for *Life on Earth* he brought to Arte just two pages (one of which was the letter to his father with which the film opens).[14] For *Heremakono*, also known as *Waiting for Happiness*, he had a synopsis of about forty pages, but the film was essen-tially improvised with the non-professional actors whom he met in Nouadhibou, who played versions of themselves in the film and provided much of the dialogue.[15] His working method was to bring a mass of people into his film 'by inviting them to tell their own stories as well'. The film was the happy

Figure 14.3   Abderrahmane Sissako: *Heremakono* (*Waiting for Happiness*)

result of these encounters: 'I admit I was very lucky with them, they were extra-ordinary. I had confidence in them and they in me'.[16]

Heremakono is Sissako's most elusive film, a narrative (like Haroun's *Bye Bye Africa*) from which all the normal signposts have been removed, and where the boundaries between actuality and pure fiction are not immediately appar-ent. The film begins in typical enigmatic fashion with a man (whom we later learn is Makan) burying his radio (carefully wrapped) in the sand and striding off into the desert. After the title credit, Makan is seen searching for the radio which is now missing. No explanation is given for either the burial or the loss, and instead the film cuts to a stationary taxi with a loaded roof-rack and an open bonnet. It has broken down and the passengers are sheltering in the shade. Eventually the taxi recommences its journey, taking a disparate band of men through an anonymous border crossing. One of these passengers is the film's protagonist, but at this stage there is nothing to distinguish him from the others, nor any way of identifying the place at which the car stops. In fact, he is the seventeen-year-old Abdallah, who has come back to say goodbye to his mother before going abroad, and the fishing village at which they have stopped is Nouadhibou, on the Mauritanian coast. In typical Sissako fashion, we do not see the meeting of mother and son, and our first view of the two of them together is when she rebukes him for smoking.

Sissako has said that 'exile precedes the departure. We make true exile within ourselves even before we depart. It's a sort of interior exile, which isn't just limited to Africans'.[17] This is certainly true of Abdallah, who is already in a sort of exile in Nouadhibou, since he does not speak the local dialect, Hassanye, does not wear the local traditional dress, and hardly ever goes out. Twice he goes to visit people who are presumably relatives. The first time there is no-one to greet him, though the television is switched on to show him a French TV quiz show, 'the intrusion of a false civilisation in a place of authentic living', as Sissako put it.[18] On his second visit, this time in traditional dress, he finds that the material he has chosen is identical to that of the refurbished curtains and drapes in the room (one of the film's many little understated gags). Visits to other relatives find him first caught up in a curious flirting ritual between men and women who sit opposite each other in the room and then, on the second occasion, being openly mocked by a gathering of women for his inability to speak the local language.

Abdallah, we learn, still lacks a passport and his linguistic problems are exploited by a little boy, Khatra, who deliberately jumbles words when ostensibly teaching him the local language. Sissako has said that Khatra's role grew during the shooting because the child 'imposed himself on the film because he wanted to act, so I was there to follow him. All the time I found him in front of the camera, because he wanted to be filmed as much as possible'.[19] In the film that finally emerged, Khatra provides much of the humour which Sissako finds so essential, particularly in his role as assistant to Maata, the ex-sailor and would-be electrician who never seems able to get a light-fitting to work.

The scenes in which Abdallah appears are intercut with scenes which, if we are to believe Sissako, feature people he encountered in Nouadhibou. Among these are an old woman, a real-life griotte, who is teaching her not very talented granddaughter to sing, and a Japanese man, who always seems to be giving away, rather than selling, the objects from his sample case. He also indulges his passion for karaoke at home in front of an audience of one. Abdallah also encounters Nana, whose story of how she visited Europe to tell her ex-lover Vincent that their daughter was dead, is accorded the only flashback sequence in the film, but seems fictitious. Another fictional story features the local photographer's studio, where Michael, who is going away, has himself photographed in turn with each of his friends, including Makan. Two weeks later, Makan reckons he must already be in Spain, but the truth is very different, since Michael's body is washed up on the beach, the photos still intact in a waterproof pouch.

The same pattern continues throughout the second half of the film. Nana receives a male visitor, the grandmother continues her teaching, Khatra peels the metal strip out of a banknote and loses it in the wind. Meanwhile, Abdallah sits at his ground-level window, watching feet go by, is woken by the sounds of the women of the village clapping and dancing at a party of some kind, and spends a night with Nana. Maata takes two unexplained trips with a light to the sea, the first with Khatra, the second alone. He dies on the second trip. The taxi is seen in operation again, with a new group of men intent on crossing borders, while Abdallah begins to make his preparations for departure. Khatra throws a lightbulb out to sea and collects it when the waves return it to the beach, but it works no better than any of the others. Abdallah sets off up the hill, only to turn back and sit down at the foot of the dunes, alone with his suitcase. This is our last image of him, as the film ends with scenes featuring Khatra, who shows off his kaleidoscope, breaks a streetlight with his catapult and watches an overcrowded train depart. When he falls asleep, he dreams of a kaleidoscope of lights all suddenly illuminated. Our last sight of Khatra (or is it Abdallah?) is when a figure vanishes in extreme long-shot behind the dunes.

Though clearly a fiction, *Heremakono* is an intensely personal and lyrical piece, held together by the strength of Sissako's emotions rather than by any sort of purely narrative logic. But because the film lacks the customary voice-over commentary by the director, these emotions always remain implicit, just as the geographical locations are vague (it is only from publicity material that we know this is Nouadhibou – Heremakono is merely the nearest town, which the film never visits). Similarly, we never learn where Abdallah is coming from or where he is bound for, though we assume it is Spain. With its exquisite photography and quirky sense of humour, *Heremakono* is compulsive viewing. But it remains elusive, built not out of the grim realities of exile but through tentative allusions and fleeting emotional links. The title given to the film abroad (*Waiting for Happiness* in English, *En attendant le bonheur* in French) prompted one interviewer to ask Sissako for his definition of happiness. His response captures perfectly the flavour of the film: 'I think that happiness is in anticipation. In the conduct of a day. In the little everyday details. And that's why there is this atmosphere of serenity in the film'.[20]

NOTES

1. Abderrahmane Sissako, 'Nous sommes riches de nos différences', interview in www.bulletin de la Guilde africaine des réalisateurs et producteurs 9 – internet publication (May 2003).
2. Abderrahmane Sissako, interview, *Cinécrits* 17 (Tunis, ATPCC, 1999), p. 47.
3. Melissa Thackway, *Africa Shoots Back: Alternative Perspectives in Sub-Saharan Francophone African Film* (London: James Currey, 2003), p. 199.
4. Abderrahmane Sissako, *Cinécrits* interview, p. 49.
5. Abderrahmane Sissako, interview, *Qantara* 46 (Paris, 2002), p. 29.
6. Ibid.
7. Ibid.
8. Abderrahmane Sissako, *Cinécrits* interview, p. 45.
9. Ibid., p. 52.
10. Hajer Bouden, 'Sissako ou l'appareil circulatoire', *Cinécrits* 17 (Tunis: ATPCC, 1999), p. 63.

11. Abderrahmane Sissako, *Cinécrits* interview, p. 51.
12. Ibid., p. 52.
13. Abderrahmane Sissako, *Qantara* interview, p. 29.
14. Abderrahmane Sissako, *Cinécrits* interview, p. 48.
15. Abderrahmane Sissako, *Qantara* interview, p. 29.
16. Ibid.
17. Ibid.
18. Ibid.
19. Ibid.
20. Ibid.

BIBLIOGRAPHY

Africultures (from 1997). Paris: L'Harmattan.

Ahmida, Ali Abdullatif (ed.) (2000) *Beyond Colonialism and Nationalism in the Maghrib: History, Culture and Politics*. New York: Palgrave.

Ait Hammou, Youssef (1996) *Lecture de l'image cinématographique*. Marrakesh: El Watanya.

Alaoui, A. Mdarhri and Zeggaf, A. (ed.) (1994) *L'Interculturel au Maroc*. Casablanca: Afrique Orient.

Allen, Roger, Kilpatrick, Hilary and de Moor, Ed (ed.) (1995) *Love and Sexuality in Modern Arabic Literature*. London: Saqi Books.

Allouache, Merzak (1987). *Omar Gatlato* (script). Algiers: Cinémathèque Algérienne/ Editions LAPHOMIC.

Allouache, Merzak (1996) *Salut Cousin!* (script). Paris: *L'Avant-Scène du Cinéma* 457.

Amarger, Michel (2002) 'Ruptures de l'espace identitaire', Paris: *Qantara* 44, pp. 22–5.

Amarger, Michel, Diop, M'Bissine and Ruelle, Catherine (2002) 'Islam, croyances et négritude dans les cinémas d'Afrique'. Paris: *Africultures* 47, pp. 5–67.

Amin, Samir (1970) *The Maghreb in the Modern World*. Harmondsworth: Penguin.

Anderson, Benedict (1991, new edn) *Imagined Communities: Reflections on the Origin and Spread of Nationalism*. London and New York: Verso.

Andrade-Watkins, Claire (1992) 'France's Bureau of Cinema: Financial and Technical Assistance between 1961 and 1977'. London: *Framework* 38–9, pp. 27–46.

Arab Cinema and Culture: Round Table Conferences (1965) 3 vols. Beirut: Arab Film and Television Center.

Araib, Ahmed and de Hullessen, Eric (1999) *Il était une fois . . . Le cinéma au Maroc*. Rabat: EDH.

Arasoughly, Alia (ed.) (1998) *Screens of Life: Critical Film Writing from the Arab World*. Quebec: World Heritage Press.

Ardener, Shirley (ed.) (1981) *Women and Space: Ground Rules and Social Maps*. London: Croom Helm.

Armbrust, Walter (1996) *Mass Culture and Modernism in Egypt*. Cambridge: Cambridge University Press.

Armbrust, Walter (ed.) (2000) *Mass Mediations: New Approaches to Popular Culture in the Middle East and Beyond*. Berkeley: University of California Press.

Armes, Roy (1985) 'Black African Cinema in the Eighties'. London: *Screen* 26: 3–4, pp. 60–73 (page order displaced).

Armes, Roy (1987) *Third World Film Making and the West*. Berkeley: University of California Press.

Armes, Roy (1994) 'The Group as Protagonist: *Ceddo*', in Roy Armes, *Action and Image: Dramatic Structure in Cinema*. Manchester: Manchester University Press, pp. 155–70.

Armes, Roy (1995) 'Cinema', in John Esposito (ed.) *The Oxford Encyclopedia of the Modern Islamic World*. New York and Oxford: Oxford University Press, pp. 286–90.

Armes, Roy (1996) *Dictionary of North African Film Makers/Dictionnaire des cinéastes du Maghreb*. Paris: Editions ATM.

Armes, Roy (1996) 'The Arab World', in Geoffrey Nowell-Smith *The Oxford History of World Cinema*. Oxford: Oxford University Press, pp. 661–7.

Armes, Roy (1998) *Omar Gatlato*. Trowbridge: Flicks Books.

Armes, Roy (2000) 'Reinterpreting the Tunisian Past: *Les Silences du palais*', in Kevin R. Lacey and Ralph M. Coury *The Arab-African and Islamic Worlds: Interdisciplinary Studies*. New York: Peter Lang, pp. 203–14.

Armes, Roy (2001) 'Cinema in the Maghreb', in Oliver Leaman, Companion Encyclopedia of Middle Eastern and African Film. London and New York: Routledge, pp. 429–517.

Armes, Roy (2002) 'History or Myth: *Chronique des années de braise*', in Ida Kummer (ed.) *Cinema Maghrébin*. Saratoga Springs: special issue of *Celaan* 1: 7–17.

Armes, Roy (2004) 'Imag(in)ing Europe: The Theme of Emigration in North African Cinema', in Tudor Parfitt and Yulia Egorova (eds), *Mediating the Other: Jews, Christians, Muslims and the Media*. London and New York: Routledge Curzon.

Armes, Roy (2005) *Postcolonial Images: Studies in North African Film*. Bloomington: Indiana University Press.

Awde, Nicholas and Samano, Putros (1986) *The Arabic Language*. London: Saqi Books.

Awed, Ibrahim M., Adam, Dr Hussein M. and Ngakane, Lionel (eds) (1983) *First Modadishu Pan African Film Symposium*. Mogadishu: Mogpafis Management Committee.

Aziza, Mohamed (1977) *Patrimonie culturel et création contemporaine en Afrique et le monde arabe*. Dakar: Les Nouvelles, Éditions Africaines.

Bachy, Victor (1978) *Le Cinéma de Tunisie*. Tunis: STD.

Bachy, Victor (1983, 2nd edn) *La Haute Volta et le cinema*. Brussels: OCIC.

Bachy, Victor (1983, 2nd edn) *Le Cinéma en Côte d'Ivoire*. Brussels: OCIC.

Bachy, Victor (1983, 2nd edn) *Le Cinéma au Mali*. Brussels: OCIC.

Bachy, Victor (1986) *Le Cinéma au Gabon*. Brussels: OCIC.

Bachy, Victor (1987) *To Have a History of African Cinema*. Brussels: OCIC.

Bakari, Umruh and Cham, Mbye (eds) (1996) *African Experiences of Cinema*. London: BFI.

Balogun, Françoise (1984) *Le Cinéma au Nigéria*. Paris: OCIC.

Barlet, Olivier (1998) 'Cinémas d'Afrique noire: Le Nouveau malentendu'. Paris: *Cinémathèque* 14, pp. 107–16.

Barlet, Olivier (2000) *African Cinemas: Decolonizing the Gaze*. London: Zed Books.

Barlet, Olivier (2001) 'Les Nouvelles stratégies des cinéastes africains'. Paris: *Africultures* 41, pp. 69–76.

Barrot, Pierre (ed.) (2005) *Nollywood: Le Phénomène vidéo au Nigeria*. Paris, Budapest and Turin: L'Harmattan.

Bataille, Maurice-Robert and Claude Veillot (1956) *Caméras sous le soleil: Le Cinéma en Afrique du nord*. Algiers.

Bazenguissa, Rémy and Nantet, Bernard (1995) *L'Afrique: Mythes et Réalités d'un Continent*. Paris: Le Cherche Midi Editeur.

Beaugé, Gilbert and Clément, Jean-François (eds) (1995) *L'Image dans le monde arabe*. Paris: CNRS Editions.

Béji, Hélé (1982) *Désenchantement national: Essai sur la décolonisation*. Paris: François Maspero/*Cahiers Libres* 368.

Ben Aissa, Anouar (ed.) (1996) *Tunisie: Trente ans de cinéma*. Tunis: EDICOP.

Ben Aissa, Khelfa (1990) *Tu vivras, Zinet!: Tahia ya Zinet!*. Paris: L'Harmattan.

Benali, Abdelkader (1998) *Le Cinéma colonial au Maghreb*. Paris: Éditions du Cerf.

Ben el Haj, Bahri (1980) *Une politique africaine du cinéma*. Paris: Éditions Dadci.

Bensalah, Mohamed (2005) *Cinéma en Méditerranée: Une passerelle entre les cultures*. Aix-en-Provence: Édisud.

Bensalem, Himmich (1997) *Au pays de nos crises: Essai sur le mal marocain*. Casablanca: Afrique Orient.

Bensmaïa, Réda (2003) *Experimental Nations:, Or, the Invention of the Maghreb*. Princeton: Princeton University Press.

Bergmann, Kristina (1993) *Filmkultur und Filmindustrie in Ägypten*. Darmstadt: Wissenschaftliche Buchgesellschaft.

Bernstein, Matthew and Studlar, Gaylyn (eds) (1997) *Visions of the East: Orientalism in Film*. London and New York: I. B. Tauris.

Berrah, Mouny, Bachy, Victor Salama, Mohand Ben and Boughedir, Ferid (eds) (1981) *Cinémas du Maghreb*. Paris: *CinémAction* 14.

Berrah, Mouny, Lévy, Jacques and Cluny, Claude-Michel (eds) (1987) *Les Cinémas arabes*. Paris: *CinémAction* 43/Cerf/IMA.

Biennale des cinémas arabes à Paris (from 1992) catalogues. Paris: Institut du Monde Arabe.

Bjornson, Richard (1994) *The African Quest for Freedom and Identity: Cameroonian Writing and the National Experience*. Bloomington: Indiana University Press.

Bossaerts, Marc and Van Geel, Catherine (eds) (1995) *Cinéma d'en Francophonie*. Brussels: Solibel Édition.

Bosséno, Christian (1979) 'Des maquis d'hier aux luttes d'aujourd'hui: Thématique du cinéma algérien'. Paris: *La Revue du cinéma – Image et son* 340, pp. 27–52.

Bosséno Christian (1983) 'Le Cinéma tunisien'. Paris: *La Revue du cinéma* 382, pp. 49–62.

Bosséno, Christian (ed.) (1985) *Youssef Chahine l'alexandrien*. Paris: *CinémAction* 34.

Boudjedra, Rachid (1971) *Naissance du cinéma algérien*. Paris: François Maspéro.

Boughedir, Ferid (1984) *Le Cinéma en Afrique et dans le monde*. Paris: *Jeune Afrique Plus*.

Boughedir, Ferid (1987) *Le Cinéma africain de A à Z*. Brussels: OCIC.

Boughedir, Ferid (1999) *Halfaouine: L'enfant des terrasses* (script). Paris: *L'Avant-Scène du Cinéma* 483.

Boulanger, Pierre (1975) *Le Cinéma colonial*. Paris: Seghers.

Bouzid, Nouri (1994) *Sources of Inspiration, Lecture: 22 June 1994, Villepreux*. Amsterdam: Sources.

Brahimi, Denise (1997) *Cinémas d'Afrique francophone et du Maghreb*. Paris: Nathan.

Brahimi, Denise (1997) 'A propos de Tala ou *L'Opium et le bâton* du roman au film'. Paris: *Awal* 15, p. 66.

Brossard, Jean-Pierre (ed.) (1981) *L'Algérie vue par son cinéma*. Locarno: Festival International du Film de Locarno.

Brown, Stewart (ed.) (1995) *The Pressures of the Text: Orality, Texts and the Telling of Tales*. Birmingham: Birmingham University Press.

Calvocoressi, Peter (1985) *Independent Africa and the World*. London and New York: Longman.

Cesca (1984) *Camera nigra: Le Discours du film africain*. Brussels: OCIC.

Chagnollaud, Jean-Paul (ed.) (2002) *Sexualité et sociétés arabes*. Paris: *Confluences Méditerranée*. 41.

Chahine et le cinéma égyptien (1984). Montreal *Dérives*: 43.

Chamkhi, Sonia (2005) *Cinéma tunisien nouveau*. Tunis: Sud Éditions.

Chanan, Michael (ed.) (1983) *Twenty-Five Years of the New Latin American Cinema*. London: BFI.

Châtillon, Georges and Lambert, Edwige (eds) (1982) *Algérie*. Paris: *Autrement* 38.

Chebel, Malek (1984) *Le Corps dans la tradition au Maghreb*. Paris: Presses Universitaires de France.

Cherfi, Abdelmajid et al. (eds) (1998) *Aspects de la civilisation tunisienne*. Tunis: Faculté de Lettres de Manouba.

Cheriaa, Tahar (1964) *Cinéma et culture en Tunisie*. Beirut: Unesco.

Cheriaa, Tahar (1979) *Ecrans d'abondance . . . ou cinémas de libération en Afrique?*. Tunis: STD.

Chikhaoui, Tahar (ed.) (1998) *Souleymane Cisse*. Tunis: ATPCC/*Cinécrits* 16.

Chikaoui, Tahar (2002) 'Le Cinéma tunisien des années 90: permanences et spécifités'. Toulouse: *Horizons Maghrébins* 46, pp. 113–19.

Choukroun, Jacques and de La Bretèche, François (2004) *Algérie d'hier et d'aujour-d'hui*. Perpignan: Institut Jean Vigo/*Cahiers de la Cinémathèque* 76.

Cinéma et libertés: Contribution au thème du Fespaco 93 (1993). Paris: Présence Africaine.

Cinéma et monde musulman (2001). Paris: *EurOrient* 10.

Cinéma: Production cinématographique 1957–1973 (1974). Algiers: Ministère de l'Information et de la Culture.

Cinémas de Africa (1995). Lisbon: Cinemeteca Portugesa/Culturgest.

Cinquante ans de courts métrages marocains 1947–1997 (1998). Rabat: CCM

Cisse, Soulemane (1998) *Yeelen* (script). Paris: *L'Avant-Scène du Cinéma* 476.

Clawson, Patrick (1981) 'The Development of Capitalism in Egypt'. London: *Khamsin* 9, pp. 77–116.

Clerc, Jeanne-Marie (1997) *Assia Djebar: Ecrire, Transgresser, Résister*. Paris and Montreal: L'Harmattan.

Cluny, Claude-Michel (1978) *Dictionnaire des nouveaux cinémas arabes*. Paris: Sindbad.

Côte, Marc (1998) *Le Maghreb*. Paris: *La Documentation Française*.

Convents, Guido (1986) *A la recherche des images oubliés*. Brussels: OCIC.

Convents, Guido (2003) *L'Afrique? Quel cinéma!: Un siècle de propagande coloniale et de films africains*. Antwerp: Editions EPO.

Cruise O'Brien, Donal B. (2003) *Symbolic Confrontations: Muslims Imagining the State in Africa*. London: Hurst & Co.

Cruise O'Brien, Donal B., Dunn, John and Rathbone, Richard (eds) (1989) *Contemporary West African States*. Cambridge: Cambridge University Press.

Dadci, Younès (1970) *Dialogues Algérie-Cinéma: Première histoire du cinéma algérien*. Paris: Editions Dadci.

Dadci, Younès (1980) *Première histoire du cinéma algérien, 1896–1979*. Paris: Editions Dadci.

Dahane, Mohamed (ed.) (1995) *Cinéma: Histoire et Société*. Rabat: Publications de la Faculté des Lettres.

Daoud, Zakya (1997) *Marocains des deux rives*. Paris: Les Éditeurs de l'Atelier/Éditions Ouvrières.

Davidson, Basil (1966) *The African Past*. Harmondsworth: Penguin.
Davidson, Basil (1973) *The Africans: An Entry to Cultural History*. Harmondsworth: Penguin.
Davidson, Basil (1978) *Africa in Modern History*. Harmondsworth: Penguin.
Davidson, Basil (1994, 3rd edn) *Modern Africa: A Social and Political History*. London and New York: Longman.
Davidson, Basil (1994) *The Search for Africa: A History in the Making*. London: James Currey.
De Arabische Film (1979). Amsterdam: Cinemathema.
Despierre, P. -G. (ed.) (2004) *Le Griot, le psychanalyste et le cinéma africain*. Paris: Grappaf/L'Harmattan.
Dialmy, Abdessamad (1995) *Logement, sexualité et Islam*. Casablanca: Éditions EDDIF.
Dialmy, Abdessamad (1995) *Sexualité et discours au Maroc*. Casablanca: Afrique Orient.
Diawara, Manthia (1991) 'African Cinema Today'. London: *Framework* 37, pp. 110–28.
Diawara, Manthia (1992) *African Cinema: Politics and Culture*. Bloomington: Indiana University Press.
Dictionnaire du cinéma africain (1991). Paris: Karthala.
Dine, Philip (1994) 'Thinking the Unthinkable: The Generation of Meaning in French Literary and Cinema Images of the Algerian War'. London: *The Maghreb Review* 19: 1–2, pp. 123–32.
Diop, Papa Samba, Fuchs, Elisa, Hug, Heinz and Riesz, János (eds) (1994) *Ousmane Sembène und die senegalesche Erzählliteratur*. Munich: Edition Text + Kritik.
Djebar, Assia (1999) *Ces voix qui m'assiègent*. Paris: Albin Michel.
Dossier: Spécial Cinémas d'Afrique (1991). Paris: CNC.
Dourari, Abderrezak (ed.) (2002) *Cultures populaires et culture nationale en Algérie*. Paris: L'Harmattan.
Downing, John D. H. (ed.) (1987) *Film and Politics in the Third World*. New York: Praeger.
Dwyer, Kevin (2002) ' "Hidden, Unsaid, Taboo" in Moroccan Cinema: Adelkader Lagtaa's Challenge to Authority'. Detroit: *Framework* 43: 2, pp. 117–33.
Dwyer, Kevin (2004) *Beyond Casablanca: M. A. Tazi and the Adventure of Moroccan Cinema*. Bloomington: Indiana University Press.
Ebanda, De B'béri Boulou (ed.) (2000) *Ecritures dans les cinémas d'Afrique noire*. Montreal: Cinémas.
Eke, Maureen N., Harrow, Kenneth W. and Yewah, Emmanuel (eds) (2000) *African Images: Recent Studies and Text in Cinema*. Trenton, NJ and Asmara, Eritrea: Africa World Press.
El Khodari, Khalid (2000) *Guide des réalisateurs marocains*. Rabat: El Maarif Al Jadida.
El Saadawi, Nawal (1980) *The Hidden Face of Eve: Women in the Arab World*. London: Zed Books.
El Yamlahi, Sidi Mohamed (1997) *Bachir Skiredj: Biographie d'un rire*. Casablanca: Najah el Jadida.
Espaces et sociétés du monde arabe (1989). Paris: *Maghreb-Machrek* 123.
Esposito, John (ed.) (1995) *The Oxford Encyclopedia of the Modern Islamic World*. New York and Oxford: Oxford University Press.
Etoke, Nathalie (2003) 'Karmen Gei: Une Censure à l'arme blanche'. Paris: *L'Arbre à Palabres* 14, pp. 92–7.
Europe – Afrique: Regards croisés (1998). Perpignon: Confrontation Cinématographique 34.
Fage, J. D. (1969) *A History of West Africa*. Cambridge: Cambridge University Press.

Fanon, Frantz (1967) *The Wretched of the Earth*. Harmondsworth: Penguin.

Fanon, Frantz (1970) *Toward the African Revolution*. Harmondsworth: Penguin.

Farid, Samir (1973) 'Les Six générations du cinéma égyptien'. Paris: *Écran* 15, pp. 38–49.

Farid, Samir (1979) *Arab Cinema Guide*. Cairo.

FEPACI (1995) *L'Afrique et le centenaire du cinéma/Africa and the Centenary of Cinema*. Paris: Présence Africaine.

Fertat, Ahmed (2000) *Une passion nommée cinéma: Vie et oeuvres de Mohamed Osfour*. Tangier: Altopress.

FESPACO (from 1969) catalogues. Ouagadougou.

Festival Cinema Africano (from 1991) catalogues. Milan: COE.

Festival du film arabe (from 1983) catalogues. Paris.

Festival: Images du monde arabe (1993). Paris: Institut du Monde Arabe.

Festival International de Montpellier (from 1985) catalogues et actes. Montpellier.

Festival National du Film Marocain (from 1982) catalogues. Morocco.

Film in Algerien ab 1970 (1978). Berlin: *Kinemathek* 57.

Finnegan, Ruth (1976) *Oral Literature in Africa*. Nairobi: Oxford University Press.

Fonkoua, Romuald-Blaise (ed.) (2004) *Cinquante ans de cinéma africain/Hommage à Paulin Soumanou Vieyra*. Paris: *Présence Africaine* 170.

Frodon, Jean-Pierre (ed.) (2004) *Au Sud du Cinéma*. Paris: Cahiers du Cinéma/Arte Editions.

Gabous, Abdelkrim (1998) *Silence, elles tournent!: Les femmes et le cinéma en Tunisie*. Tunis: Cérès Editions/CREDIF.

Gabriel, Teshome H. (1982) *Third Cinema in the Third World*. Ann Arbor, MI: UMI Research Press.

Gadjigo, Samba, Faulkingham, Ralph H., Cassirer, Thomas and Sander, Reinhard (eds) (1993) *Ousmane Sembene: Dialogues with Critics and Writers*. Amherst: University of Massachusetts Press.

Gakwandi, Shatto Arthur (1977) *The Novel and Contemporary Experience in Africa*. London: Heinemann.

Ganda, Oumarou (1981) *Cabascabo* (with *Moi un noir*) (script). Paris: *L'Avant-Scène du Cinéma* 265.

Garcia, Jean-Pierre (1996) *Sous l'arbre à palabres: Guide pratique à l'usage des cinéastes africains*. Amiens: Festival International du Film d'Amiens; (2001, 2nd edn). Givenchy: Caravane Editeurs.

Garcia, Jean-Pierre (1997) *Itinéraires: Les cinéastes africains au festival de Cannes*. Paris: Ministère de la Coopération.

Gardies, André (1989) *Cinéma d'Afrique noire francophone*. Paris: L'Harmattan.

Gardies, André and Haffner, Pierre (1989) *Regards sur le cinéma négro-africain*. Brussels: OCIC.

Garon, Lise (2003) *Dangerous Alliances: Civil Society, the Media and Democratic Transition in North Africa*. London and New York: Zed Books.

Gaulme, François (ed.) (2001) *Afrique contemporaine*. Paris: La Documentation Française.

Ghazoul, Ferial J. (ed.) (1995) *Arab Cinematics: Towards the New and the Alternative*. Cairo: *Alif* 15.

Ghoussoub, Mai and Sinclair-Webb, Emma (ed.) (2000) *Imagined Masculinities: Male Identity and Culture in the Modern Middle East*. London: Saqi Books.

Givanni, June (ed.) (2000) *Symbolic Narratives/African Cinema: Audiences, Theory and the Moving Image*. London: BFI.

Gordon, David C. (1978) *The French Language and National Identity*. The Hague: Mouton Publishing.

Guellali, Amna (ed.) (1998) *Idrissa Ouedraogo*. Tunis: ATPCC/*Cinécrits* 15.

Gugler, Josef (2003) *African Film: Re-Imagining a Continent*. London: James Currey.
Guide du cinéma africain (1989–1999) (2000). Paris: Ecrans Nord-Sud.
Gupta, Dhruba (1994) *African Cinema: A View from India*. Jamshedpur: Celluloid Chapter.
Gutberlet, Marie-Hélène and Metzler, Hans-Peter (eds) (1997) *Afrikanisches Kino*. Bad Honnef: Horlemann/ARTE.
Gutmann, Marie-Pierre (ed.) (1999) *Le Partenariat euro-méditerranéen dans le domaine de l'image*. Morocco: Service de coopération de l'action culturelle de l'Ambassade de France au Maroc.
Hadj-Moussa, Rahiba (1994) *Le Corps, l'histoire, le territoire: Les rapports de genre dans le cinéma algérien*. Paris/Montreal: Publisud & Edition Balzac.
Haffner, Pierre (1978) *Essai sur les fondements du cinéma africain*. Paris: NEA.
Haffner, Pierre (1989) *Kino in Schwarzafrika*. Munich: French Institute/*Cicim* 27–8.
Haffner, Pierre (1994) 'The Hypothesis of Suspense'. Milan: *Écrans d'Afrique/African Screen* 7, pp. 16–21.
Haffner, Pierre (2000) 'D'une fleur double et de quatre mille autres: Sur le développement du cinéma africain'. Paris: La Documentation Française, pp. 27–35.
Hall, Stuart (1989) 'Cultural Identity and Cinematic Representations'. London: *Framework* 36, pp. 68–81.
Harrow, Kenneth W. (ed.) (1996) *The Marabout and the Muse: New Approaches to Islam in African Fiction*. Portsmouth NH and London: Heinemann/James Curry.
Harrow, Kenneth W. (ed.) (1997) *With Open Eyes: Women and African Cinema*. Amsterdam and Atlanta, GA: Rodopi/*Matutu* 19.
Harrow, Kenneth W. (ed.) (1999) *African Cinema: Post-Colonial and Feminist Readings*. Trenton, NJ and Asmara, Eritrea: Africa World Press.
Hayes, Jarrod (2000) *Queer Nations: Marginal Sexualities in the Maghreb*. Chicago: Chicago University Press.
Hayes, Jonathan (ed.) (1997) *Nigerian Video Films*. Jos: Nigerian Film Corporation.
Hennebelle, Guy (ed.) (1972) *Les Cinémas africains en 1972*. Paris: Société Africaine d'Edition.
Hennebelle, Guy (1975) *Quinze ans de cinéma mondial*. Paris: Éditions du Cerf.
Hennebelle, Guy (ed.) (1979) *Cinémas de l'émigration*. Paris: *CinémAction* 8.
Hennebelle, Guy and Soyer, Chantal (ed.) (1980) *Cinéma contre racisme*. Paris: *CinémAction* (hors série)/*Tumulte* 7.
Hennebelle, Guy (ed.) (1983) *Cinémas noirs d'Afrique*. Paris: CinémAction 23.
Hennebelle, Guy and Ruelle Catherine (1978) *Cinéastes de l'Afrique noire*. Paris: FESPACO/*CinémAction* 3/*L'Afrique Littéraire et Artistique* 49.
Hennebelle, Guy, Berrah, Mouny and Stora, Benjamin (eds) (1997) *La Guerre d'Algérie à l'écran*. Paris: Corlet/Télérama/*CinémAction* 85.
Hitchcott, Nicki (ed.) (2001) *Gender and Francophone Writing*. Nottingham: *Nottingham French Studies* 40: 1.
Hjort, Mette and Mackenzie Scott, (ed.) (2000) *Cinema and Nation*. London and New York: Routledge.
Hobsbawm, Eric, and Ranger, Terence (eds) (1983) *The Invention of Tradition*. Cambridge: Cambridge University Press.
Horne, Alastair (1979) *A Savage War of Peace: Algeria 1954–1962*. Harmondsworth: Penguin.
Hull, Richard W. (1980) *Modern Africa: Change and Continuity*. Englewood Cliffs, NJ: Prentice-Hall.
Ibo, Ousmane (1993) *Le Cinéma au Niger*. Brussels: OCIC.
Iliffe, John (1993) *The Emergence of African Capitalism*. London: Macmillan.
Image(s) du Maghrébin dans le cinéma français (1989). Paris: *Grand Maghreb* 47.

Images et Visages du Cinéma Algérien (1984). Algiers: ONCIC/Ministry of Culture and Tourism.

Irele, Abiola (1981) *The African Experience in Literature and Ideology*. London: Heinemann.

Issa, Maïzama (1991) *Omarou Ganda, Cinéaste nigérien: Un regard de dedans sur la société en transition*. Dakar: Ena-Édition.

Jaïdi, Moulay Driss (1991) *Le Cinéma au Maroc*. Rabat: Collection al majal.

Jaïdi, Moulay Driss (1992) *Public(s) et cinéma*. Rabat: Collection al majal.

Jaïdi, Moulay Driss (1994) *Vision(s) de la société marocaine à travers le court métrage*. Rabat: Collection al majal.

Jaïdi, Moulay Driss (1995) *Cinégraphiques*. Rabat: Collection al majal.

Jaïdi, Moulay Driss (2000) *Diffusion et audience des médias audiovisuels*. Rabat: Collection al majal.

Journées Cinématographiques de Carthage (from 1966) catalogues. Tunis.

Jung, Fernand (1997) *Südlich der Sahara: Filme aus Schwarzafrika*. Munich: Kopäd Verlag.

Kamba, Sébastien (1992) *Production cinématographique et parti unique: l'exemple du Congo*. Paris: L'Harmattan.

Kaye, Jacqueline (ed.) (1992) *Maghreb: New Writing from North Africa*. (York: Talus Editions/University of York.

Kaye, Jacqueline and Zoubir, Abdelhamid (1990) *The Ambiguous Compromise: Language, Literature, and National Identity in Algeria and Morocco*. London and New York: Routledge.

Kemp, Tom (1983) *Industrialization in the Non-Western World*. London and New York: Longman.

Khayati, Khémais (1996) *Cinémas arabes: Topographie d'une image éclatée*. Paris and Montreal: L'Harmattan.

Khelil, Hédi (1994) *Nouvelles du cinéma*. Sousse: Éd. Saïdane.

Khelil, Hédi (1994) *Résistances et utopies: Essais sur le cinéma arabe et africain*. Tunis: Édition Sahar.

Khelil, Hédi (2002) *Le Parcours et la Trace: Témoignages et documents sur le cinéma tunisien*. Salammbô: MediaCon.

Khlifi, Omar (1970) *L'Histoire du cinéma en Tunisie*. Tunis: STD.

Khuri, Fuad I. (1990) *Tents and Pyramids: Games and Ideology in Arab Culture fromBackgammon to Autocratic Rule*. London: Saqi Books.

Khuri, Fuad I. (2001) *The Body in Islamic Culture*. London: Saqi Books.

Kummer, Ida (ed.) (2002) *Cinéma Maghrébin*. Saratoga Springs: special issue of *Celaan* 1: 1–2.

La Semaine du cinéma arabe (1987). Paris: IMA.

La Tunisie: Annuaire 1995 (Etats des lieux du cinéma en Afrique) (1995). Paris: Association des Trois Mondes/FEPACI.

Lacey, Kevin R. and Coury, Ralph M. (eds) (2000) *The Arab-African and Islamic Worlds: Interdisciplinary Studies*. New York: Peter Lang.

Lacoste, Camille and Lacoste, Yves (1995) *Maghreb: Peuples et populations*. Paris: Éditions la Découverte.

Lamchichi, Abderrahim and Ballet, Dominique (eds) (2001) *Maghrébins de France: Regards sur les dynamiques de l'intégration*. Paris: *Confluences Méditerranée* 39.

Landau, Jacob M. (1958) *Studies in the Arab Theater and Cinema*. Philadelphia: University of Pennsyvania Press.

Landy, Marcia (1996) 'Folklore, Memory, and Postcoloniality in Ousmane Sembene's Films', in Marcia Landy, *Cinematic Uses of the Past*. Minneapolis: University of Minnesota Press, pp. 30–66.

Laroui, Abdallah (1997) *Islamisme, Modernisme, Libéralisme*. Casablanca: Centre Culturel Arabe.

Lazreg, Marnia (1994) *The Eloquence of Silence: Algerian Women in Question*. London and New York: Routledge.

Le Clap ou à la connaissance des cinéastes africains et de la diaspora (2001). Ouagadougou: Sykif.

Le Droit à la Mémoire (2000). Toulouse: *Horizons Maghrébins* 46.

Le Rôle du cinéaste africain dans l'éveil d'une conscience de civilisation noire (1970). Paris: *Présence Africaine* 90.

Leaman, Oliver (2001) *Companion Encyclopedia of Middle Eastern and North African Film*. London and New York: Routledge.

Legall, Michael and Perkins, Kenneth (eds) (1997) *The Magrib in Question*. Austin: University of Texas Press.

Lelièvre, Samuel (ed.) (2003) *Cinémas africains, une oasis dans le désert?*. Paris: Corlet/Télérama/*CinémAction* 106.

Lequeret, Elisabeth (2003) *Le Cinéma africain: Un continent à la recherche de son propre regard*. Cahiers du cinéma/Scérén/CNDP.

Les Cinémas d'Afrique: Dictionnaire (2000). Paris: Éditions Karthala/Éditions ATM.

Lewis, Bernard (1998) *The Multiple Identities of the Middle East*. London: Weidenfeld and Nicolson.

Liauzu, Claude, Meynier, Gilbert, Sgroi-Dufresne, Maria and Signoles, Pierre (eds) (1985) *Enjeux urbains au Maghreb*. Paris: L'Harmattan.

L'Individu au Maghreb (1993). Tunis: Éditions TS.

Lionnet, Françoise and Scharfman, Ronnie (eds) (1993) *Post/Colonial Conditions: Exiles, Migrations and Nomadisms*. New Haven and London: Yale University Press/*Yale French Studies* 82 and 83.

Littératures de Tunisie (1997). Paris: *Ifriquiya* 1.

Lloyd, P. C. (1969) *Africa in Social Change*. Harmondsworth: Penguin.

Maarek, Philippe J. (ed.) (1983) *Afrique noire: quel cinéma?*. Paris: Association du Cinéclub de l'Université de Paris X.

Maherzi, Lotfi (1980) *Le Cinéma algérien: Institutions, imaginaire, idéologie*. Algiers: SNED.

Malkmus, Lizbeth and Armes Roy (1991) *Arab and African Film Making*. London: Zed Books.

Malti-Douglas, Fedwa (1991) *Woman's Body, Woman's Word: Gender and Discourse in Arabo-Islamic Writing*. Princeton: Princeton University Press.

Manning, Patrick (1988) *Francophone Sub-Saharan Africa 1880–1985*. Cambridge: Cambridge University Press.

Mansour, Guillemette (2000) *Samama Chikly: Un tunisien à la rencontre du XXième siècle*. Tunis: Simpact Editions.

Mansouri, Hassouna (2000) *De l'identité, ou Pour une certaine tendance du cinéma africain*. Tunis: Éditions Sahar.

Maquet, Jacques (1972) *Civilisations of Black Africa*. New York: Oxford University Press.

Martin, Angela (1982) *African Films: The Context of Production*. London: BFI.

Martineau, Monique (ed.) (1979) *Le Cinéma au féminisme*. Paris: *CinémAction* 9.

McDougall, James (ed.) (2003) *Nation, Society and Culture in North Africa*. London and Portland, OR: Frank Cass.

Meddour, Azzedine (1999) *La Montagne de Baya, ou la 'diya'* (novel). Algeria: Editions Marinoor.

Megherbi, Abdelghani (1982) *Les Algériens au miroir du cinéma colonial*. Algiers: SNED.

Megherbi, Abdelghani (1985) *Le Miroir aux alouettes*. Algiers and Brussels: ENAL/ UPU/GAM.

Memmi, Albert (1974) *The Colonizer and the Colonized*. London: Souvenir Press.

Memmi, Albert (1985) *Portrait du colonisé, précédé de Portrait du colonisateur*. Paris: Gallimard.

Mernissi, Fatima (1985, 2nd edn) *Beyond the Veil: Male Female Dynamics in Muslim Society*. London: Al Saqi Books.

Mernissi, Fatima (1991) *Women and Islam: An Historical and Theological Enquiry*. Oxford: Blackwell.

Mernissi, Fatima (1993) *Islam and Democracy: Fear of the Modern World*. London: Virago.

Mernissi, Fatima (1996) *The Harem Within: Tales of a Moroccan Girlhood*. London: Bantam Books.

Miller, Christopher L. (1998) *Nationalists and Nomads: Essays on Francophone African Literature and Culture*. Chicago: University of Chicago Press.

Millet, Raphaël (1998) '(In)dépendance des cinémas du Sud &/vs France'. Paris: *Théorème 5*, pp. 141–77.

Millet, Raphaël (2002) *Cinémas de la Méditerranée: Cinémas de la mélancolie*. Paris: L'Harmattan.

Mimoun, Mouloud (ed.) (1992) *France-Algérie: Images d'une guerre*. Paris: Institut du Monde Arabe.

Mitterrand, Frédéric and Elyes-Ferchichi, Soraya (1995) *Une saison tunisienne*. Arles: Actes Sud/AFAA.

Mondolini, Dominique (ed.) (2002) *Cinémas d'Afrique*. Paris: ADPF/*Notre Libraire* 149.

Moumen, Touti (1998) *Films tunisiens: Longs métrages 1967–98*. Tunis: Touti Moumen.

Mudimbe, V. Y. (1988) *The Invention of Africa*. Bloomington: Indiana University Press.

Mulvey, Laura (1996) 'The Carapace that Failed: Ousmane Sembene's *Xala*', in Laura Mulvey, *Fetishism and Curiosity*. London: BFI, and Bloomington: Indiana University Press.

Murison, Katharine (2002) *Africa South of the Sahara*. London: Europa Publications.

Murphy, David (2000) *Sembene: Imagining Alternatives in Film and Fiction*. Oxford: James Currey, and Trenton, NJ: Africa World Press.

Naficy, Hamid (2001) *An Accented Cinema: Exilic and Diasporic Filmmaking*. Princeton: Princeton University Press.

Ngakane, Lionel and Shiri, Keith (1991) *Africa on Film*. London: BBC.

Ngansop, Guy Jérémie (1987) *Le Cinéma camerounais en crise*. Paris: L'Harmattan.

N'Gosso, Gaston Samé and, Ruelle, Catherine (1983) *Cinéma et télévision en Afrique*. Paris: Unesco.

Ngugi wa Thiong'o (1986) *Decolonising the Mind: The Politics of Language in African Literature*. London: John Currey.

Niang, Sada (ed.) (1996) *Littérature et cinéma en Afrique francophone: Ousmane Sembène et Assia Djebar*. Paris: L'Harmattan.

Niang, Sada (2002) *Djibril Diop Mambety: Un Cinéaste à Contre-Courant*. Paris: L'Harmattan.

Nicollier, Valéri (1991) *Der Offene Bruch: Das Kino der Pieds Noirs*. munich: *Cinim* 34.

Nieuwkerk, Karin van (1995) '*A Trade Like Any Other*': *Female Singers and Dancers in Egypt*. Austin: University of Texas Press.

Nowell-Smith, Geoffrey (1996) *The Oxford History of World Cinema*. Oxford: Oxford University Press.

N'zelomona, Berthin (ed.) (2001) *La Francophonie*. Paris: *Recherches Africaines* 5.
Okot p'Bitek (1973) *Africa's Cultural Revolution*. Nairobi: Macmillan.
Olaniyan, Richard (ed.) (1982) *African History and Culture*. Lagos: Longman.
Oliver, Roland (1999) *The African Experience*. London: Weidenfeld and Nicolson.
Ossman, Susan (1998) *Miroirs maghrébins: Itinéraires de soi et paysages de rencontre*. Paris: CNRS Éditions.
Ostle, Robin, de Moor, Ed and Wild, Stefan (ed.) (1998) *Writing the Self: Autobiographical Writing in Modern Arabic Literature*. London: Saqi Books.
Otten, Rik (1984) *Le Cinéma au Zaire, au Rwanda et au Burundi*. Brussels: OCIC.
Où va le cinéma algérien? (2003). Paris: *Cahiers du Cinéma*, hors-série.
Ouédraogo, Hamidou (1995) *Naissance et évolution du FESPACO de 1969 à 1973*. Ouagadougou: Hamidou Ouédraogo.
Panorama du cinéma marocain (2004). Rabat: Centre Cinématographique Marocain.
Perkins, Kenneth J. (2004) *A History of Modern Tunisia*. Cambridge: Cambridge University Press.
Petty, Sheila (ed.) (1996) *A Call to Arms: The Films of Ousmane Sembene*. Trowbridge: Flicks Books.
Pfaff, Françoise (1984) *The Cinema of Ousmane Sembene*. Westport: Greenwood Press.
Pfaff, Françoise (1988) *25 Black African Film Makers*. New York: Greenwood Press.
Pfaff, Françoise (ed.) (2004) *Focus on African Films*. Bloomington: Indiana University Press.
Pommier, Pierre (1974) *Cinéma et développement en Afrique noire francophone*. Paris: Pedone.
Pontcharra, Nicole de and Maati Kabbal (ed.) (2000) *Le Maroc en mouvement: Créations contemporaines*. Paris: Maisonneuve et Larose.
Pour une promotion du cinéma national (1993). Rabat: CCM.
Pourtier, Roland (ed.) (1999) *Villes africaines*. Paris: La Documentation Française.
Puaux, Françoise (ed.) (2001) *Le machisme à l'écran*. Paris: Corlet/Télérama/*CinémAction* 99.
Quarante Ans de Cinéma Algérien (2002). Algiers: Dar Raïs Hamidou.
Reader, John (1998) *Africa: A Biography of the Continent*. Harmondsworth: Penguin Books.
Regard sur le cinéma au Maroc (1995). Rabat: CCM.
Remacle, Xavière (2002) *Comprendre la culture arabo-musulmane*. Brussels: Centre Bruxellois d'Action Interculturelle/Editions Vista/Lyon: Chronique Sociale.
Reporters sans Frontières (ed.) (1995, 2nd edn) *Le Drame algérien: Un peuple en otage*. Paris: Éditions la Découverte.
Reynolds, Dwight F. (ed.) (2001) *Interpreting the Self: Autobiography in the Arabic Literary Tradition*. Berkeley: University of California Press.
Robinson, Cedric (1980) 'Domination and Imitation: *Xala* and the Emergence of the Black Bourgeoisie'. London: *Race and Class* 22: 2, pp. 147–58.
Robinson, David (2004) *Muslim Societies in African History*. Cambridge: Cambridge University Press.
Rodney, Walter (1972) *How Europe Underdeveloped Africa*. London: Bogle-L'Ouverture.
Roitfeld, Pierre (1980) *Afrique noire francophone*. Paris: Unifrance.
Roque, Maria-Àngels (ed.) (1996) *Les Cultures du Maghreb*. Paris: L'Harmattan.
Rouissi, Moncer (1983) *Population et société au Maghreb*. Tunis: Cérès Productions.
Ruelle, Catherine (ed.) (2005) *Afriques 50: Singularités d'un cinéma pluriel*. Paris: L'Harmattan.
Sadoul, Georges (1966) *The Cinema in the Arab Countries*. Beirut: Interarab Center for Cinema and Television/Unesco.

Salhi, Abdel-Illah (2002) 'Sissako, Bricoleur de petites existences'. Paris: *Qantara* 46, pp. 28–9.

Said, Edward W. (1993) *Culture and Imperialism*. London: Vintage.

Sakr Naomi (ed.) (2004) *Women and Media in the Middle East: Power Through Self-Expression*. London and New York: I. B. Tauris.

Salah, Rassa Mohamed (1192) *35 ans de cinéma tunisien*. Tunis: Éditions Saharx.

Salmane, Hala, Hartog, Simon and Wilson, David (eds) (1976) *Algerian Cinema*. London: BFI.

Sayad, Abdelmalek (1999) *La Double absense: Des illusions de l'émigré aux souffrances de l'immigré*. Paris: Seuil.

Schmidt, Nancy (1988 and 1994) *Sub-Saharan African Films and Film Makers: An Annotated Bibliography*, 2 vols. London: Zell.

Seguin, Jean-Claude (1999) *Alexandre Promio ou les énigmes de la lumière*. Paris: L'Harmattan.

Sembene, Ousmane (1977) Interview with Robert Grelier. Paris: *La Revue du Cinéma/Image et Son* 322, pp. 74–80.

Sembene, Ousmane (1979) *Borom Sarret* (script, with Jacques Chapreux's *Bako, L'Autre Rive*). Paris: *L'Avant-Scène du Cinéma* 229.

Sene, Papa (2001) *Djibril Diop Mambety: La caméra au bout . . . du nez*. Paris: L'Harmattan.

Serceau, Daniel (ed.) (1985) *Sembène Ousmane*. Paris: *CinémAction* 34.

Serceau, Michel (ed.) (2004) *Cinémas du Maghreb*. Paris: Corlet/Télérama/*CinémAction* 111.

Shafik, Viola (1998) *Arab Cinema: History and Cultural Identity*. Cairo: The American University in Cairo Press.

Shaka, Femi Okiremuete (2004) *Modernity and the African Cinema*. Trenton, NJ and Asmara, Eritrea: Africa World Press.

Sherzer, Dina (1996) *Cinema, Colonialism, Postcolonialism: Perspectives from the French and Francophone Worlds*. Austin: University of Texas Press.

Shiri, Keith (1993) *Africa at the Pictures*. London: National Film Theatre.

Shiri, Keith (2003) *Celebrating African Cinema*. London: Africa at the Pictures.

Shoat, Ella and Stamm, Robert (1994) *Unthinking Eurocentrism: Multiculturalism and the Media*. London and New York: Routledge.

Signaté, Ibrahima (1994) *Med Hondo – Un cinéaste rebelle*. Paris: Présence Africaine.

Slavin, David Henry (2001) *Colonial Cinema and Imperial France, 1919–1939*. Baltimore: The Johns Hopkins University Press.

Slyomovics, Susan (ed.) (2001) *The Walled Arab City in Literature, Architecture and History*. London: Frank Cass.

Souiba, Fouad and el Zahra el Alaoui, Fatima (1995) *Un siècle de cinéma au Maroc*. Rabat: World Design Communication.

Soyinka, Wole (1976) *Myth, Literature and the African World*. Cambridge: Cambridge University Press.

Spass, Lieve (2000) *The Francophone Film: A Struggle for Identity*. Manchester: Manchester University Press.

Steven, Peter (ed.) (1975) *Jump Cut: Hollywood, Politics and Counter-Cinema*. Toronto: Between The Lines.

Stollery, Martin (2001) 'Masculinities Generations, and Cultural Transformation in Contemporary Tunisian Cinema'. Glasgow: *Screen* 42: 1, pp. 49–63.

Stora, Benjamin (1994) *Histoire de l'Algérie depuis l'indépendance*. Paris: Éditions La Découverte.

Stora, Benjamin (1998) *La Gangrène et l'oubli: La mémoire de la guerre d'Algérie*. Paris: Éditions La Découverte.

Stora, Benjamin (2001) *La Guerre invisible: Algérie, années 90*. Paris: Presses de Sciences PO.

Stora, Benjamin (2001) *Algeria 1830–2000: A Short History*. Ithaca and London: Cornell University Press.

Stora, Benjamin and Ellyas, Akram (1999) *Les 100 Portes du Maghreb*. Paris: Les Éditions de l'Atelier/Éditions Ouvrières.

Taboulay, Camille (1997) *Le Cinéma métaphorique de Mohamed Chouikh*. Paris: K Films Editions.

Talha, Larbi (ed.) (1987) *Monde arabe: Migrations et identités*. La Calade: Edisud.

Tamzali, Wassyla (1979) *En attendant Omar Gatlato*. Algiers: EnAP.

Tanizaki, Junichiro (2001) *In Praise of Shadows*. London: Vintage.

Tarr, Carrie (2005) *Reframing Difference: Beur and Banlieue Film Making in France*. Manchester: Manchester University Press.

Teicher, Gaël (2003) *Moustapha Alassane Cinéaste*. Paris: Les Éditions de l'Oeil.

TenKoul, Abderrahman (ed.) (1991) *Ecritures Maghrébines: Lectures croisées*. Casablanca: Afrique Orient.

Thackway, Melissa (2003) *Africa Shoots Back: Alternative Perspectives in Sub-Saharan Francophone African Film*. London: James Currey.

Thiers-Thiam, Valérie (2004) *À chacun son griot*. Paris: L'Harmattan.

Tlatli, Moufida (2004) *Les Silences du palais*. Paris: *L'Avant-Scène du Cinéma* 536.

Tomaselli, Keyan (1981) *The South African Film Industry*. Johannesburg: University of Witwatersrand.

Tomaselli, Keyan (ed.) (1986) *Le Cinéma sud-africain est-il tombé sur la tête?*. Paris: *L'Afrique littéraire* 78/*CinémAction* 39.

Tomaselli, Keyan (1989) *The Cinema of Apartheid*. London: Routledge.

Tomaselli, Keyan (ed.) (1993) *African Cinema*. Natal: *Critical Arts* 7: 1–2.

Toumi, Mohsen (1982) *Le Maghreb*. Paris: Presses Universitaires de France.

Troin, Jean-François (ed.) (1985) *Le Maghreb: Hommes et espaces*. Paris: Armand Colin.

Troin, Jean-François (ed.) (1995) *Maghreb Moyen-Orient Mutations*. Paris: Sedes.

Turégano, Teresa Hoefert de (2005) *African Cinema and Europe: Close-up on Burkina Faso*. Florence: European Press Academic.

Turvey, Gerry (1995) '*Xala* and the Curse of Neo-Colonialism: Reflections on a Realist Project'. London: *Screen* 26: 3–4, pp. 75–87.

Ukadike, Nwachukwu Frank (1994) *Black African Cinema*. Berkeley: California University Press.

Ukadike, Nwachukwu Frank (2002) *Questioning African Cinema: Conversations with Filmmakers*. Minneapolis: University of Minnesota Press.

Vautier, René (1998) *Caméra citoyenne: Mémoires*. Rennes: Editions Apogée.

Vautier, René (2001) *Afrique 50* (script). Paris: Éditions Paris Expérimental.

Venturini, Fabrice (2005) *Mehdi Charef: Conscience esthétique de la génération 'beur'*. Biarritz: Séguier.

Vermeren, Pierre (2001) *Le Maroc en transition*. Paris: Éditions La Découverte.

Videau, André (ed.) (2001) *Mélanges culturelles*. Paris: *Hommes et Migrations*.

Vieyra, Paulin Soumanou (1969) *Le Cinéma et l'Afrique*. Paris: Présence Africaine.

Vieyra, Paulin Soumanou (1972) *Sembène Ousmane cinéaste*. Paris: Présence Africaine.

Vieyra, Paulin Soumanou (1975) *Le Cinéma africain des origines à 1973*. Paris: Présence Africaine.

Vieyra, Paulin Soumanou (1983) *Le Cinéma au Sénégal*. Brussels: OCIC.

Vincendeau, Ginette (1998) *Pépé le Moko*. London: BFI.

Visions du Maghreb (1985) Aix-en-Provence: Edisud.

Wassef, Magda (ed.) (1995) *Egypte: Cent ans de cinéma*. Paris: IMA.

Werbner, Richard and Ranger, Terence (eds) (1996) *Postcolonial Identities in Africa*. London: Zed Books.

Wynchank, Anny (2003) *Djibril Diop Mambety, ou Le Voyage du Voyant*. Ivry-Sur Seine: Éditions A3.

Zannad, Traki (1984) *Symboliques Corporelles et Espaces Musulmans*. Tunis: Ceres Productions.

Zannad Bouchrara, Traki (1994) *Les Lieux du corps en Islam*. Paris: Publisud.

Zeleza, Paul Tiyambe (ed.) (2003) *Encyclopedia of Twentieth Century African History*. London and New York: Routledge.

Zuhur, Sherifa (ed.) (1998) *Images of Enchantment: Visual and Performing Arts of the Middle East*. Cairo: The American University in Cairo Press.

INDEX

This index is limited to filmmakers and their films. Numbers in italic type indicate illustrations; those in bold type refer to whole chapters devoted to the particular filmmaker.